BrightRED Study Guide

Curriculum for Excellence

N5

RMPS
RELIGIOUS, MORAL AND PHILOSOPHICAL STUDIES

David Jack

First published in 2018 by:
Bright Red Publishing Ltd
1 Torphichen Street
Edinburgh
EH3 8HX

Copyright © Bright Red Publishing Ltd 2018

Cover image © Caleb Rutherford

All rights reserved. No part of this publication may be reproduced, stored in a retrieval system, or transmitted in any form or by any means, electronic, mechanical, photocopying, recording or otherwise, without prior permission in writing from the publisher.

The rights of David Jack to be identified as the author of this work has been asserted by him in accordance with Sections 77 and 78 of the Copyright, Designs and Patents Act 1988.

A CIP record for this book is available from the British Library.

ISBN 978-1-849483-13-1

With thanks to:
Sue Lyons (editorial) and PDQ Digital Media Solutions (layout)
Cover design and series book design by Caleb Rutherford – e i d e t i c.

Acknowledgements
Every effort has been made to seek all copyright-holders. If any have been overlooked, then Bright Red Publishing will be delighted to make the necessary arrangements.

Permission has been sought from all relevant copyright holders and Bright Red Publishing are grateful for the use of the following:

Festival of Faiths (CC BY 2.0)[1] (p 6); Catholic Diocese of Saginaw (CC BY-ND 2.0)[2] (p 6); israeltourism (CC BY-SA 2.0)[3] (p 6); Jean-Pierre Dalbéra (CC BY 2.0)[1] (p 9); Photo Dharma (CC BY 2.0)[1] (p 14); Hintha (CC BY 2.0)[1] (p 15); Wellcome Images (CC BY 4.0)[4] (p 22); saamiblog (CC BY 2.0)[1] (p 24); Staffan Scherz (CC BY 2.0)[1] (p 28); Mr.Peerapong Prasutr (CC BY-SA 4.0)[5] (p 30); Dennis Jarvis (CC BY-SA 2.0)[3] (p 31); Diagram reproduced by permission of James Kennedy (https://jameskennedymonash.wordpress.com/) (p 32); Boundary Commission for Scotland (OGL)[6] (p 33); Andyso (CC BY-SA 3.0)[7] (p 61 & 70); domdomegg (CC BY 4.0)[4] (p 61 & 71); Logo reproduced by permission of SACRO (p 77); vnliti/iStock.com (p 82); Chris Potter (CC BY 2.0)[1] (p 84); Extract from the article 'The Trouble With Prison' by Kenneth Hartman in Counterpunch, 25 May 2009 (https://www.counterpunch.org/2009/05/25/the-trouble-with-prison/) © CounterPunch (p 85); Sowlos (Own work) (CC BY-SA 3.0)[7] (p 88); Extract from the article 'Big Ideas: Evolution' by Richard Dawkins in New Scientist, 14 September 2005 (https://www.newscientist.com/article/mg18725171-500-big-ideas-evolution/) © New Scientist (p 128); Extract from the article 'Yes, the universe looks like a fix. But that doesn't mean that a god fixed it' by Paul Davies in The Guardian, 26 June 2007 (https://www.theguardian.com/commentisfree/2007/jun/26/spaceexploration.comment). Courtesy of Guardian News & Media Ltd (p 128)

(CC BY 2.0)[1] https://creativecommons.org/licenses/by/2.0/deed.en
(CC BY-ND 2.0)[2] https://creativecommons.org/licenses/by-nd/2.0/
(CC BY-SA 2.0)[3] https://creativecommons.org/licenses/by-sa/2.0/
(CC BY 4.0)[4] https://creativecommons.org/licenses/by/4.0/deed.en
(CC BY-SA 4.0)[5] https://creativecommons.org/licenses/by-sa/4.0/deed.en
(OGL)[6] https://www.nationalarchives.gov.uk/doc/open-government-licence/version/1/
(CC BY-SA 3.0)[7] https://creativecommons.org/licenses/by-sa/3.0/deed.en)

Printed and bound in the UK by Ashford Colour Press Ltd.

CONTENTS

INTRODUCTION
Course overview 4

WORLD RELIGIONS

TOOLKIT
Impact on feelings 6
Impact on lifestyle 8
Impact on actions and relevance 10

BUDDHISM
Starting points 12
Life of the Buddha, part 1 14
Life of the Buddha, part 2 16
The First Noble Truth 18
The Second Noble Truth 20
The Third Noble Truth 22
The Fourth Noble Truth 24
The Eightfold Path 26
Three Jewels or Refuges 28
The relevance of Buddhism 30
Summary and consolidation 32

CHRISTIANITY
Starting points 34
Humanity, a special creation 36
Jesus: Holy week 38
Jesus: Final days 40
Jesus: His nature and teaching 42
Jesus: Beginnings 44
God and His people 46
Celebrating Jesus 48
Communion 50
Living the Life 52
RMPS skills 54
The relevance of Christianity 56

MORALITY AND BELIEF

TOOLKIT
Making moral decisions 58

MORALITY AND JUSTICE
Causes of crime 1 60
Causes of crime 2 62
Moral issues 64
The purposes of punishment 1 66
The purposes of punishment 2 68
Religious views on punishment 70
Non-religious views on punishment 72
Purposes of punishment and causes of crime 74

UK responses to crime 76
The death penalty 1 78
The death penalty 2 80
Whole life terms 1 82
Whole life terms 2 84

MORALITY AND MEDICINE
The value of life 86
The value of life: Religious and non-religious views . 88
Medical ethics: Rights and choices 90
The morality of personal autonomy 92
The status and uses of the human embryo 94
The issues raised by using embryos 96
Thinking about embryo use 98
End-of-life decisions 100
Palliative care: Case studies 102
Assisted dying 104
Assisted dying law 106
Dying choices 108
The euthanasia debate 110

RELIGIOUS AND PHILOSOPHICAL QUESTIONS

TOOLKIT
RPQ basics 1 112
RPQ basics 2 114
RPQ basics 3 116

ORIGINS
Origins of the Universe: The debate 118
Origins of the Universe: Big Bang or infinite? .. 120
Origins of the Universe: God did it 1 122
Origins of the Universe: God did it 2 124
Origins of life: The debate 1 126
Origins of life: The debate 2 128
Origins of life: The debate 3 130

THE EXISTENCE OF GOD
The starting point 132
The cosmological argument: Aquinas 134
The cosmological argument: Kalam 136
The teleological argument 1 138
The teleological argument 2 140

GLOSSARY   142

INTRODUCTION

COURSE OVERVIEW

Although the modern world may be less religious today, religions and their cultures have shaped our world. On a daily basis we grapple with choices between right and wrong, and humanity faces major moral issues. Everyone uses philosophy in its various forms as part of their thinking, to help them make sense of the world, and to give them some ideas about how we fit into the Universe.

THE BENEFITS OF NATIONAL 5 RMPS

National 5 RMPS is a course that enables you to develop an in-depth understanding of many of the most important and interesting issues related to religion, morality and philosophy.

This course will provide you with a range of skills. These include carrying out effective research, understanding and analysing subjects from a range of perspectives, and presenting your knowledge, understanding, analysis and criticism of the topics in the course.

THE COURSE ASSESSMENT

The course assessment will determine your grade for National 5 RMPS. This course can be passed from grade A to grade D.

THE EXTERNAL ASSESSMENT: COMPONENT 1 – QUESTION PAPER

The question paper is worth 80 marks (80% of the total). You have two hours and 20 minutes to complete the question paper. The question paper has three sections and each section has a number of parts. Each part has a minimum of 25 marks available. There are four to six questions in each part, and each of those questions is worth 3–8 marks.

The question paper measures the breadth and application of your learning, and challenge you to show how much you understand the course.

Challenge

You will be expected to show an understanding of what you are being asked about. Answers to questions of knowledge and understanding should give detailed explanations and descriptions.

Skills questions involve:

- Analysis, in which you break down an idea and explain how it works or show how it is connected to other ideas.
- Evaluation, in which you comment on a belief, practice or viewpoint, and support it with evidence.

Knowledge, understanding and skills

World religions

You may be asked to do the following, at a straightforward level, in relation to the religion you have studied:

contd

Introduction – Course overview

- Describe, explain and analyse aspects of the religion and their relationship.
- Present reasoned views on religion and evaluate the importance, relevance and impact of aspects of the religion.

Morality and belief

You may be asked to do the following, at a straightforward level, in relation to the moral issue you have studied:

- Describe, explain and analyse aspects of the issue.
- Describe, explain and analyse religious and non-religious responses to the issue.
- Present reasoned views on and evaluate the issues, and religious and non-religious responses to them.

Religious and philosophical questions

You may be asked to do the following, at a straightforward level, in relation to the religious and philosophical question you have studied:

- Describe, explain and analyse aspects of the religious and philosophical question.
- Describe, explain and analyse religious and non-religious responses to the question.
- Present reasoned views on and evaluate the question, and religious and non-religious responses to it.

(Refer to https://www.sqa.org.uk/files_ccc/RMPSCourseSpecN5.pdf for further details.)

THE EXTERNAL ASSESSMENT: COMPONENT 2 – ASSIGNMENT

The assignment is worth 20 marks (20% of the total).

Unlike the question paper, the assignment has marks available for skills other than knowledge and understanding.

You will have one hour to complete the assignment.

HOW WILL THIS GUIDE HELP YOU MEET THE CHALLENGES?

This guide is designed to give you the best possible chance to succeed in National 5 RMPS. One of the key parts of this book are the toolkits. These may be unfamiliar to you and may not have been used in class, but this doesn't mean that your teacher has not taught the course properly. Sometimes you will be given special tools to do a better job of the project you are working on. This is what the toolkits are all about. They will help you do even better.

Preparation

It is important to realise that reading books in the week before the final exam will not be enough to pass the exam. You need to work steadily throughout the year. Spending time on the internet looking at websites and watching videos covering the topics you are studying will help you understand those topics. Spend time practising answering the questions raised in the toolkits.

An important note about this book

There are 15 options across all of the units in RMPS and they are not all in this book, although the toolkits can be applied to any topic in the course. The two most popular options from each unit are covered in this book. The three units can be approached from a variety of directions so do not worry if you have not covered all the information in this book. Throughout the book it is assumed that you have a set of class notes to refer to.

ONLINE

This book is supported by the BrightRED Digital Zone – log on at www.brightredbooks.net for a world of tests, activities, videos and more!

World Religions

TOOLKIT

IMPACT ON FEELINGS

RELIGION IS COMPLEX

You may have heard various stories about Jesus or Buddha during your course and sat there wondering: 'Really? You expect me to believe that? You expect me to believe this is for real?' Well, no, nobody is expecting that of you. Most religions were founded when history was not recorded as we record it today. Therefore it is difficult to be certain of historical details about particular individuals, events and teachings. Experts try to work out what is likely (or unlikely) to be true. What has to be remembered is that much of what we see in religion today, including in Christianity and Buddhism, is the result of discussion and debate which has been moulded into a religion by a number of people over many years. Different traditions of Christianity and Buddhism demonstrate that there have been disagreements about certain beliefs or practices, and that some individuals have left the original group and gone their own way. Debates continue today within religions with individuals and groups voicing their own opinions.

However, it is clear that in world religions there is agreement on several core beliefs and practices. At National 5 (N5) level, religion is presented as complete without having been added to for hundreds of years: but this could not be further from the truth! Religion is dynamic, continually changing and responding to the world in which it exists. It is not a relic from the past like a museum exhibit. A more in-depth study of religion is fascinating but at N5 that level of understanding isn't required. What we are trying to do at N5 is give you an accurate feel for each religion studied, rather than its entire and complicated history.

At N5 you are expected to analyse and evaluate the religion being studied. One way to do this is to look at the impact and relevance of each religion. Impacts can be good and bad and it is important to be aware of each type. Religion impacts on:

- feelings
- lifestyle
- actions

Let's start by looking at its impact on feelings or **emotions**.

IMPACT ON FEELINGS

In theory, religion should change people in some way, usually for the better, although that is not always certain. The psychological impact (impact on feelings) will differ from person to person. For some individuals religion will make a noticeable difference to them and how they behave, but for others it will be a more private matter and no outward differences in their behaviour may be observed.

If an individual is labelled as a Christian, Buddhist or a member of any religious movement, some people may regard them as adherents to their faith and will have an expectation of how they will behave. But this is not necessarily how it works.

What might the **psychological** impact of religious belief be? Here are some possibilities:

- Feelings of security because a special individual (i.e. a god) is with them – and therefore they no longer feel alone in the Universe. The believer feels secure knowing that their god is (in some way) nearby.
- Feelings of hope for an afterlife – with which some (or all) of the fear of death disappears because the believer thinks that existence will continue in another dimension free from suffering, mortality and guilt.
- Feelings of belonging to a community and a tradition – the believer feels part of, and has the support of, the community to which they belong.
- Feelings of having a better understanding of both the world and of themselves – the believer enjoys a better understanding of other people and of their own place in the world.
- Feelings of responsibility towards others – the believer feels compassion towards others, and is more accepting of their faults.
- Feelings of confidence in coping with challenges – when faced with difficulties in life, the believer trusts that the help and guidance their religion provides will enable them to overcome these challenges.
- Feelings that life has a purpose.

But the psychological impact of religious belief may not always be positive, it can also have a negative impact; for example:

- Feelings of shame, guilt and anxiety – when the believer feels unworthy, or guilty about the things they do.
- Feelings of superiority to others – the believer feels that the religious message they believe in is the truth, and that this is the only message which others need to understand. This can make the believer feel more worthy because they believe they have achieved salvation.
- Self-delusion – when the believer convinces themselves that their understanding of life and that the actions they take are right, even when their views and actions appear wrong to both other believers from the same religion as well as non-believers.
- Attraction to extremism – when the believer is attached to splinter groups holding extreme or unconventional beliefs which only focus on small aspects of the religion.
- Attraction to superstitious ideas – when the believer stops using reasoning or logic and instead adopts old ideas like magic.
- Susceptibility to extraordinary experiences – in which the believer sees visions or hears voices and interprets these as religious, reinforcing belief in their god and what is expected of them.

TOOLKIT

IMPACT ON LIFESTYLE

If you are religious then your religious beliefs are going to have an impact on your lifestyle. Similar to the psychological effect, the impact on lifestyle of religion will vary from person to person, from country to country, and from culture to culture. For some individuals there will be no discernible difference in their behaviour after they become religious: outwardly they will conduct themselves as before; indeed, somebody who behaved in a decent way before becoming religious will continue to behave in a decent way and therefore the impact on their lifestyle is not obvious to others, apart from possible attendance at faith meetings or the practice of worship related to their religion.

By contrast, there will be others whose lifestyle changes dramatically after they become religious. Possible differences could be the clothes they wear, what they eat and drink, the new friends they have, the places they go, the way they behave towards others, what they say and consider important in life. It could be some of these or other lifestyle changes. As with other aspects of life, people respond and change in different ways, and no stereotype will fit all the possibilities.

POSITIVE IMPACT

What might the positive impact of religious belief have on an individual's lifestyle? Here are some possibilities:

- Less materialistic – the believer cares less about possessions and finds more satisfaction in observing their religion.

- Change of habits – a believer's behaviour may change in one way or another. For example, they may stop swearing or criticising others, or perhaps begin living a healthier life.

- New friends – when the believer joins a religious community they may want to spend more time with that community rather than existing, older friends.

- Less stressed – the believer finds that religious belief provides peace of mind, which in turn makes life less stressful. The believer may become less ambitious and simply accept what life throws up in a calm fashion because this is the way fate is going to play out.

- New routines – the believer's life revolves around their religious faith. This can happen in various ways. It could be that the religion's chosen holy day becomes the day for attending the sacred building to worship. It could be changes to the believer's daily routine, for instance the introduction of prayer or meditation.

- Self-denial – the believer may give up something for the religion. This could be either for a short period or permanently. It might involve not eating particular foods, or maybe doing things which are demanding to demonstrate your faith.

- Renunciation – formally rejecting something. For example, the believer may renounce any form of violence and will undertake to never speak or think any violent thoughts. Some religious groups renounce eating meat or renounce material possessions. In some religions followers have renounced the world to concentrate on God and have gone to live in an exclusively religious community.

- Making a statement – by adopting a religion and allowing it to impact on their lifestyle the believer is making a statement to others. The new lifestyle may give the believer a new identity and other people may take notice of what that identity signifies.

NEGATIVE IMPACT

However, there are also lifestyle changes which may be perceived as negative; for example:

- Sacrifice – a religion may demand that sacrifices be made. These could be extremely challenging, for example, leaving one's family to go off in search of spiritual truth, or giving away one's wealth to help the poor. Religious belief may mean that you are tortured or killed because of your faith in some countries. Making sacrifices for others may be admirable but loved ones may suffer because of the believer's sacrifice.

- Decision-making – the believer may lose the ability to make decisions in relation to particular lifestyle choices. This may be because they are waiting for a sign from their god, or because religious leaders dictate about how they must live their lives. The most extreme examples are often to be found in extremist religious groups or cults.

- Renunciation – may be the result of running away from a problem; it can be used by individuals unwilling to face up to the harsh realities of life.

- Experiencing intolerance – a believer whose religion means they adopt a distinctive lifestyle can be a target for religious bigots. There are many historical examples of members of religious groups being raped, tortured, discriminated against or murdered because of their religious beliefs and lifestyle.

- Non-integration – some religious groups prescribe a lifestyle which may be difficult to transfer into a different host culture. The religion may have food, dress and social codes that are not the norm in the country being lived in. These can result in the believer being vulnerable to attacks from those who fail (or choose) to understand the demands of the religion.

- Daily living – the believer's religion may affect activities like shopping, eating out, fashion, entertaining, and leisure pursuits. One possible difficulty may be having to shop at specialist food stores which stock acceptable products. Eating out could also be problematic because certain ingredients are banned by one's religion. This can apply to fashion as well, particularly clothing made from animals. Although not every believer strictly follows every rule their religion has, activities like gambling, drinking alcohol, and taking part in blood sports may be prohibited by the rules of the religion.

TOOLKIT

IMPACT ON ACTIONS AND RELEVANCE

The relevance and importance of religion in a person's life can be seen by their actions. Some believers may be involved in religious activity more than once a week, for others it may be a daily occurrence. Another individual or group who describe themselves as belonging to a religion may only perform religious actions at certain times of the year, or because of major events like weddings or funerals. If you live in a Christian or Buddhist country then it may be that religious actions take place every day, as part of the culture.

It is important to avoid stereotyping and the generalisation that 'all religious' people say, do or believe something. There is a wide range of religious beliefs and a variety of ways in which people perform their religious actions.

POSITIVE IMPACT

What might the positive impact of religious actions be on an individual? Here are some possibilities:

- *Motives* – a motive is the reason for doing something. With some of the actions they perform, believers state their motivation for carrying them out as being religious. This means:
    - They will do something because their religion expects it of them. This is usually a positive thing and may include helping others, being more considerate, being less selfish and making sacrifices for others.
    - The motivation behind the acts they perform is religious rather than selfish or personally driven.
    - The good acts they perform are similar to the good acts others (non-believers) perform, and each will have a similar effect on the recipients, but it is the motivation behind the acts which makes them different from each other.
    - Believers will possibly look for more opportunities to perform good acts in the name of their religion.
    - They want their religion to be seen in a good light through their good acts.

- *Acts of devotion* – acts of devotion or worship are part of every religion and take many different forms. These include:
    - Following the example of, or instructions given by, important figures in the religion.
    - Participating regularly in weekly worship.
    - Taking part in special festivals.
    - Meditating and/or praying.
    - Chanting and/or singing.
    - Reading from sacred texts.
    - Holding ceremonies for key life events.

- *Worldview* – a **worldview** shows how a believer perceives the world. This affects their actions through:
    - Seeing them as part of a duty towards their religion.
    - Having a greater awareness of the consequences of their actions.
    - Being more positive and compassionate towards others.
    - Appreciating the natural world more.
    - Accepting what life throws up rather than complaining about it.
    - Trying to improve the world on the basis of their religious values.

NEGATIVE IMPACT

There are others who argue that religious actions can have negative impacts; for instance:

- *Bad motives* – believers may be motivated for the wrong reasons to carry out certain religious acts. These acts might appear good at first but what they may actually be doing is the opposite. These actions might be performed to:

  o Look good (not conducted for the benefit of others or their religion).
  o Control people.
  o Lure people into the religion.
  o Give individuals more power.
  o Ease a bad conscience.

- *Acts of devotion* – any act of worship could be seen as a harmless activity which helps people feel better. Nevertheless, certain aspects of worship or devotion can create problems. For instance, an act of devotion might:

  o Lead an individual to seek solutions only through their faith rather than taking practical steps.
  o Increase superstitious beliefs in an individual.
  o Become an obsession and take priority over other responsibilities.
  o Lead to an overdependence on meditation or prayer.
  o Lead to a narrow and restrictive lifestyle.
  o Create tensions between friends or family members not involved in the religion.
  o Cause a believer to be more introspective.

- *Distorted worldview* – when an individual's view of the world becomes distorted they start to perceive it in a manner different to others. This can lead to a believer:

  o Seeing the world in an unhealthy and dangerous manner, approaching a state of paranoia.
  o Adopting an extreme version of their religion (possibly involving brainwashing and violence).
  o Seeing the world full of sin, a place that must be destroyed.
  o Expecting the world to adopt and follow their religious beliefs.
  o Losing respect for the sanctity of human life.
  o Doing evil things in the name of their religion.
  o Having unrealistic expectations of other people.
  o Reject modern scholarship on aspects of their religion which are doubtful.

RELEVANCE

Relevance means how closely something relates to what is currently going on. One thing can help explain other things it is linked with. Relevance also means that something has importance (to a certain extent) to people living in the world today. Let's take a closer look at this idea. What is it that makes something relevant?

- It affects the lives of individuals today.
- It affects the community today.
- It has an impact on the world in different ways.
- It helps explain why people behave in a certain way.
- It is something that is noticeable.
- It helps to make the world a better place.
- It gives people hope.
- It gives people good values to live by today.
- It promotes a fairer and more **compassionate** society.
- It is used for evil purposes.
- It causes problems in the world today.
- It shows how humanity has developed.

IRRELEVANCE

Irrelevance means that something has little connection to what is currently going on. It doesn't help explain anything about the world because so few people are interested in it. Irrelevance also means that it is of little importance to most people because it has little (or nothing) to do with their lives or how they perceive the world. What is it which makes religion irrelevant?

- Fewer people have any interest in it.
- It does not make much (if any) difference to the way people live.
- It is old-fashioned and out-of-date.
- It is superstitious.
- It is a belief based on hope and not fact.
- It is a practice that serves no benefit of any sort to anyone.
- It is not taken seriously.
- It is considered to be untrue.
- It is based on ancient customs and traditions.
- It provides guidance that is unreasonable.
- It is based on so-called facts that are disputed by modern research.

World Religions

BUDDHISM

STARTING POINTS

Buddhism is an ancient religion which is about 2500 years old. In its early days it grew then spread across many kingdoms and several different languages were used to express its ideas. **Siddhatta (Siddhartha) Gautama**, also known as **Shakyamuni**, or the **Buddha**, never wrote anything down. No biographies were written about him when he was alive, which means it is difficult to be certain about his life and his teachings. However, experts are able to confirm (with some certainty) that he did exist, describe what his key teachings were, and explain how his teachings grew into a religion.

To understand Buddhism there are four main ideas you need to understand:

- **Vedic religion**
- the **Buddha**
- the **Dhamma** (Dharma)
- the **Sangha** (Samgha)

VEDIC RELIGION

Modern Hinduism emerged from the religion of the Vedas. The Vedas are the four sacred texts of Hinduism based on:

- **rituals**
- the role of the priests
- keeping the gods happy

Originally the ancient Indians were nomadic, but once they settled into cities and developed civilisations, they became dissatisfied with the Vedic religion and began to resent the role of its priests, who were called Brahmins. The Brahmins were at the top of the four castes (social groups of people). An individual was born as a Brahmin into caste rather than growing up and choosing to become a Brahmin. This led to resentment which resulted in people forming sects across India called **shramanas**. Siddhatta Gautama, like several other princes and nobles of the time, decided to go on a spiritual quest with a shramana. It is believed that he was in at least one shramana before forming his own, which later developed into Buddhism.

contd

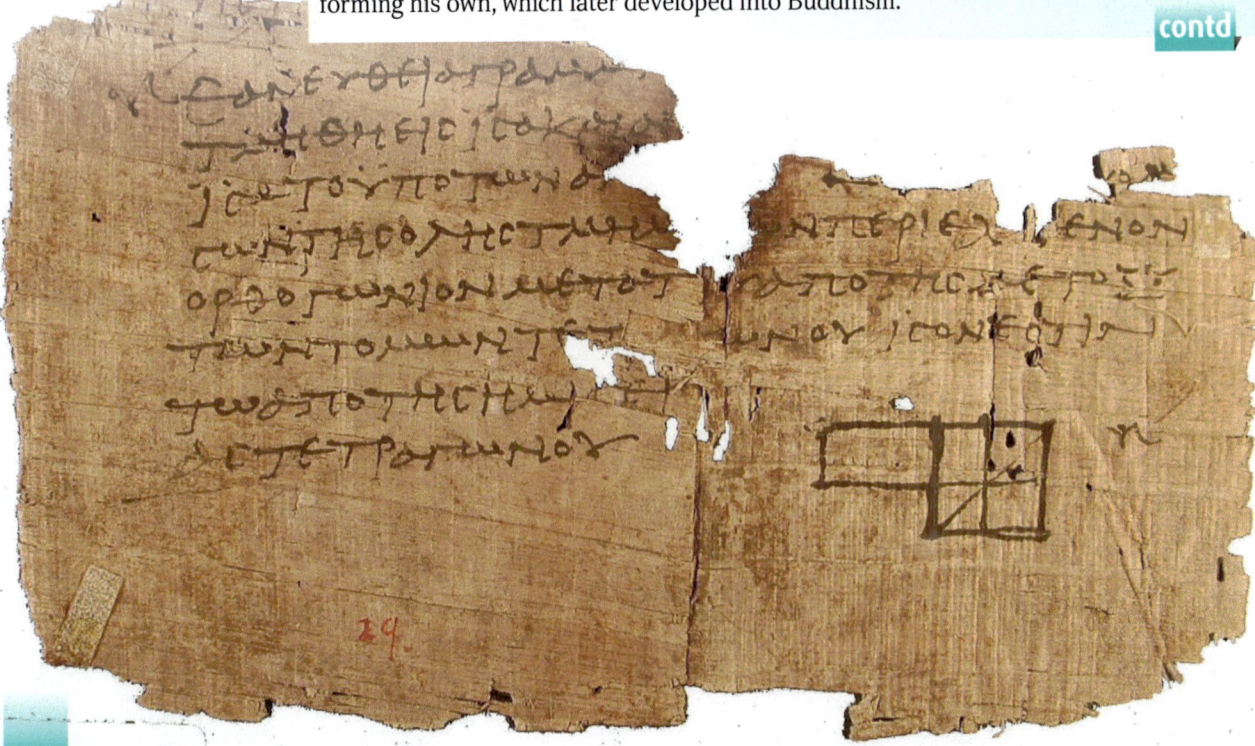

Shramanas had many different approaches to beliefs and practices, some of which can be seen in Buddhism. Some beliefs and practices were:

- there is no creator God
- there is no free will
- there is no separate soul
- there is no goal of life
- there is no caste system
- there is samsara
- meditation
- worship of perfect beings
- several steps to liberation.

In India there were schools of philosophy, one of which, the **samkhya** school, existed around the time of Siddhatta Gautama. Its explanations of life fell into 25 realities, 3 **gunas** and 11 powers. Samkhya was atheistic but not atheist: God's existence was not denied but it was believed that God's existence could not be proved, and therefore humans should spend time tackling the biggest problem they faced, which was **dukkha** (suffering). The Samkhya school believed that **meditation** was the best way to end suffering. By drawing on his own ideas and ancient traditions the teacher **Patanjali** developed his eight limbs of **yoga** which led to the end of suffering. It is believed that Samkhya and Buddhism borrowed ideas from each other.

DON'T FORGET

Buddhism, like other religions, began as a reaction against what was happening in older established religions in the area, so many of its ideas are influenced by other faiths.

VIDEO LINK

Learn more about Buddhism by watching the video at the Digital Zone.

ONLINE TEST

Test your knowledge of Buddhism at www.brightredbooks.net

THINGS TO DO AND THINK ABOUT

Always refer to the World Religions Toolkit on page 6 when tackling questions. The information there will help you develop your skills of analysis and evaluation.

1. From what you already know about Buddhism, what ideas do you think Buddhism developed from the shramanas and samkhya school?
2. Do you think religious teachings become any less valuable if the ideas have been borrowed and adapted?
3. Does it really matter if some of the Buddha's ideas were not his?
4. Would there be any problem caused by not knowing the background of the Buddha?

BUDDHISM

LIFE OF THE BUDDHA, PART 1

Although historians agree that Siddhatta Gautama existed, there is a problem with his biography. The Buddha never wrote down any of his teachings and nobody wrote a detailed biography of his life. It wasn't until many years after his death that various stories about his life were combined to give the biography which exists today. Although his life story may appear simple and straightforward on the surface, it is actually a complicated mix of myth, legend, history, symbolism, philosophy, cultural influences and beliefs.

THE CONCEPTION AND BIRTH OF THE BUDDHA

Buddha was born a prince named Siddhatta Gautama. His precise birth date, birth place and circumstances of his birth, are unknown. One tradition states that his mother, Queen Maya, dreamed a white elephant entered her womb, and when the King consulted wise men they told him that his son, Siddhatta, would be a great king or holy man. Queen Maya gave birth to Siddhatta through her side so that he remained pure; he could walk and talk from birth. The King provided Siddhatta with a life of luxury to discourage him from becoming a holy man. At the time, being a member of a royal family gave Siddhatta credibility in the eyes of many.

Siddhatta's name contains symbolism. It comes from two **Sanskrit** words, 'siddha' meaning accomplished and 'atta' meaning goal. So his name means 'one who has accomplished the goal'. It was not unusual for significant religious figures to have names linked to their mission or character; for example, Jesus means 'he who saves', Muhammad means 'the praiseworthy one' and Abraham means 'the father of many'.

To complicate matters further this was not the first birth of Siddhatta. According to Buddhist scriptures, the Buddha spoke of his previous births, the jatakas. There is a collection of books in Buddhist traditions called the Jataka Tales which contain stories of Siddhatta's past lives.

Associated with this is the question of whether or not Siddhatta was human. Buddhism is split into three main branches and these three branches are subdivided into many more branches in different countries with different cultures at different times, so getting agreed answers to questions about the Buddha is not easy.

Some Buddhists believe that Siddhatta is in the **tusita** heaven where all buddhas and gods are before they come to Earth so it appears that some Buddhists view him almost as a god. However, some believe that he was a human with supernatural powers, and others believe that he was a human who had unique insights into the Universe. The acts of devotion seen in many branches of Buddhism resemble the acts of worship of God or gods in other religions, except that the devotion is in the form of deep reverence for the Buddha, rather than seeing him as God.

Buddha in his earthly form is called Shakyamuni because he belonged to the shakya clan. The 'muni' part of his title means 'sage' or 'wise man'. The birth of the Buddha is celebrated in the **Wesak** festival (Vesakha, Vaisakha). It is a colourful, fun-filled festival during which:

- Homes are cleaned.
- Temples are visited.
- Monks are given food.
- Statues of the Buddha are bathed.
- Gifts are laid before statues to express gratitude to the Buddha.
- Lanterns are made in Thailand and Indonesia.
- In China there are dancing dragons.
- In several countries there are mass releases of wild birds.

VIDEO LINK

For more background on the life of the Buddha, watch the documentary at the Digital Zone.

DON'T FORGET

Wesak combines celebrations of Buddha's birth, Enlightenment and death.

THE GREAT RENUNCIATION

On four trips away from home, Siddhatta saw the **Four Sights**: the old man, the sick man, the dead man and the **ascetic**. He decided that the life of the ascetic was for him and joined a shramana which followed the Samkhya philosophy. Siddhatta joined with others in rejecting the religion of the Vedas which was dominated by priests and performing rituals for the gods. In the shramana he learned how to meditate and developed an atheistic approach to the Universe, but he was still unhappy. He went to another shramana and developed further insights but remained attached to the world and unhappy. He also left that shramana and decided to go his own way. In time five other ascetics joined him, impressed as were they by his strict self-discipline. Unfortunately, as with previous attempts to ultimately find peace and happiness, this effort also failed.

ONLINE TEST

Test your knowledge of Buddhism at www.brightredbooks.net

THE ENLIGHTENMENT

After six years of trying different methods to seek ultimate peace and happiness, Siddhatta experienced enlightenment while sitting under a banyan tree. In Hinduism, the banyan tree was seen as a **sacred** tree; because it has a long life and provides shade. It was compared to gods protecting their followers. It is seen as a tree of immortality because its roots create other trunks. Grass cannot grow beneath it because it doesn't permit regeneration in its shade. It represents the three main gods in Hinduism, with the bark being Vishnu (to protect it), the branches being Shiva and the roots being Brahma. Some links with Buddhist beliefs can be seen here. Can you spot them?

Siddhatta's enlightenment occurred near Gaya, before which he was tempted away from his quest by the demon, Mara. Siddhatta became known as Buddha. His enlightenment came in three stages:

- Discovery of his past lives.
- Discovery of the law of **kamma** and the **Eightfold Path**.
- Discovery of the Four Noble Truths and attaining **Nibbana** (Nirvana).

This led him to declare: 'My heart, thus knowing, thus seeing, was released from the fermentation of sensuality, released from the fermentation of becoming, released from the fermentation of ignorance. (Maha-Saccaka Sutta, *The Longer Discourse to Saccaka*).

Bodh Gaya still exists today although the river has long since changed its course. As with many religious sites, it is difficult to know exactly where the Enlightenment took place. A temple was built on one possible site by Emperor **Ashoka**, who made Buddhism the religion of his empire. Ashoka's name means "without sorrow", which may be related to his association with Buddhism.

DON'T FORGET

Stories of the birth of the Buddha were not written down until hundreds of years after his death.

VIDEO LINK

Learn more about Bodh Gaya by watching the video at the Digital Zone.

THINGS TO DO AND THINK ABOUT

1. In what ways does the name "Siddhatta" reflect the life of Buddha?
2. If Buddha is not a god, why then is his birth celebrated?
3. Is the nature of the Buddha important?
4. Why might some people think that the story of Siddhatta's birth is symbolic?
5. Does it matter whether or not the Buddha's life story is completely true?
6. Why might Buddha's birth make Buddhists thankful?
7. In what ways might Buddha's birth make people see the world differently?
8. Why do you think Hinduism is so important in understanding Buddhism?
9. What do you think put Siddhatta off the religion he had been brought up to believe in?
10. In what ways might Siddhatta's rejection of religion inspire people today?
11. Why did Siddhatta's rejection of the old religion lead him to change his lifestyle?
12. In what ways might Siddhatta's rejection of his old religion lead people today to live their lives differently?

BUDDHISM
LIFE OF THE BUDDHA, PART 2

THE GREAT DISCOURSE

Siddhatta's five followers had deserted him before his enlightenment but he went back and told them what he had discovered. This was his first sermon and its **Pali** name is Dhammachakkappavattana Sutta, translated literally as the Setting in Motion the Wheel of the Dhamma. Although it is claimed that these are the actual words spoken by the Buddha, given that they weren't written down until a few centuries after the Buddha's death, it seems unlikely that they are the exact words. However, even if they are not the actual words of the Buddha, they contain enough evidence to show that this was what the Buddha taught. This event is also known as the Sermon at Benares.

AFTER THE ENLIGHTENMENT AND DEATH

The Buddha spent the remaining years of his life teaching in various places and instructing his followers to spread his word. His family converted to Buddhism, as did other royal families and wealthy merchants, which enabled him to build monasteries. After a while, he reluctantly agreed to allow women into his order, too. When he was aged 79 his health began to fail and he felt that the end was near.

The *Mahaparinibbana Sutta* details this event. Three months before he died he said to his disciples: 'Behold now, O Brethren, I exhort you. All component things are subject to decay. Work your salvation with diligence. The final passage of the Tathagatha will take place soon. At the end of three months hence the Tathagatha will die.' He died near a place called Kusinara, a town named after a type of grass called kush, which was considered to have purifying powers. The Buddha sat on a mat made from kush when he received enlightenment and once again when he lay down to die. He passed on to higher states of consciousness before entering **parinibbana**. This is the final state for a person who has achieved nibbana during their life and spent all of their kamma. His head pointed to the north and the earth shook as he passed away.

His body was cremated shortly afterwards and his remains were divided into eight portions and distributed among his own and other tribes. They were housed in mounds of earth called stupas which eventually became more substantial buildings. These days there are thousands of stupas in Buddhist countries and beyond, and each is said to

contain relics (remains) of the Buddha, possessions of the Buddha (or bits of them), and to also represent important events in his and his disciples' lives as well as teachings of the Buddha. One of the most famous stupas is the Temple of the Tooth in Sri Lanka which attracts thousands of pilgrims every year. Whether or not the relics have actually survived is a matter for debate.

So where did the Buddha go after he died? **Mahayana** Buddhism has a belief in the doctrine of Trikaya, or the three bodies of the Buddha, which are:

- The **dhammakaya** (dharmakaya) or truth body, which is the Dhamma without any shape or form. Dhammakaya contains the word 'Dhamma' which has many meanings in Indian religions, but one common meaning is that it is the substance which holds the Universe together – it is not God, though. It is where everything comes from and ultimately where everything returns to after many rebirths.

contd

- The **nirmanakaya** is the physical body of the Buddha that lived and died.
- The **sambhogakaya** is the divine enjoyment body which exists in the tusita heaven waiting to appear on Earth. This is where the Buddha was before he came to Earth and where **Metteyya** (Maitreya) is just now, awaiting appearance on earth. Given that anyone can be a Buddha, it is possible for people who have undergone enlightenment to experience sambhogakaya. Sambhogakaya Buddha can be a focus of deep meditation and may appear in visions.

Siddhatta was in the sambhogakaya form before his birth and once born he took on the nirmanakaya form; on his death he passed into the dhammakaya body, which is the body without form. There is a variety of teachings on this, though. **Therevada** Buddhism does not accept **trikaya**, but Mahayana and **Vajryana** Buddhism do. In each of these two branches of Buddhism there are different versions of trikaya, which almost suggest the dhammkaya Buddha is God, but this is frequently denied despite the acts of worship that are carried out.

VIDEO LINK

Watch the videos at the Digital Zone to explore the story of Buddha further.

THINGS TO DO AND THINK ABOUT

'It's complicated.'

1. What evidence is there that beliefs about the Buddha are complicated?
2. Suppose you have been asked to do a presentation on "The Life of the Buddha Made Simple".

   What would you put in your presentation?
3. What positive impact might the story of the Buddha have on the lives of Buddhists?
4. What negative impact might the story of the Buddha have on the lives of Buddhists?
5. 'Whether Buddhists believe the life story of the Buddha or not, it will affect how they live their lives.'

   What do you think? Support your answer with reasons.
6. What might the good and bad effects be of becoming a Buddhist?

ONLINE TEST

Test your knowledge of Buddhism at www.brightredbooks.net

DON'T FORGET

There was and is a debate in Buddhism about what the Buddha was. There are different opinions ranging from him being an ordinary human being to a god-like figure.

BUDDHISM
THE FIRST NOBLE TRUTH

THE DHAMMA

The Buddha's teachings are called the Dhamma and are found in the Buddhist sacred scriptures called the **tripitaka**. Buddha's teachings were written down by his followers. Buddhist tradition says this happened shortly after his death and 500 followers agreed that they were accurate. However, experts suggest that they were put together many years after the Buddha's death.

Buddha taught that there were **Four Noble Truths**:

1. All existence is suffering
2. The cause of suffering is **tanha** which means craving
3. There is a cure for suffering
4. The way to end desire is the middle way

1. All Existence is Suffering

The Buddha noticed that everyone had two basic experiences of reality which were dukkha (suffering) and **anicca** (impermanence). He wondered what could be behind this. He realised that to understand suffering you have to understand human nature. This is achieved through understanding the **Three Marks of Existence**.

The first mark is dukkha. It includes:

- anguish
- unsatisfactoriness
- imperfection

Buddhism identifies three kinds of suffering:

- Suffering which includes old age, sickness, death, being separated from what you want, being with what you don't want.
- Suffering of change which includes anything that is impermanent.
- The suffering of conditioning which arises from simply being a human being with five **skandhas**.

The American Theravadin monk, Thanissaro, translated the Buddha's word dukkha as stress: 'Now this, monks, is the noble truth of stress: birth is stressful, ageing is stressful, death is stressful; sorrow, lamentation, pain, distress and despair are stressful; association with the unbeloved is stressful, separation from the loved is stressful, not getting what is wanted is stressful. In short, the five clinging-aggregates are stressful.'

The second mark of existence is anicca. Recitations from the Mahaparinibbana Sutta at Theravadin funerals make clear what impermanence is:

'Impermanent are all component things,

They arise and cease, that is their nature:

They come into being and pass away,

Release from them is bliss supreme.'

In Buddhist shrines, the flowers and lamps in front of images of the Buddha symbolise anicca as they fade away. Anicca involves believing that:

- Everything changes all the time.
- Everything is impermanent.
- Conscious thoughts mislead us into seeing permanence in things that are impermanent.
- Everything is part of a process and changes even if we cannot see it.
- There is nothing underlying it all that is permanent (the Hindu view is that things are impermanent, but that behind everything is the unchanging, permanent **Brahman**).
- Anicca is the root of human suffering.
- Since anicca is the problem then humans have to find something permanent that will bring bliss, and that is Nibbana.

The final mark of existence is **anatta**. This is the belief that there is no soul. Buddha belonged to a shramana that rejected belief in a human soul. The Buddha viewed humans as a collection of parts. These parts are known as the five skandhas.

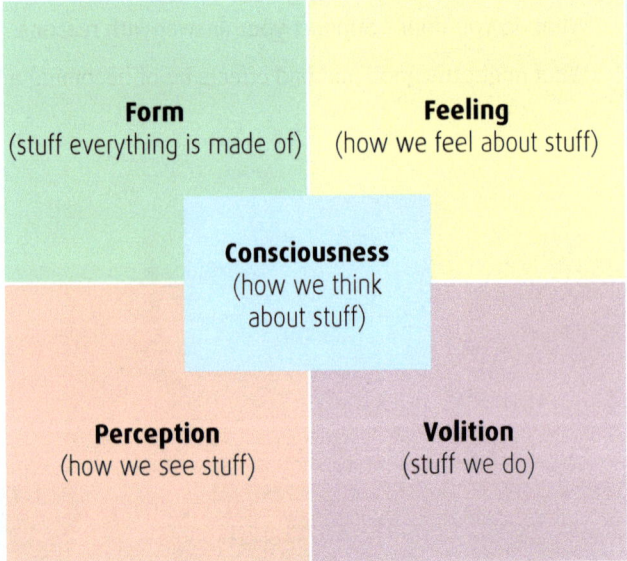

The problem is that humans think that the five skandhas are what they are. Buddha said that this is not the case. Humans have no soul, which means there is no self. Everything changes every microsecond of the day. So, although humans may think that they and the world are permanent, they are deceiving themselves. The whole idea of permanence is an illusion.

contd

Buddhism – The First Noble Truth

One Buddhist teacher, **Nagasena**, when teaching King **Milinda**, compared a human being to a chariot. Nagasena wondered at which point a chariot became, or ceased to be, a chariot. He said that it was a matter of opinion. He also wondered which part made the chariot a chariot, and stated that there was no single part, or combination of several parts, that made the chariot a chariot. Nagasena concluded that the chariot didn't actually exist: it was a concept created in our minds to call the construction a chariot. It is the same with humans. They are made up of five skandhas which are collectively called a human being. In some Mahayana schools this is called Dependent Origination, that everything is interconnected and depends on other things for their existence.

In the Anattalakkhana Sutta, the Buddha explains that humans cling to the skandhas and that this causes cravings for things, leading to suffering and the second Noble Truth. The Buddha was unclear about what humans were if they had no soul. There is also the question of what is it that accumulates kamma, is reborn and achieves Nibbana, if there is no soul. All Buddhist schools accept the idea of anatta but Mahayanan schools refer to **sunatta**, which means emptiness, that although things exist they do not have any individual identity or self. Mahayana Buddhist schools also emphasis that everyone has a buddha-nature. The buddha-nature is not a soul but is the potential to become a Buddha. The leader of Tibetan Buddhist, the **Dalai Lama**, believes everyone possesses the seed of enlightenment within themselves, which could be considered to be a kind of soul, but isn't.

In general, Buddhists believe that humans are a collection of parts with an ego which must be overcome so that the potential for enlightenment within can be released. There are differences between Theravada and Mahayana Buddhism, and further differences in the beliefs within different Mahayana schools.

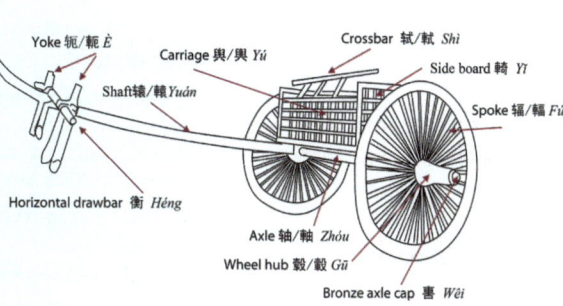

DON'T FORGET

Anicca is impermanence and anatta is the belief that there is no soul.

ONLINE

Follow the link at www.brightredbooks.net for a good source of resources on Buddhism.

ONLINE TEST

Head to www.brightredbooks.co.uk to test your knowledge of Buddhism.

THINGS TO DO AND THINK ABOUT

1. 'All existence is suffering.' Really? Imagine a dialogue between a believer and a doubter. Write it down like this:

   Believer: Our lives are full of suffering.
   Doubter: I don't think it is that bad. We have happy times too!
   Believer: Do we really? Don't you feel sad when the happy times are over?
   Doubter: Well, yes I do, everyone does.
   Believer: So, would you agree that if you are sad you are suffering?
   Continue with their dialogue and see how long you can keep it going!

2. Perform the same exercise for this statement: 'Buddhism has such a depressing outlook on life.'

3. Describe how the Three Marks, the skandhas and the First Noble Truth can be connected.

4. Copy out the table below and then look at the World Religions Toolkit. See if you can add in two positive and two negative impacts about belief in the Three Marks of Existence.

Impact	Positive Impact	Negative Impact
Feelings		
Lifestyle		
Actions		

BUDDHISM

THE SECOND NOBLE TRUTH

2. THE CAUSE OF SUFFERING IS CRAVING (TANHA)...

This brings us to the second noble truth which identifies the cause of suffering as craving or desire. The Buddha taught that there are three types of tanha or desire:

- Tanha-kamma, sensual desires which can be anything that brings pleasure.
- Bhava-tanha, the desire to be a being with a personal identity.
- Vibhava-tanha, a craving to avoid anything unpleasant in this or future lives.

But there is something else behind these forms of tanha, and Buddhist teaching identifies these as greed, anger and delusion. Mahayana Buddhist schools call them the **Three Poisons** and Therevada Buddhists call them the Three Unwholesome Roots. We will refer to them as the Three Poisons.

The craving is about how humans react to the world around them and also things that happen to them. They react by using either **skilful or unskilful actions**.

Skilful actions (kusala)	Unskilful actions (akusala: 3 poisons/fires)
· Generosity · Compassionate love · Wisdom	· Greed · Hatred · Ignorance

The Buddha was very clear about what humans had to do and it was written in Anguttara Nikaya:

'Abandon what is unskilful, monks. It is possible to abandon what is unskilful. If it were not possible to abandon what is unskilful, I would not say to you: Abandon what is unskilful. But because it is possible to abandon what is unskilful, I say to you: Abandon what is unskilful. Develop what is skilful, monks. It is possible to develop what is skilful. If it were not possible to develop what is skilful, I would not say to you: Develop what is skilful. But because it is possible to develop what is skilful, I say to you: Develop what is skilful.'

Kamma

Actions produce kamma. Indian religions tell us that the law of kamma is a natural law, just like the law of gravity. Buddhism is no different. The Dhammapada describes it thus: 'If one speaks or acts with a wicked mind, because of that, pain follows one. If one speaks or acts with a good mind, because of that, happiness follows one.'

However, not everything that happens can be attributed to kamma. Buddhists believe that kamma is one of five natural forces at work in the universe. There are laws that govern:

- seasonal changes
- biological changes
- moral changes (kamma)
- natural forces
- psychological changes

This means that as a natural law kamma:

- Is not controlled by a god of any kind.
- Operates without any interference from any external source.
- Does not require prayer to a god to influence its effects.
- Is not predestination because we have control over (much of) it.
- Helps to explain the injustices of the world.
- Is unbiased.
- Is not a religious law.
- Does not belong to any one religion.

Kamma is often described as a kind of energy that is everywhere and which permeates the **Universe**. The following attempts have been made to describe how it works:

- It has no beginning. It is like electricity. It operates when the conditions are right.
- It is not simply purely action.
- The motive for actions in kamma is often seen as more important than the action itself.
- Does not apply to buddhas or arahants because they are beyond kamma.
- Is both past and present actions.

The teachings about kamma do not stop there.

What types of kamma are there?

- Reproductive kamma – this is the kamma that is produced when a person is conceived and is retained throughout a person's life.
- Supportive kamma – this is the kamma that makes the reproductive kamma take effect.
- Obstructive kamma – this is the kamma that can get in the way of reproductive kamma taking effect.
- Destructive kamma – this the kamma that stops reproductive kamma from having its effect.

contd

Some Buddhist teachers use the story of Buddha's brother-in-law, Devadatta, to explain how kamma works. His good reproductive kamma meant that he was born into a royal family. His comfortable life and wealth were the result of his reproductive and supportive kamma. His eventual removal from the Sangha began when the obstructive kamma started working and the destructive kamma forced its way in, causing a split in the Sangha and ending in the avici hell which is reserved for those who kill their parents or an arhat, shed the blood of a Buddha, or cause a split in the Sangha.

How does kamma affect a person?

- Weighty kamma – this is the serious good or bad kamma which produces its effect in this or the next life.
- Proximate kamma – this is the kamma done as a person approaches death. There is a custom is many Buddhist countries of the dying person trying to perform good kamma up to the last moment to secure a better rebirth.
- Habitual kamma – this is someone's default kamma performed regularly by habit, or it may be a kamma which is performed once and is recollected and remembered all the time.
- Unspecified kamma – this is the kamma that once done is soon forgotten.

When does kamma take effect?

- Immediate effect – takes effect in this life.
- Subsequent effect – takes effect in the next life.
- Indefinite effect – takes effect in the third life and all future lives after that.
- Defunct – the kamma which no longer has an effect.

Where does kamma take effect?

Buddhists divide the Universe into three worlds. The **kammalokha** is the world humans live in. The kammalokha is split into two planes, the happy plane and the woeful plane. The happy plane is full of bliss and joy and the woeful plane is full of misery and suffering. Good kamma takes place in the happy plane of the kammalokha and perhaps the world above that, but bad kamma only ever takes effect in the woeful plane of the kammalokha. In summary, the effects of kamma are experienced mainly here on Earth by people and, as the Buddha said, nobody can ever escape any of the consequences of their actions.

Kamma generates an energy which is passed on when you die, like the flame of a dying candle being used to light the wick of a new candle, so that energy is reborn in another form. This is called samsara.

DON'T FORGET
Kamma includes thoughts, words and actions and it will always have an effect in this or future lives.

VIDEO LINK
Learn more about the three marks of existence by watching the video on the Digital Zone.

THINGS TO DO AND THINK ABOUT

1. In what ways might kamma be connected to other Buddhist beliefs?
2. Why might the law of kamma make people feel better about the things that happen to them in life?
3. Why might people think that the law of kamma is unfair?
4. What harm might belief in kamma cause to people?
5. Some people think that the law of kamma just doesn't make sense. What beliefs would they point to as being confusing about kamma?

ONLINE TEST
Head to www.brightredbooks.net to test yourself on your knowledge of Buddhism.

BUDDHISM
THE THIRD NOBLE TRUTH

SAMSARA

The Buddha believed that the situation we were in with all this suffering was not hopeless and in his third noble truth he said that the cure is to escape from samsara (nibbana). Let's think first about samsara.

Samsara means rebirth and it comes from the Hindu idea of samsara: a person's atman (soul) moves from being to being as it progresses towards moksha (liberation from rebirth). Its new body depends on how good its kamma is. But the Buddha stated that there is no soul (anatta). So, if there is no soul, what is it that gets reborn? This has presented a problem which continues today.

There are six realms that beings can be reborn into. There are heavens and hells, with the hells being somewhat unpleasant. All of them are temporary and imperfect and because of this all of them involve dukkha which, of course, everyone wants to escape. Manusya-Gati is the human realm and it is the only realm from which beings can escape samsara. In Mahayana Buddhism, bodhisattas are often depicted in the realms helping beings to move through them.

DON'T FORGET

Mahayana Buddhist schools believe in the various heavens and hells of samsara. Not all Buddhist schools believe in the heavens and hells.

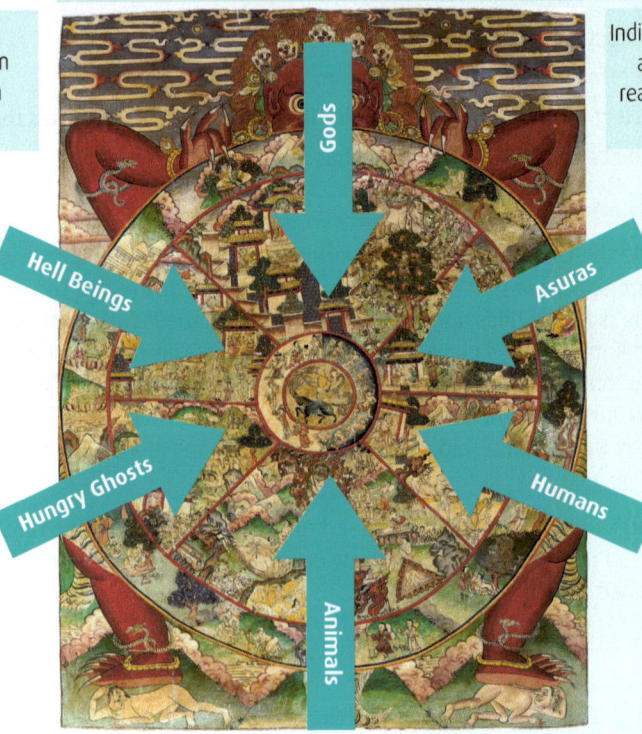

Six realms of rebirth

Death is the transition from one life form to another

Individuals move up and down the realms depending on kamma

Gods, Asuras, Humans, Animals, Hungry Ghosts, Hell Beings

This cycle of samsara can go on forever because:
- We crave things.
- We perform unskilful actions.
- We do not realise we have no soul.
- We depend too much on impermanent things and suffer.
- We have not realised the truth.

VIDEO LINK

Learn more about this topic by watching the video on the Digital Zone.

3. THERE IS A CURE FOR SUFFERING

The Buddha reckoned he had found a way out of this endless cycle of misery and suffering by achieving Nibbana which means:

Nibbana means → blowing out desire
→ freedom from samsara
→ end of craving

The whole world is in flames. By what fire is it kindled? By the fire of lust, hatred and ignorance, by the fire of birth, old age, death, pain, lamentation, sorrow, grief and despair it is kindled.

Where there is nothing, where there is no clinging, the only island, it is called Nibbana. It is devoid of old age, devoid of death.

So, what is Nibbana? It is quite frustrating to understand. It is not like heaven, nor is it a place. It is something that cannot be put into words. It is, perhaps, like describing the colour yellow to someone who cannot see. Nibbana is an experience, impossible to describe and a state of mind. It is not the total destruction of a being. It is only something that can be experienced.

DON'T FORGET

Nibbana is not a place like heaven. It is a state of mind that is beyond description.

THINGS TO DO AND THINK ABOUT

1. What effect might belief in rebirth have on individuals?
2. In what ways is samsara connected to other Buddhist teachings?
3. Would belief in rebirth do individuals more good than harm?
4. What might the positive effects be on a person's actions if they believed in rebirth?
5. Some people say that the Buddhist belief in rebirth is full of contradictions. Give some examples of the contradictions.
6. Connect kamma, samsara and nibbana.
7. Copy out the table below and then look at the World Religions Toolkit. See if you can write in two positive and two negative impacts about believing in kamma and samsara.

Impact	Positive Impact	Negative Impact
Feelings		
Lifestyle		
Actions		

8. One of the hardest beliefs to understand in Buddhism is Nibanna. What makes it so hard for ordinary Buddhists to understand it?
9. 'The Buddha did not make a good job of explaining Nibbana.' What do you think?
10. 'There is nothing attractive about believing in anything which says that after you die, the person you are is completely destroyed.' What do you think?

VIDEO LINK

Watch the video on the Digital Zone for an overview of the four noble truths.

Head to www.brightredbooks.net to test yourself on your knowledge of Buddhism.

BUDDHISM
THE FOURTH NOBLE TRUTH

4. THE WAY TO END DESIRE IS THE MIDDLE WAY

The Buddha knew that it was not enough to say that there was suffering and that he knew the cause of it. He had to provide the solution, which is the Middle Way or the Magga (marga). This is the way to overcome suffering and escape rebirth. It was the Middle Way between the extremes of wealth and extreme asceticism. There are eight steps in the Middle Way, which are collectively called the Eightfold Path and they are divided into three main groups:

- Wisdom to help individuals escape from the endless cycle of birth and rebirth.
- Morality to improve the kamma that is being gathered.
- Meditation to help individuals see the true nature of reality and the self.

The steps do not need to take place in sequence but they all must be done before nibbana can be achieved. Among the various Buddhist schools there is little disagreement about the Eightfold Path (although the exact words used vary from school to school). There are other paths to enlightenment taught in different Buddhist schools but for our purposes we will look at the Eightfold Path.

The steps to do with wisdom are right view and right intention. These steps involve the individual accepting the Buddha's teaching so that they have the right view of the world; they then go on to accept that to obtain release from the world they need to change their ways and avoid harmful thoughts and actions.

The steps to do with morality are about having the right speech, action and livelihood. To take these steps Buddhists must not be involved in any activity that causes harm because this will increase their bad kamma and the suffering of others.

The three steps to do with meditation are right effort, mindfulness and concentration. When taking these steps Buddhists are trying to control their thinking. They are making the effort to control emotions, to avoid negative thoughts and to become detached from the self and from the world by concentration.

Underlying the Eightfold Path are rules about behaviour which will help individuals make progress along the Eightfold Path. There are differences between the different Buddhist schools but there is general agreement on what the precepts are. There are two groups of precepts. The first five are for the laity and there are five more for monks.

Buddhism – The Fourth Noble Truth

The laity

Every Buddhist should try to live by the **Five Precepts** and by doing this they will gain control of the Three Poisons and in time may be able to master the art of meditation when their minds are pure. The five precepts are:

1. Not harming living things
2. Not stealing
3. No sexual misconduct
4. No lying or gossiping
5. No taking of intoxicating substances, such as drugs or drink.

The monks

Monks, or arhats, have more demands placed on them and they have to follow an additional five precepts so they have **Ten Precepts** to master. As well as the original five precepts, monks follow these additional five precepts:

6. No big meals after midday.
7. No dancing, singing or listening to music.
8. No use of perfumes and personal adornments.
9. No use of luxurious beds and seats.
10. No accepting and holding of money, gold or silver.

DON'T FORGET

The Eightfold Path does not need to be followed sequentially and most Buddhists do not complete it in one lifetime.

VIDEO LINK

Learn more about the Eightfold Path by watching the video on the Digital Zone.

THINGS TO DO AND THINK ABOUT

1. In what ways might the Eightfold Path improve the lives of individuals?
2. How practical is the Eightfold Path in this day and age?
3. Why might the Eightfold Path create difficulties for some people?
4. Explain the positive effect that the Eightfold Path could have on a person's actions?
5. If you were following the Eightfold Path, how would it affect your lifestyle?

ONLINE TEST

Head to www.brightredbooks.net to test yourself on your knowledge of Buddhism.

BUDDHISM
THE EIGHTFOLD PATH

TRAINING MINDS: MEDITATION

The last three parts of the Eightfold path are about concentration or **meditation**. It has two main forms.

Vipissana meditation is the oldest form of meditation in Buddhism. It is the type practised in Theravada Buddhism and Buddhist monasteries by monks and nuns. It means insight or clear sightedness. One way to understand vipissana meditation is to look at what vipissana mediation courses consist of. These take place in meditation centres in South East Asia. Here, for example, is what one such course in Cambodia offers:

- A way of transforming yourself through self-observation.
- A focus on physical sensations.
- To see things as they really are.
- An exploration of the connection between mind and body.
- Production of a balanced mind.

But the course is not a cure for any illness, a time-out, or an escape from life's challenges.

It teaches the following methods:

- Breathing to help concentrate the mind.
- Observation of the Three Marks of Existence.
- How to follow the Five Precepts to calm the mind.
- A focus on suffering and its causes to enable freedom from suffering.

It requires considerable practice to perfect these techniques.

Methods vary from school to school and depend to a large extent on each meditation master's own ideas. As with many Indian religions it is the goal that matters most, while the method is decided by the individual.

Samatha meditation is the most commonly practised form of meditation. Although both forms of meditation are believed to be needed to achieve Nibbana, in Mahayana countries in particular many Buddhists perform samatha meditation because it is less demanding than vipassana. Samatha meditation is aimed at calming the mind, and a wide variety of techniques are used to achieve this.

One branch of Mahayana Buddhism is Nicheren Buddhism (also known as Soka Gakkai). Samatha meditation is based on chanting the words 'Nam-myoho-renge-kyo' and parts of the Lotus Sutra. There is focus on a Gohonzon based on the Lotus Sutra. The chanting and focusing leads to a calming of the mind and cultivation of love and respect for others.

In Zen Buddhism, which is practised mainly in Japan, individuals sit upright with their eyes open without slouching to meditate. The palms of their hands face upwards with their thumbs touching. Their wrists touch their thighs and the edge of each hand is placed on the stomach. As with other forms of meditation, breathing is very important. The focus is on slow rhythmic breathing and allowing thoughts to pass without dwelling on them. Individuals are advised to face a wall to minimise distraction. Beginners should attempt 15–30 minutes each day to improve their meditation skills.

In Buddhism it is believed that vipassana meditation can begin once samatha meditation has been mastered.

Linked to meditation is **puja** or worship. Some argue that Buddhists don't worship because they don't pray to a separate divine being called God. When making offerings, praying, chanting and decorating statues Buddhists don't expect the Buddha to hear them.

However, for Buddhists worship involves showing respect to someone they admire, and they perform several actions when they perform puja, including:

- Using idols or images of Buddha or bodhisattas.
- Using incense.
- Lighting candles.
- Placing offerings of flowers before statues or images of the Buddha.
- Using symbols to signify beliefs.
- Performing rituals like bowing before statues.
- Reciting verses from sacred texts.
- Using **mandalas** (designs).
- Using **mantras** (chants).
- Using music.
- Listening to sermons.
- Chanting the Three Jewels.
- Meditating.

There is no set routine:

- Worship can take place at home or in the temple.
- In temples there are shrine rooms containing images of the Buddha. Many Buddhist homes also have shrines with images of the Buddha.
- People bow before the image sitting with their feet tucked under their legs.
- Worship usually begins with chanting the Three Jewels.
- Monks may give a sermon or read from the Tripitaka.
- Offerings will be placed in front of the statue.

contd

Remember that the Buddha and bodhisattas are not worshipped as gods (although it may look like that). Reasons for worship include:

- Showing respect to the Buddha and bodhisattas.
- Using the life of the Buddha and bodhisattas as an inspiration.
- Building up good kamma.
- Reminding oneself of the teachings of Buddhism.
- Showing gratitude to the Buddha and bodhisattas for their teaching.
- Bringing the community together for shared devotion.
- Learning more about the Buddha, the Three Jewels and bodhisattas.
- Celebrating the achievements of the Buddha and bodhisattas.

So when you look at how Buddhists worship, you could be forgiven for thinking that Buddhists believe in God. In fact, wondering about the existence of God in Buddhism is one of the Four Imponderables (acintya). The imponderables are ideas beyond human understanding. The Four Imponderables are:

- The powers that buddhas develop once they have achieved Nibbana.
- The powers individuals gain when practising meditation.
- The exact mechanics of how kamma works.
- How the Universe came to exist.

The last two are closely related to God. Buddha did not believe that God or gods had anything to do with kamma: it was a natural law. He also believed that there was no creator (God) because the Universe is **eternal**. As for these imponderables, he said that humans cannot get an answer to them and that they will be an obstacle to achieving nibbana. There is a debate in Buddhism about whether or not the Buddha denied the existence of God. Quite a number of scholars argue that he never voiced an opinion on this but others claim he either clearly accepted or rejected belief in God. It would be fair to argue that if the Buddha did accept or deny the existence of God then he would have explained his stance, but he didn't. We know that he rejected the gods of the Vedic religion because he saw how they were used by brahmins to retain power and influence. The Buddha's main focus was on removing suffering and attaining nibbana rather than discussing something where the answer was never going to be clear.

 DON'T FORGET

A **bodhisatta** is an individual who has delayed entry into nibbana to help others. This is mainly believed by Mahayana Buddhists.

VIDEO LINK

Learn more about Mahayana Buddhism by watching the video on the Digital Zone.

 THINGS TO DO AND THINK ABOUT

1. How do you think meditation makes people feel?
2. Would meditation change your outlook on the world? Explain your answer.
3. Some Buddhist meditation websites warn people with mental illnesses to seek advice before meditating. Why is this?
4. In what ways might meditation appear to be harmful?
5. Do you see any differences between the worship of God and Buddhist worship? Explain your answer.
6. How might meditation affect your actions in a good way?
7. How might meditation affect your actions in bad way?

 ONLINE TEST

Head to www.brightredbooks.net to test yourself on your knowledge of Buddhism.

BUDDHISM
THREE JEWELS OR REFUGES

SANGHA

At the start we mentioned that understanding Hinduism was important to understanding Buddhism. We also mentioned the Buddha, the Dhamma and the Sangha, known as the **Three Jewels or Refuges** in Buddhism. They are at the heart of Buddhism and in our discussion of The Buddha and his teachings we explored two of the Three Jewels in depth. The remaining Jewel is the Sangha. The Buddhist Sangha was not unique at the time of the Buddha; nor was it unusual for the shramanas to have communities of followers who lived together and practised self-denial and meditation.

There are different understandings of the Sangha:

- It is the whole community of Buddhists according to Mahayana schools of Buddhism.
- It is those who have achieved at least one of the four stages of enlightenment according to some Theravada schools.
- It is only monks and nuns according to other Theravada schools.

We'll look firstly at the Sangha as a community of individuals. Theravada and Mahayana Buddhism differ in some key areas and their understanding of the Sangha is one of these key areas. In Theravada Buddhism the definition of the Sangha is quite narrow. It refers only to ordained monks and nuns. The names for them are **bhikku** (bikhsu) and **bhikkhuni** (bikhsuni). In general, nobody under the age of 20 can be ordained, but it is possible to spend time in a **monastery** up to the age of 20 learning the ropes of monastic life. Once a person has gone through the four stages of enlightenment (which is rare) then they become an arhat (arahant) meaning, that although they are still in their body, they have achieved Nibbana.

Theravadin monasteries have some common features but there are variations depending on local traditions and customs:

- It is common for many men in Theravadin countries to spend a few months living in a monastery to improve their kamma.
- Joining the monastery involves re-enacting the Great Renunciation, having one's head shaved, receiving a new name and reciting the vows of the monastery.
- Monks and nuns are expected to stick to the rules and set an example to local people.
- Monks and nuns are expected to help the laity in ceremonies, provide education in rural areas, support adult education in rural places and support community projects.
- Monks and nuns are supported by local people because it brings good kamma.
- Monks and nuns wear saffron or maroon robes although in Thailand both sexes wear saffron. The colours vary depending on the sect they belong to.
- Monks and nuns have to follow the Ten Precepts.
- Monks and nuns have a further 227 rules to follow (although not every monk or nun knows each one).
- Monks and nuns cannot ask for support, it must be offered.
- Living quarters should be basic.
- Daily routines in monasteries include a very early rise in the morning, two meals, several hours of study and meditation, and performing domestic tasks.
- Monks and nuns attain Nibbana through self-effort and meditating on the Dhamma. Nobody helps monks and nuns become arahants. They revere Sakyamuni Buddha and see him as an inspiration along with the previous 27 buddhas recorded in their sacred books. They await the arrival of Mettreyya who is the only bodhisatta they accept.

ONLINE
Learn more about Theravada Buddhism by following the link at the Digital Zone.

DON'T FORGET
Only monks and nuns can attain Nibbana in Theravada Buddhism.

contd

- Monks and nuns are part of an ancient community that has preserved, protected and developed the Dhamma.
- There are significantly more males than females but efforts are being made to address this imbalance.

In Mahayana Buddhism there is debate about what the Sangha is. There are those who argue that the Sangha is everyone in the Buddhist community whilst others argue it is only those who are on the path. The debate centres around the definition of a word which means 'assembly'. The meaning is vague and could mean both people on the path or anyone who is devoted to the Buddha. In the western world, Buddhists are comfortable with Sangha meaning all Buddhists, while in the homelands of Buddhism, it is traditional to understand the Sangha as lay male and female followers who have accepted the Three Jewels and have started on the path to Enlightenment but who are not, as yet, ordained monks or nuns.

VIDEO LINK

Learn more about Mahayana Buddhism by watching the video on the Digital Zone.

One of the biggest differences between Mahayana and Theravada Buddhism is the Mahayana belief in the **bodhisatta**, an individual who delays entry into Nibbana in order to help others achieve enlightenment. They believe that this is what the Buddha did. They believe that everyone has a buddha-nature and can therefore be helped. After the First Buddhist Council hundreds of years ago, there was a split and the more traditional Theravada Buddhists did not accept the concept of the bodhisatta (amongst other things). Their concern was keeping the tradition of monasteries as the places to attain Nibbana. The Mahayanist Buddhists disagreed and, because of their belief in the bodhisatta, were more concerned with the spiritual development of ordinary people. Therefore, unlike Theravada, the Mahayana Sangha included monks and nuns and lay men and women who were true believers in the Middle Way.

There are many different disciplines and rules in the Mahayana monasteries but they are similar to the Theravada Sanghas except that:

- There are images of Buddhas and bodhisattas.
- The images tend to be used for worship rather than meditation.
- The rituals and ceremonies are more complex and numerous.
- There is a closer relationship with the laity.

THINGS TO DO AND THINK ABOUT

1. 'Shutting yourself away from the world does not do anyone any good apart from yourself.' Do you agree?
2. What positive impact can you see Buddhist monks and nuns having on the community?
3. Some people argue that the Sangha should include all Buddhists; others say it should only include those in the monastery. What do you think?
4. It is quite common in some Buddhist countries for people to spend some time in the Sangha. Explain the positive and negative impacts of doing this.
5. In some Buddhist countries democracy is not particularly strong. Why do you think they might see the Sangha as a threat?
6. 'Monks and nuns just sponge off the lay community and actually bring them no real benefits.' How would you defend the monks and nuns against this accusation?

ONLINE TEST

Head to www.brightredbooks.net to test yourself on your knowledge of Buddhism.

BUDDHISM

THE RELEVANCE OF BUDDHISM

So how do you know how relevant Buddhism is today? Very often religion is seen as something that belongs to the past and no longer has relevance in a scientific world. It may be true that for some people it is irrelevant but for millions of people Buddhism remains very relevant today. What is it that makes Buddhism relevant? What is it that makes some people believe Buddhism is no longer relevant?

IMPACTS OF BUDDHISM

It is too easy to say that religion is no longer relevant and it would be a poor exam answer that tried to argue that case. Whether you believe in Buddhism or not, it is relevant. You may believe that the things like the Sangha is an outdated institution with outdated ideas but again that does not mean to say it is not relevant. Something that has had the impact of Buddhism is a long way off from being irrelevant and unimportant.

In a positive way Buddhism has:

- Shaped much of the Eastern world
- Contributed to the social, moral and cultural development of humanity
- Contributed to the progress of civilisation
- Changed the lives of countless millions of people

But it is not all good. Buddhism has had a negative impact on the world:

- Wars have been fought because of it
- People have lost their lives because they rejected it
- It abused its power
- It developed moral positions which were harmful to the innocent

Buddhism is still something that its opponents 'go after'. You get humanists who want religion in general and Buddhism in particular to have their influence reduced by not having automatic places on the committees of public bodies. Or you get individuals who go after Buddhism because they believe it constrains people and has double standards. You could also have people who object to some Buddhist views on moral issues like non-violence, vegetarianism and asceticism.

contd

Buddhism – The relevance of Buddhism

If individuals feel the need to go after Buddhism then clearly it is still relevant. If it was irrelevant, nobody would bother with it. Furthermore, if individuals, whether for or against Buddhism, feel the need to respond to its beliefs or practices, that also makes it relevant. Once again, if it was irrelevant, nobody would raise an eyebrow over anything that it said or did.

On a more personal level there are individuals who have gained a lot from their commitment to Buddhism. It could be anything from the dramatic change that takes place in a serial killer or drug addict through to the company and comfort Buddhism offers those who are lonely or confused. These things happen. These things are real. Whether you believe Buddhism is true or not, the fact is that the individual sees it as being highly relevant to them.

That being said, there are those who see its relevance in a more negative way at a personal level. They may have been disillusioned by attitudes towards the laity or their doubts about some Buddhist teachings for example. They may have been hurt by the actions of other Buddhists or the pronouncements of the Buddhist leaders on issues like the Five Precepts, attitudes towards non-Buddhists and the power of clergy over the laity. Even though the experience was negative it still remains relevant because it influences individuals and communities in the way they understand the world.

 **DON'T FORGET**

The key things to remember when thinking about religion are impact, importance and relevance.

 ONLINE

Head to the Digital Zone for a video on the Buddha.

THINGS TO DO AND THINK ABOUT

1. Pick out two beliefs in Buddhism that you think are especially relevant to today and explain your choice.
2. Pick out two practices in Buddhism that you think are especially relevant today and explain your choice.
3. Buddhism is often thought to be a religion that has a special appeal to younger people. Why do you think this might be?
4. What might make people think that Buddhism is irrelevant?

 ONLINE TEST

Test yourself on the relevance of Buddhism at www.brightredbooks.net

BUDDHISM
SUMMARY AND CONSOLIDATION

Buddhism is as complex a religion as Christianity. It is practised all over the world but started in India and spread north, south and east of India, where it eventually died out. There are two main translations of scripture which were translated into the languages of the countries in the Far East. Buddhism developed Hindu ideas, innovated new ideas of its own and took over existing customs and traditions where it spread. This has happened with other major world religions and is not unique. It might help to tie this together by using two diagrams:

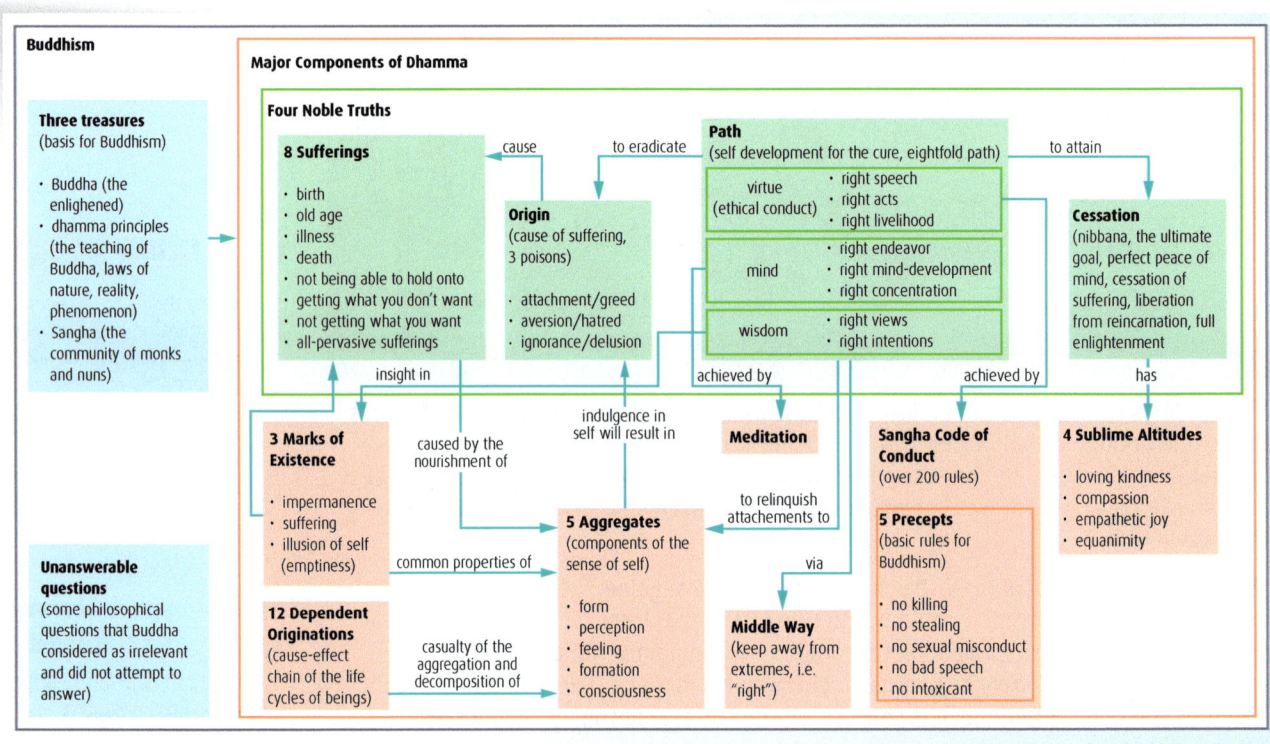

Hinduism and Buddhism

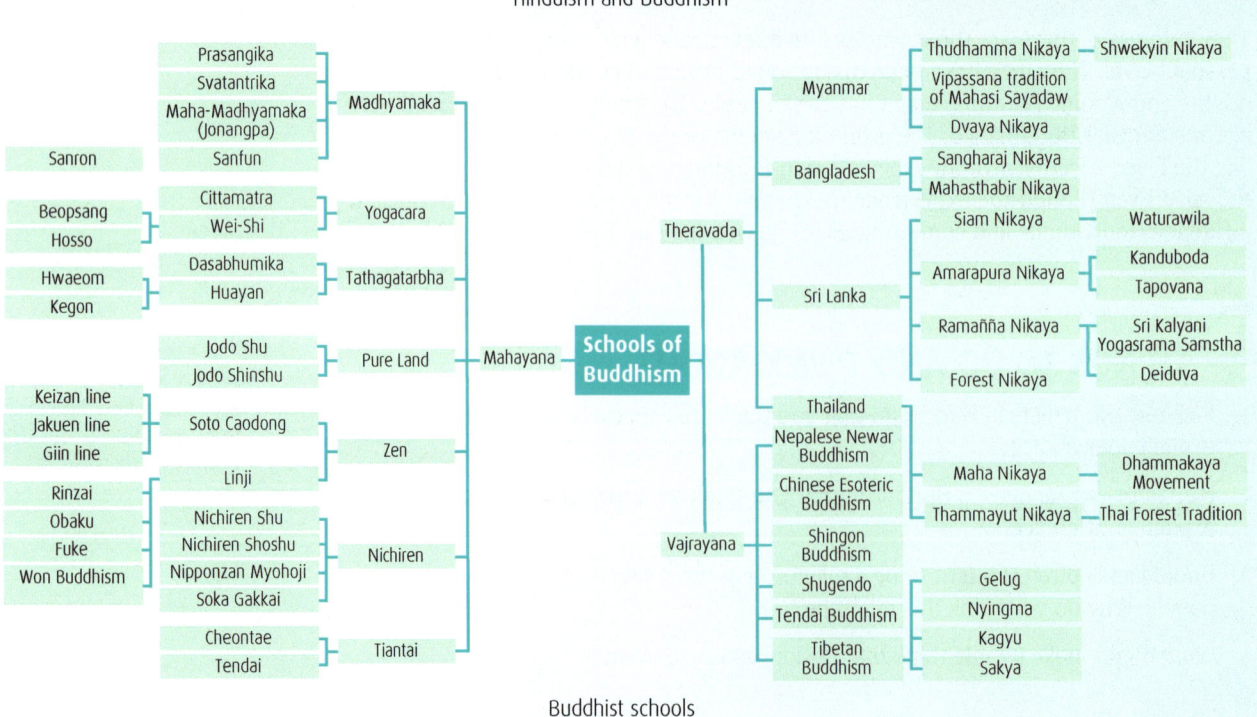

Buddhist schools

Buddhism – Summary and consolidation

 THINGS TO DO AND THINK ABOUT

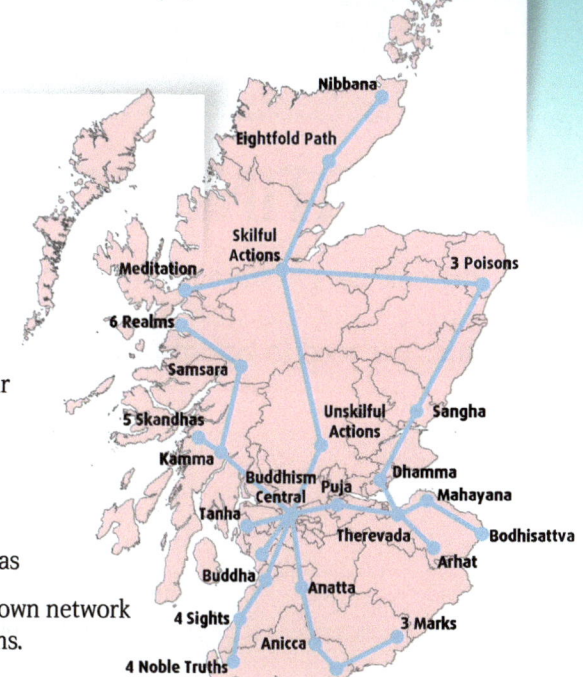

1. Below is a very basic map of the rail network in Scotland. Rather than having stations we have Buddhist beliefs and practices. What you have to do is to try to make different journeys across the map by making connections between the beliefs and practices. Some of the journeys are easy, the connections are obvious, but others require a bit of thinking. Remember, to get to each 'station' you have to make the connection between your destination and your 'home' station.

   Try these journeys:
   - Buddhism Central to Nibbana
   - Meditation to Six Realms
   - Buddhism Central to Three Marks
   - Eightfold Path to Skilful Actions
   - Anicca to Five Skandhas

   Alternatively, get a blank map from your teacher and make up your own network ensuring that there is a clear connection between each of the stations.

   To finish, write out your journeys like an answer in the exam.

2. This activity is designed to get you making connections to show the importance of a belief. The minimum number of connections you have to make is four, hence the title 'Connect Four'. You need to explain what the connection is in each case. Write in Dhamma in the circle at the bottom of the first column. Now try to connect three beliefs or practices to it. If you can get more, then great; if not then try the next column with another belief or practice.

   When you have done a few, write an answer explaining why the belief or practice in the bottom line is important.

3. **The Impact-o-meter**

   To begin with, divide your page into three columns with the headings Belief/Practice, Impact and Explanation. In the first column, note down the beliefs and practices of Buddhism that give people a feeling of security. Then explain your answer. Go on to Hope and write in the first column those things in Buddhism that give a person hope, and so on until you get to the bottom of the grid, making sure each time that you explain your answer.

   You could do the exercise a different way and add in a Yes/No column after the Belief/Practice column. Then you would put a tick or a cross in the Yes/No column and focus on only one belief at a time. So you could write in Three Marks of Existence in the first line, then place a tick or a cross to say whether or not they make people feel secure, and then explain the reason for your choice. You would then repeat the exercise for the Three Marks of Existence for each of the other different impacts.

 **DON'T FORGET**

Buddhism is one religion with many traditions.

 **ONLINE TEST**

Head to www.brightredbooks.net to test yourself on your knowledge of Buddhism.

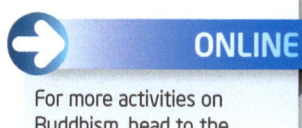 **ONLINE**

For more activities on Buddhism, head to the Digital Zone.

Belief/Practice	Impact	Explanation
Buddha	Security	Belief in Buddha might make people feel secure because…
Kamma, Samsara	Hope	
Sangha, Eightfold Path, puja	Belonging	
	Understanding	
	Responsibility	
	Coping	
	Guilt	
	Superiority	
	Delusion	
	Extreme	
	Superstitious	
	Experience	

33

World Religions

CHRISTIANITY

STARTING POINTS

It would be a mistake just to launch straight into Christianity without first setting the scene. Simply telling the story of Jesus is not enough. To help make sense of things which will crop up later we need to look at four key things:

- God
- Judaism
- humanity
- Jesus.

GOD

God is a spiritual being and has no physical body. He is **eternal** and has always existed. He is personal which means that He wants to have a relationship with intelligent beings like humans.

God created the Universe out of nothing. He knows everything that can be known and has the power to do anything that can be done.

God is **immanent** and deeply involved in the world by manipulating events in history, but at the same time He is **transcendent** and does not depend on the world.

God is good and hates evil. He is also all loving and forgiving. Because He is good He is also just. This means that He is fair in all his dealings with humanity.

And humanity knows God is like this because God has revealed Himself to humanity in various ways.

God reveals Himself in three main ways. He reveals Himself in the Bible, in history through His chosen people (the Jews) and through Jesus.

Trinity

Add to these attributes a belief in the **Trinity**. God is made up of three equal parts, the Father, the Son and the Holy Spirit. They are the same substance. Exactly how this operates has been debated for hundreds of years by the Church because Bible teaching on it was not clear. It is a very important part of Christian belief.

DON'T FORGET

The Trinity is the belief that God is made up of three equal parts, Father, Son and Holy Spirit.

ONLINE

Learn more about the conceptions of God by following the link at www.brightredbooks.net

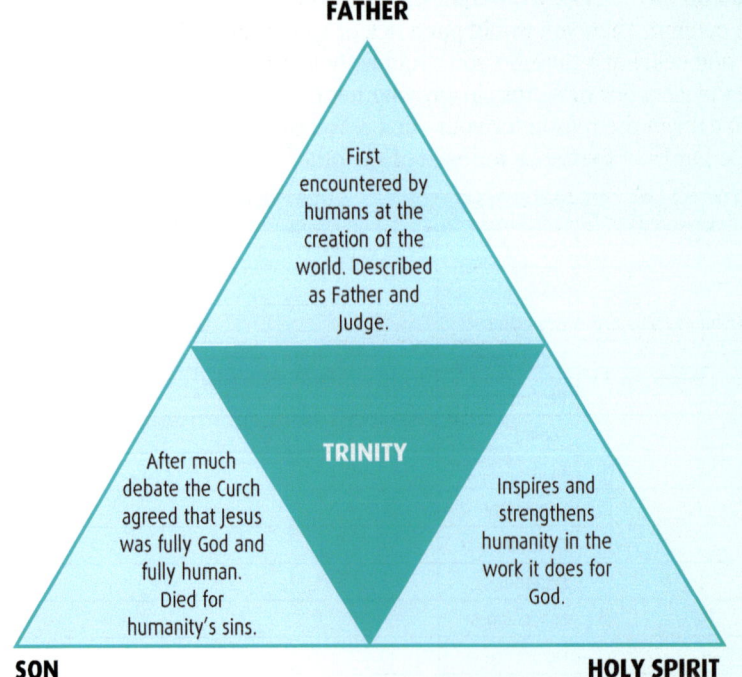

Christianity – Starting points

JUDAISM

You cannot understand Christianity unless you have some understanding of the Jewish religion. Jewish beliefs about God are similar to, but not exactly the same as, Christian beliefs about God, except for the Trinity which is completely rejected by **Jews**. There are a few Jewish beliefs that need to be explained so that Christian beliefs make more sense; these are:

- Atonement
- Sacrifice
- Covenant
- Messiah

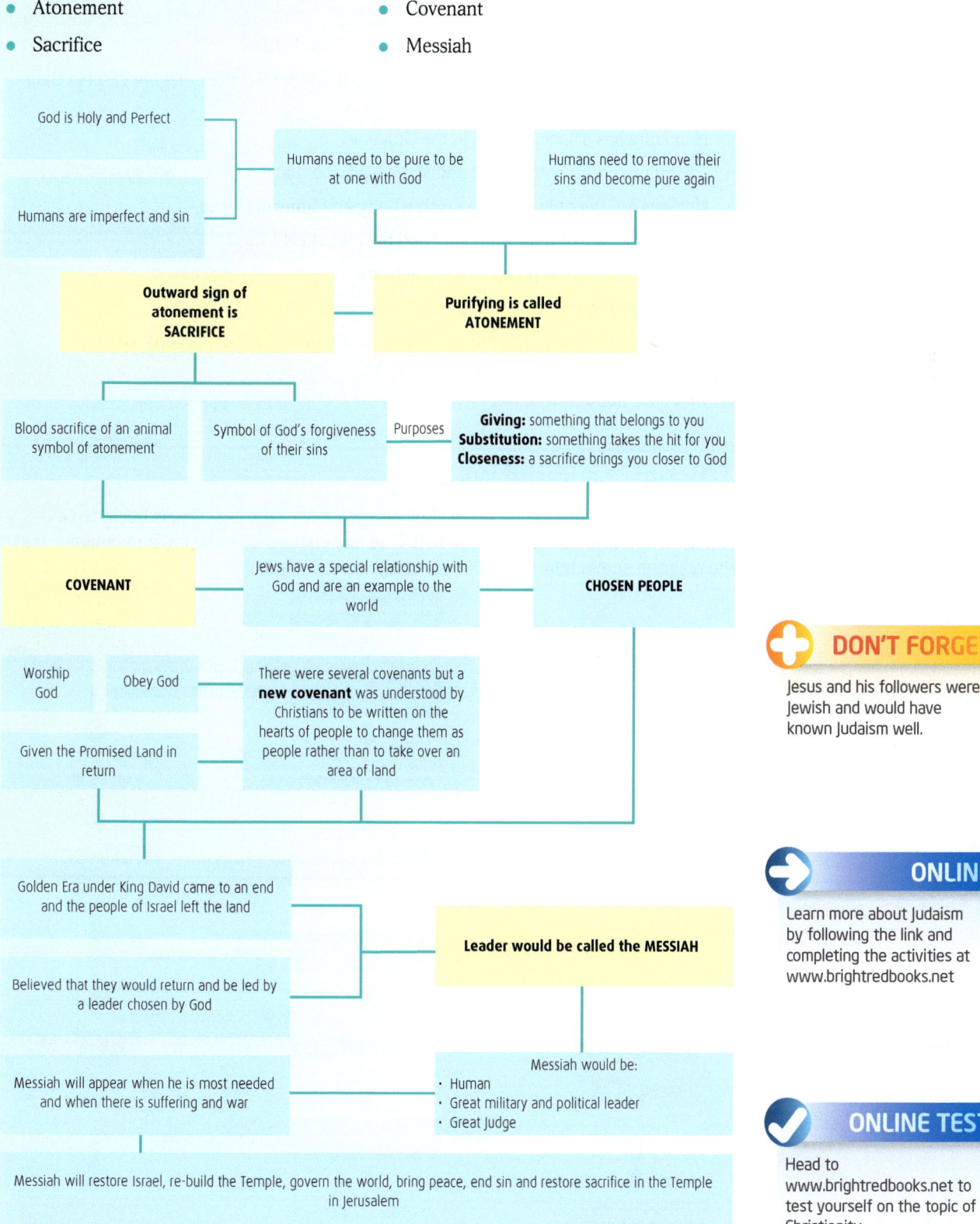

DON'T FORGET

Jesus and his followers were Jewish and would have known Judaism well.

ONLINE

Learn more about Judaism by following the link and completing the activities at www.brightredbooks.net

ONLINE TEST

Head to www.brightredbooks.net to test yourself on the topic of Christianity.

CHRISTIANITY

HUMANITY, A SPECIAL CREATION

Christians believe that humanity is a special creation of God. It is different from anything else in the world and here is why.

HUMANITY WAS CREATED IN GOD'S LIKENESS

Coming out of this belief are the following points and ideas:

- Humanity was created in God's likeness and therefore worthy of higher respect than any other creature.
- Humanity has a special place in the Universe.
- Only humans are able to love and serve God and that is why they are so special.
- Humans are the only creatures with a body and **immortal** soul.
- God created a world for humanity and they must care for it.
- Humans are God's representatives on Earth.
- God created humans, male and female.
- Humans must remain humble and always remember that God is Lord over the Universe.
- God gave humans free will.

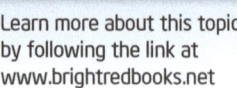

ONLINE

Learn more about this topic by following the link at www.brightredbooks.net

THE GIFT OF FREE WILL

The reason that humans can make choices and obey or disobey God is because God decided to give human beings **free will**. God had choices when he created humans, and the diagram shows how these choices could have worked.

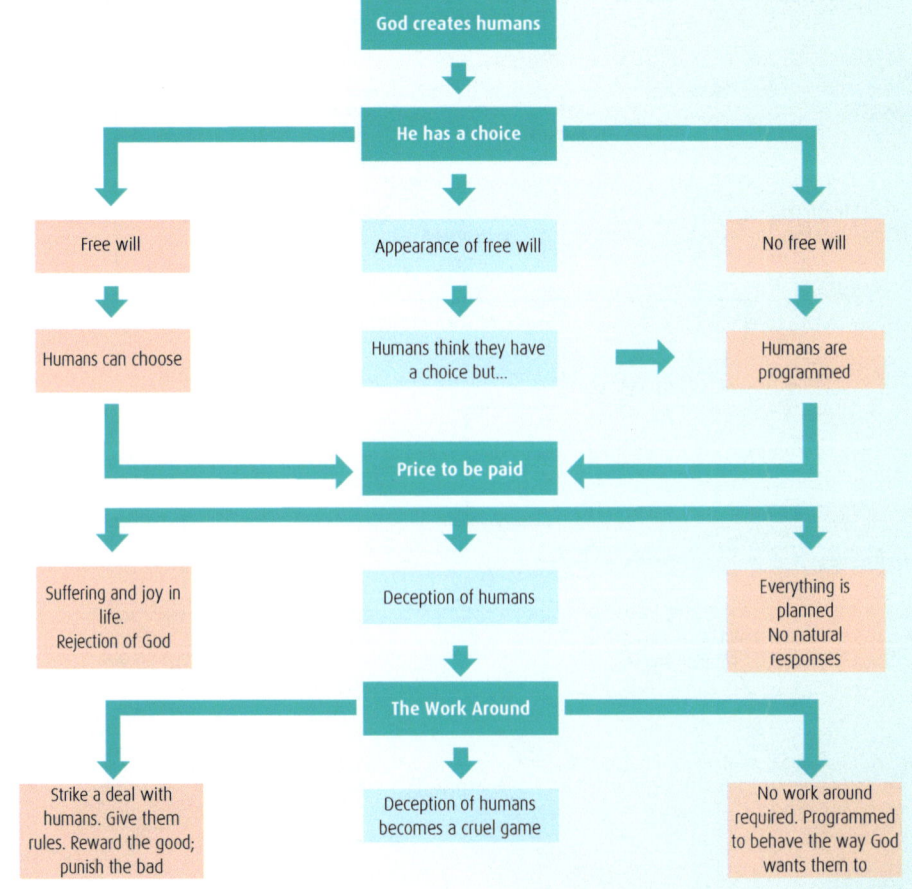

DON'T FORGET

Free will is understood in different ways by different Christians.

contd

36

Christianity – Humanity, a special creation

Christians believe that God chose to give them the gift of free will. This free will allows humans to make choices and to accept or reject God's commands. When a person disobeys God's commands it is called **sin**. There has to be consequences of sin. People need to be rewarded or punished because God is a just God. He has set the Universe up so that good is rewarded and evil is punished.

Christians have different ways of understanding free will. What follows is a brief summary of the main views.

The Bible: tells us that Adam and Eve used their free will to disobey God which indicates that the Bible supports the idea of complete freedom to choose.

Roman Catholic Church: follows the Bible in that it believes humans have complete free will so that they can enter freely into a relationship with God.

Protestant Church: there is agreement that humans have free will but some Protestant Christians believe that God has planned everything. Others believe that God knows all the possible outcomes but he lets humans choose, and others believe that humans are totally free.

Orthodox Church: the Orthodox Church speaks of something called "synergy". What this means is that God always respects the choices humans make. God has set up an arrangement where, working as a team with God, humans can be saved from their sins. God does not force this choice on humans. The offer of help from God is freely given and humans can freely choose to accept or reject God's help.

DON'T FORGET

Many Christians consider the story of Adam and Eve to be symbolic of man's disobedience and not historical.

VIDEO LINK

Watch the video at www.brightredbooks.net to learn more about original sin.

ORIGINAL SIN

So, in summary:

- Humans have free will.
- Humans have a sinful nature.
- God wanted humans to have free will.
- Humans abused this free will by disobeying and rejecting God.
- Humans can choose whether or not they wish to be saved by God.
- Augustine, a religious scholar, proposed a solution to this.

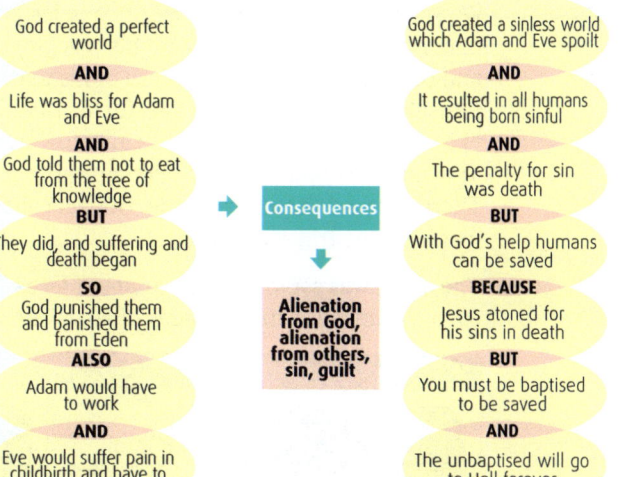

THINGS TO DO AND THINK ABOUT

Always refer to the World Religions Toolkit on page 6 when tackling questions. The information there will help you develop your skills of analysis and evaluation

Three words dominate Christian teaching about humans and they are:

Likeness   Free will   Sin

1. Make up a mind map for each one. Make sure each mind map is on the same sheet of paper and well apart from the others.
2. Draw connecting lines between Likeness, Free will and Sin and explain the connections.
3. In what ways might Christian beliefs about humans be a positive thing?
4. Overall, are Christian views on humans positive or negative?

ONLINE TEST

Test yourself on this topic at www.brightredbooks.net

37

CHRISTIANITY

JESUS: HOLY WEEK

Now we are going to work backwards in the life of Jesus starting with his Death and Resurrection and end with his birth. It might seem an odd approach but it will make more sense once you've read everything. Remember that when Jesus was alive nobody wrote down anything he said or did. Later on, after his death, people in the very new Church decided that before those who knew him died, they should start writing down information about his life and teachings. This information was written down to persuade people that Jesus was indeed a very special person rather than a straightforward biography of Jesus. The people who wrote believed that Jesus was a special person and they presented information which makes a very strong case for that.

ATONEMENT

The word atonement means at-one-ment. In Christianity it means that individuals are at one with God because Jesus had changed the situation by dying on the cross and rising from the dead. Jesus, his followers and those who wrote and taught about Jesus were very aware of the whole idea of atonement and the meaning and importance of blood sacrifices to Jewish people so a lot of effort went into showing that Jesus had a very clear purpose in life.

VIDEO LINK

Check out the clip on the Digital Zone for a brief overview of Holy Week.

THE DEATH OF JESUS

We will start with the blood sacrifice of Jesus. He had spent between one and three years making a name for himself with his teachings, growing in popularity around Galilee and building up a following. Word of his teachings spread and he eventually arrived in Jerusalem where the most powerful Jewish religious teachers were based. They did not like what they were hearing. The eventual outcome of this was that Jesus was sentenced to death and crucified by the Romans after one of his disciples, Judas, betrayed him. There is broad agreement in the **Gospels** about what happened but only one Gospel mentions the trial with Herod.

The scene was set for the execution of Jesus. There are several key characters and events involved in the last week of Jesus' life.

The Characters			
	**Peter** Peter was Jesus' closest disciple. Jesus predicted that Peter would deny knowing him three times. His prediction proved to be right.		**Judas Iscariot** A disciple who wanted Jesus to overthrow the Romans. Paid by the Sanhedrin to set Jesus up for arrest.
	Caiaphas Leader of the Jewish court (**Sanhedrin**) who put Jesus on trial and found him guilty of blasphemy. The court passed Jesus on to Herod then Pilate.		**Pontius Pilate** The Roman Governor. He had an uneasy relationship with the Sanhedrin and was not keen to get involved in religious disputes.
	**Herod** The Jewish king who interviewed Jesus after he was sent to them by the **Sanhedrin**. He passed him on to Pilate.		**Mary Magdalene** She was Jesus' closest female friend. It was Mary and other women who saw to it that Jesus was put in the tomb. She was the first to meet the resurrected Jesus and she told the disciples about his resurrection.

contd

Christianity – Jesus: Holy week

The Events
Sunday
Known as **Palm Sunday**. Jesus entered Jerusalem on a donkey and people laid down palm fronds for him.
Monday
Went to the Temple. Disgusted by the stalls selling things and threw them around: called the Cleansing of the Temple.
Tuesday
Met with Jewish leaders to explain his actions the previous day. Discussed his beliefs and ideas with them. Some loved them, some hated them.
Wednesday
Judas agrees to betray Jesus and hand him over to the Sanhedrin the next day.
Thursday
Last Supper with the disciples. Gave them bread and wine. Arrested in the Garden of Gethsemane after Judas betrayed him. Tried by Sanhedrin, Herod and Pilate.
Friday
Known as **Good Friday**. Executed by means of crucifixion. Body taken to the tomb which was sealed and guarded.

THINGS TO DO AND THINK ABOUT

1. In what ways is Jesus' death linked to the Jewish beliefs of atonement and sacrifice?
2. Why do you think Judaism and Christianity are so closely linked?
3. 'The whole blood sacrifice and atonement belief is complicated. God could have found an easier way to forgive humans.' Do you agree? Give reasons.

DON'T FORGET

There are strong links between Jesus' death and Jewish beliefs about sacrifice and atonement.

ONLINE TEST

Test yourself on this topic at www.brightredbooks.net

CHRISTIANITY

JESUS: FINAL DAYS

THE TRIALS

Jesus went through two or three trials on the Thursday night/early Friday morning by the Sanhedrin, King Herod and Pilate. The questions focused on two claims: one that he was the Messiah or **Son of God** which would see him punished on religious grounds, and the other on him being the King of the Jews which would see him punished on political grounds.

Sanhedrin		Herod		Pilate	
Question	Reply	Question	Reply	Question	Reply
He was accused of saying that he could destroy the Temple and rebuild it in 3 days. (Matthew, Mark)	No reply	No details of questions but he did question him for quite a while	No reply	Are you the King of the Jews? (Matthew, Luke)	You have said so.
Tell us if you are the Christ, the Son of God (Matthew)	You say that I am.			Have you no answer to make? See how many charges they bring against you. (Matthew)	No reply
Are you the Christ, the Son of the Blessed? (Mark)	I am.			Are you the King of the Jews? (John)	Do you say this of your own accord, or did others say it to you about me?
If you are the Christ, tell us. (Luke)	If I tell you, you will not believe, and if I ask you, you will not answer.			Am I a Jew? Your own nation and the chief priests have delivered you over to me. What have you done? (John)	My kingdom is not of this world. If my kingdom were of this world, my servants would have been fighting, that I might not be delivered over to the Jews. But my kingdom is not from the world.
Are you the Son of God? (Luke)	You say that I am.			So you are a king? (John)	You say that I am a king. For this purpose I was born and for this purpose I have come into the world—to bear witness to the truth. Everyone who is of the truth listens to my voice.
High priest asked him about his teaching (John)	I have spoken openly to the world. I have always taught in synagogues and in the temple, where all Jews come together. I have said nothing in secret. Why do you ask me?			What is the truth? (John)	No reply

You read in the Gospels that only Luke reports that he was taken to Herod. The Gospels would appear to agree that:

- Jesus' answers were vague.
- Jesus was careful not to make any claims that would upset the Romans.
- Jesus did not answer questions that would get him into trouble.
- Jesus knew that their minds were made up.
- Jesus knew that their aim was to get him executed.

Many questions remained after Jesus' death and resurrection. A few years after Jesus died a Jewish convert to Christianity, a man named Paul, along with a few others developed the original beliefs about Jesus and began to study his reported words in more depth to try to make sense of the events surrounding him. The main areas of debate were:

- The nature of the **resurrection**.
- The meaning of the resurrection.
- The nature of Jesus.

Christianity – Jesus: Final days

THE NATURE OF THE RESURRECTION

There was a debate about the form of Jesus' resurrection...

Even although their views of the purpose of Jesus' death and resurrection may vary, Christians do agree on several key points:

- Jesus' death and resurrection were no accident.
- Jesus reversed the effect of original sin.
- His death was a sacrifice that needed to be made to wash away human sin.
- Jesus knew that he had to sacrifice himself.
- There must be an acceptance of Jesus to be atoned (forgiven).
- Jesus is the Son of God and the Messiah.

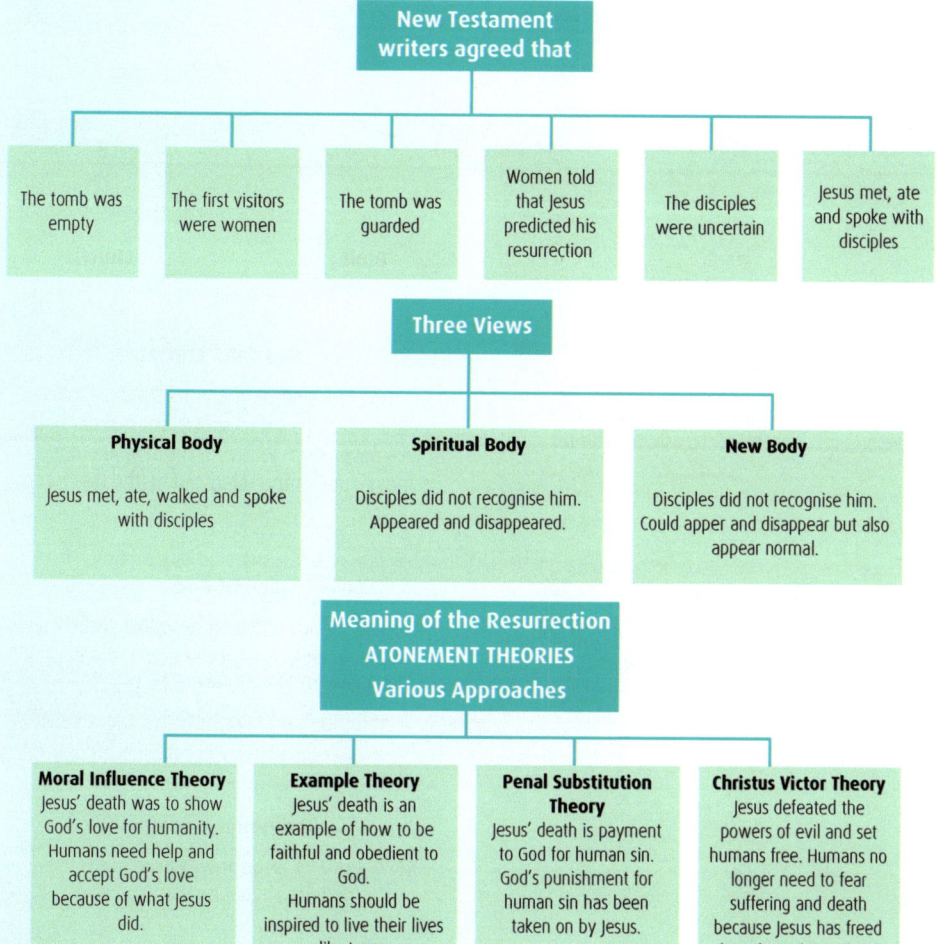

New Testament writers agreed that
- The tomb was empty
- The first visitors were women
- The tomb was guarded
- Women told that Jesus predicted his resurrection
- The disciples were uncertain
- Jesus met, ate and spoke with disciples

Three Views

Physical Body — Jesus met, ate, walked and spoke with disciples.

Spiritual Body — Disciples did not recognise him. Appeared and disappeared.

New Body — Disciples did not recognise him. Could apper and disappear but also appear normal.

Meaning of the Resurrection — ATONEMENT THEORIES — Various Approaches

Moral Influence Theory — Jesus' death was to show God's love for humanity. Humans need help and accept God's love because of what Jesus did.

Example Theory — Jesus' death is an example of how to be faithful and obedient to God. Humans should be inspired to live their lives like Jesus.

Penal Substitution Theory — Jesus' death is payment to God for human sin. God's punishment for human sin has been taken on by Jesus.

Christus Victor Theory — Jesus defeated the powers of evil and set humans free. Humans no longer need to fear suffering and death because Jesus has freed them from their power.

VIDEO LINK
Watch the documentary on this on the Digital Zone.

DON'T FORGET
The Resurrection of Jesus is believed to show that sins have been forgiven.

THINGS TO DO AND THINK ABOUT

1. Which statement do you disagree with the most?
   - 'The resurrection never happened.'
   - 'Some kind of resurrection took place.'
   - 'The resurrection is based on the superstition of ignorant ancient people.'
   - 'Something happened otherwise Christianity would never have become a religion.'
2. Why is the Resurrection such a mystery for many people?
3. Why is the Resurrection of Jesus so important?
4. 'It's complicated!'
   Why might some people think that the beliefs around the Resurrection are complicated?
5. Do you think belief in the Resurrection would change a person's lifestyle?

ONLINE TEST
Test yourself on this topic at www.brightredbooks.net

CHRISTIANITY

JESUS: HIS NATURE AND TEACHING

THE NATURE OF JESUS

The study of who Jesus was is called **Christology**. This involves working out who and what Jesus was. The main areas for study are his nature and his identity.

Jesus believed that he had a special relationship with God and that he was sent by God on a mission. He called God 'Father' which was quite different from the way that God was generally spoken about at the time.

Nature of Jesus		
They said		
Jesus	Bible	Church
Son of Man Used most often by Jesus. The meaning is uncertain but maybe it has to do with his mission.	**Messiah/ Christ** Used by friends and enemies alike. A title meaning he was God's special messenger. Jesus was never keen to accept the title and it was developed in the Bible and by the Church.	
Human or Divine Jesus never made any comment on this but he clearly felt he had a special relationship with God.	**Son of God** Used by friends and enemies alike. Jesus was never keen to accept the title and it was developed in the Bible and by the Church.	
	Redeemer/Saviour Never used by Jesus. It was used in the Bible and developed by the Church.	
	Incarnation Never used by Jesus. It was used in the Bible and developed by the Church. It means that Jesus was God in the flesh.	

THE PARABLES OF JESUS

Christians believe that Jesus had an ideal world in mind when he taught. This is referred to as the **Kingdom of God**. He used parables (stories with meanings), direct teaching and his actions to show how he thought people should live. What follows are examples of his teaching and actions to give you an idea of his message.

contd

Christianity – Jesus: His nature and teaching

Jesus wanted to put across some of the following points:

- God loves and forgives humans.
- Love your enemies; do good to those who hate you. Do to others what you would have them do to you.
- Jesus' message will start small but change every person and the world.
- Humans have free will, God will not force choices or his love on to humans.

God loves and forgives humans	
Words	**Actions**
Read the parable of the Lost Son in the Bible. A link can be found on the Digital Zone.	Read the story of Zacchaeus in Luke's Gospel. For Christians today the meaning of Jesus' words and actions have not changed: • God remains the same, prepared to love and forgive no matter what humans have done. • God will seek out and invite the lost back into the Kingdom of God. • The words and actions provide humanity with hope nobody is a lost cause. • The parable reminds Christians that a relationship with God is not about following rules and routines. It is something that is very personal, emotional, something that requires love and a desire for closeness. • It may remind Christians today that the most important part of their faith is a loving relationship with God, and not automatically following rules and responsibilities. • Zacchaeus reminds Christians that if your heart is sincere God will forgive.

Love your enemies; do good to those who hate you. Do to others what you would have them do to you.	
Words	**Actions**
Read the parable of the Good Samaritan in Luke's Gospel. A link can be found on the Digital Zone.	Read the story of when Jesus ate with tax collectors and sinners in Mark's Gospel. Christians believe that these words and actions teach the following: • Love your enemies and be good to those who hate. • Love of enemies and haters has to be done as if it is meant. • Treat others the way they should treat you. • Help anyone with no questions asked. • Go the extra mile.

Jesus' message will start small but change every person and the world.	
Words	**Actions**
Read the Parable of the Yeast in Matthew's Gospel. A link can be found on the Digital Zone.	Read how Jesus sent his disciples out to spread his message in Mark's Gospel. A link is available at the Digital Zone. Today Christians view these words and actions like this: • Faith in God is something that will grow steadily inside people. • God's message will start out small and become something big in the world. • God's message will change people from the inside. • There is duty to spread the teachings of Jesus.

Have faith	
Words	**Actions**
Read Matthew's Gospel chapter 8 for what Jesus said about the birds. A link can be found on the Digital Zone.	Read the story of the Blind Beggar in Luke chapter 18. Christians understand these stories to mean that: • It is important to have faith in God. • Faith has to be a simple faith. • God loves humanity and cares for all creation. • With faith, anything can be achieved.

DON'T FORGET

Parables are stories with meanings behind them.

ONLINE

Find the link to these parables at www.brightredbooks.net

ONLINE TEST

Test yourself on this topic at www.brightredbooks.net

CHRISTIANITY

JESUS: BEGINNINGS

ONLINE

Read this parable at www.brightredbooks.net

JESUS' TEACHINGS

In summary, Jesus taught that:

1. There is a Kingdom of God. God is the ruler of the Kingdom and He loves everyone, forgives everyone and takes people back.
2. The Kingdom will be small to begin but will steadily grow into something great.
3. To enter into God's Kingdom, humans must love their enemies, forgive others, help the needy and have faith in God and serve Him.
4. Go out and tell the world about the Kingdom of God.
5. The Kingdom of God is not a place, it is a mix of beliefs and attitudes a person has.

But there were other things that Jesus taught:

6. Humans should give thanks to God in prayer.
7. Be prepared for people to reject the message.
8. Be prepared to suffer for spreading the message.

So, how did Jesus end up going on this mission?

It all began when he went to hear a preacher named John the Baptist. He was **baptising** people and symbolically washing away their sins. John said that Jesus was the one who was going to do greater things than him.

After this Jesus went into the desert for about six weeks. The **New Testament** tells us that during this time his mission in life became clear. The Gospels say he was tempted by the Devil and that he was tempted to do three things:

- **Turn stone into bread** – Jesus was hungry and the temptation was to use his powers to make life easy for himself. He didn't, though, because that wasn't what his powers were for.
- **Become a military ruler** – If Jesus said he was the Messiah and led a revolt against the Romans he would quickly become popular. He wasn't tempted by this because God had to be first in his life.
- **Throw himself off a high tower without injury** – People would see him perched on the high tower and landing uninjured after throwing himself off it. People would immediately see that he was the Son of God. Jesus wanted to change people's hearts and not impress them into accepting him with miracles.

These are called **Jesus' Temptations** and after forty days in the desert (forty days is just an expression for a long time, it does not literally mean forty days) Jesus was clear in his mind what his mission was to be.

DON'T FORGET

This event in Jesus' life is called the Temptations.

THE CHRISTMAS STORIES

The idea of Jesus' coming to Earth on a mission leads us to the question of where he came from. According to Matthew and Luke, Jesus was born in Bethlehem.

Matthew was writing for Jewish people in the church, and this is why he does not explain any Jewish customs; his readers would have already known about them. He was sure that Jesus was the Messiah and his gospel is full of **Old Testament** prophecies he believed Jesus had made true. Luke believed that Jesus was the Messiah. He was anxious to stress that Jesus died for everyone and that he was the Messiah for everyone.

contd

Since both of these men were writing for different audiences and for different purposes, it is not such a surprise that the birth stories are so different.

Matthew	Luke
Jesus descended from King David	**Mary** was a virgin and engaged to **Joseph**
Angel visited Joseph	Joseph was a descendent of King David
Joseph became engaged to Mary who was expecting Jesus	Angels spoke to Mary
The Holy Spirit had made her pregnant	The Holy Spirit made her pregnant
Joseph took Mary home to have Jesus	A census was called so Mary and Joseph had to go to Bethlehem
Jesus was born in Bethlehem	Jesus was born in a stable because there was no room at the inn
Mary was a virgin	Angels spoke to shepherds in the fields
There was a bright star which the Wise Men followed	Shepherds visited Mary, Joseph and Jesus
Wise men from the East visited Jesus	
Herod tried to kill baby Jesus	
Escaped to Egypt when Herod was hunting them	

Whether or not Christians believe in the gospels of Matthew and Luke is another matter. There are those that believe they are literally true. However, there are Christians who, while accepting that Jesus was a real person, have their doubts about the Christmas stories, and treat them as symbolic, transmitting the authors' messages.

ONLINE

Read the story of Jesus' birth in Luke Chapter 2 and Matthew Chapter 1 on the Digital Zone.

ONLINE TEST

Test yourself on this topic at www.brightredbooks.net

THINGS TO DO AND THINK ABOUT

1. Make a list of the main events in each birth story of Jesus and their differences.
2. Look back at the Jewish beliefs earlier in this chapter. What Jewish beliefs can you see coming through in these stories?
3. Does it matter that the stories are different?
4. Does it matter if these stories are not treated as historical?
5. How might the birth of Jesus give Christians hope?
6. Does the birth story of Jesus really matter, is it not enough to know that he existed?
7. What do you think the parable of the Lost Son teaches about God?
8. What do you think Jesus' actions towards Zacchaeus teaches about God?
9. Show how the actions of Jesus are connected to the words of the parable of the Lost Son.
10. How realistic are these teachings in this day and age?
11. What do you think the parable of the Good Samaritan teaches about treatment of others?
12. What do you think Jesus' actions in eating with sinners showed?
13. Show how the actions of Jesus are connected to the words of the Good Samaritan.
14. How realistic are these teachings in this day and age?
15. What do these words and actions say about Jesus' vision for his message?

CHRISTIANITY
GOD AND HIS PEOPLE

SALVATION AND THE AFTERLIFE

Now we have reached the next group of beliefs held by Christians. Christians believe in achieving **salvation**. Salvation involves believing that you have a soul and that you are going to suffer the consequences of your sins. In Christianity, three beliefs are linked closely to salvation and they are:

- Judgement
- Heaven
- Hell

> Everyone has an eternal soul. It is spiritual and made impure by human sin.

> Salvation = the eternal soul being freed or reunited with God.

> The Roman Catholic Church identifies two types of sin: venial (less serious) and mortal (very serious) sins. Other churches teach more generally about sin.

> Sin is when a person does wrong by disobeying God's commands.

> Some believe judgement takes place when you die and that there will be a Day of Judgement at the end of the world when God will judge the living and the dead.

> God is fair and just and he makes a judgement on a person's life so there is reward or punishment at the end of it.

> God said that if people believed in Jesus, in return he would forgive sins; Jesus took the sin of the world upon himself and died for humanity's sins.

> The New Covenant is God's way of helping humans avoid punishment for sins. Jesus' sacrifice atoned for human sin.

> The Bible is not clear about what Heaven is but most Christians believe it as being in the presence of God forever.

> Those who accept Jesus will be rewarded in Heaven in the afterlife.

> The Bible is not clear about what Hell is but most Christians see Hell as not being in the presence of God forever. It is not a place: the Hell of terrible suffering and eternal torment is believed as being in the minds of artists and writers from a long time ago.

> Those who choose not to accept Jesus will be called to account for their sins. They will be punished for their sins in Hell in the afterlife.

Summary of beliefs

Christian beliefs about salvation and the afterlife can be summarised as:

- God is a loving, merciful, forgiving, fair and just God who cannot let sin go unpunished.
- Every person is made up of a body and a soul. The body is mortal. The soul is eternal.
- Every person is born with a sinful nature.
- God set up covenants between himself and humans. Humans failed to honour various covenants.
- God wanted to restore his relationship with humans and set up a New Covenant.
- The New Covenant involved God becoming human in the form of Jesus. This is called the **Incarnation**.
- Jesus was sacrificed on the cross as a sacrifice for the sins of humanity.
- Belief in Jesus is necessary if a person wants to be forgiven by God.
- Every person is judged by God. Those who believe Jesus is their **Saviour** are innocent because they believe Jesus died for their sins. This is known as atonement.
- Jesus' resurrection was proof that God had forgiven the sins of humanity.
- Those who believe in Jesus end up being in the presence of God forever in Heaven. Those who do not believe in Jesus end up being separated from God for ever in Hell.

Christianity – God and His people

WORSHIP

Now we know what the key ideas of Christianity are, how do Christians respond to them? They respond in several ways but we are going to look at two main responses, how they worship and how they put Jesus' ideas and teachings into practice.

Types of worship

There are many different ways in which Christians worship.

This provides an overview of worship in Christianity. Now we'll take a closer look at the Christian faith.

Private	Public	Annual	Regular
Prayer Bible Study	Praise Bible readings Prayer Community gatherings	Advent Christmas Holy Week Easter	Prayer Praise Bible Study Communion

Private: own time, at home, individual or small groups.

Public: church building, led by clergy, open to all, held often.

Annual: remember Jesus, special events, special customs.

Regular: church building, home, with or without others.

| Practised by some Christians but by no means all. Can be short prayers and brief Bible readings or small groups who meet in each other's homes to study, pray and enjoy each other's company. | Done regularly by most Christians. The main worship is on a Sunday and is led by a member of the clergy. It is the biggest weekly gathering of Christians. There is usually music, prayer, Bible readings and teaching. | Usually done to celebrate and remember big events in the life of Jesus. Some churches have other big annual events but these are the ones that pretty much every church celebrates. Attendance is usually high. | These are worship activities that can happen more than once a year. The most important one is communion. Some churches do it daily, others do it less often. |

VIDEO LINK

Watch the video on the Digital Zone to learn more about Christian worship.

DON'T FORGET

Most Christian churches celebrate communion.

ONLINE TEST

Test yourself on this topic at www.brightredbooks.net

Here are some of the things that happen when Christians meet to worship God:

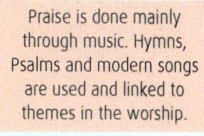

Praise is done mainly through music. Hymns, Psalms and modern songs are used and linked to themes in the worship.

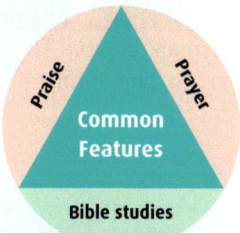

Prayer is talking to God. Prayers usually include thanks to God, praise to God, requests to God to help others and oneself.

Bible studies — Studied to learn more about the faith. Study is often linked to current events or special times of the year.

In addition, there the major celebrations tied to the key events in Jesus' life. During the celebrations and commemorations of these key events there will be Bible study, praise and prayer, all linked to the themes of Jesus' life.

47

CHRISTIANITY
CELEBRATING JESUS

CHRISTMAS CELEBRATIONS

The day

There are many **Christmas** celebrations. One custom is that Jesus' birthday is traditionally celebrated on 25 December. The truth is that nobody knows exactly when Jesus was born. Around the year 350 AD the leader of the Church (the Pope) and his advisers decided that 25 December would be the date when the birth of Jesus would be celebrated, although they knew that this was most likely not the actual date.

The reason they chose this date was because on it people celebrated Saturnalia, a festival which was not Christian. It was an old festival and it was decided that Christmas should take over from it.

Giving

Giving is widespread at Christmas. Christians give presents and cards. This is an ancient custom and is believed to have come from the festival of Saturnalia. The Church allowed the giving to carry on stating that it was symbolic of God giving the world Jesus. Giving presents to each other became a tradition.

Light

The theme of light is important at Christmas. Christmas lights decorate streets, trees and homes. Light was a theme in Saturnalia because it stood for the return of the sun. Christianity has changed the meaning of light at Christmas. Light traditionally stands for good and dark stands for evil. Jesus was seen as the light of the world because he overcame evil.

Love and Eternal Life

Another theme is eternal life. This is symbolised through the appearance of evergreens like mistletoe at Christmas time. Its origin is a story about a Norse god who was killed with an arrow made of mistletoe, after which it was decided mistletoe would never hurt anyone again. The custom was taken over by Christians who used it as a reminder of the love they should have for each other, and the love they should have for God because God is a god of love.

Holly is another custom borrowed from an old religion; it is associated with the birth and death of Jesus. The white flower stands for the purity of Mary, the leaves for the crown of thorns, and the red berries for the blood of Christ. The bark stands for the bitterness of Jesus suffering on the cross.

The Christmas fir tree is one of the best known customs of Christmas. It came from Germany and grew out of an old German religion. The fir tree became a symbol of eternal life because it was an evergreen, and in time people decorated it with fruit.

EASTER CELEBRATIONS

Easter is a very important time of the year for Christians because of the Resurrection and the beliefs associated with it.

Palm Sunday marks the beginning of Holy Week when Christians remember this as the day when Jesus entered Jerusalem. During Holy Week some churches have services every day, remembering the events of Holy Week as told in the Bible.

Good Friday was the day Jesus died. Services are sometimes held for as long as the three hours that Jesus was said to have hung on the cross. These are emotional services

contd

Christianity – Celebrating Jesus

when Christians remember the suffering that Jesus underwent for them. Ceremonies and services take place all over the world and they tend be quite solemn. People go to church throughout Good Friday.

On Holy Saturday (or Easter Eve) the mood begins to change. All the ornaments which were taken out of the church on Good Friday are cleaned and brought back into church. Colourful flowers are displayed. In some parts of Europe at midnight on Easter Eve shouts go up: 'He is risen!' This is the sign that it is now Easter Sunday, when Jesus came back from the dead. In some churches a vigil is kept all night, with Christians staying in church all night waiting for the dawn of Easter Day, the time Jesus rose again.

Easter Day services are held in all churches. These services are full of great joy because Christ is risen. The churches will be filled with bright flowers; the songs sung will remind the congregation of Jesus' victory over death, and how he saved humanity from sin. Readings from the Bible will relate the exciting events witnessed by the disciples. The sermon or homily will speak of hope for all mankind as a result of Jesus' resurrection.

EASTER CUSTOMS

Laurel

This is a shrub that is evergreen. Like many other Christian symbols the laurel has its origins in non-Christian religions. For Christians today it is a sign of everlasting life.

Eggs

This custom has been going on for a long time. Eggs are a sign of new life, and other religions that preceded Christianity used them symbolically. For Christians their meaning is very significant. From the outside an egg looks dead but contains life. The rolling of eggs symbolises rolling away the stone.

Paschal candle

In many churches there is a special candle known as the Paschal candle. The name comes from the Hebrew word Pesach which means Passover. The paschal candle burns for forty days, from Easter until Ascension Day, the day Jesus entered Heaven. The flame is a reminder that Jesus is the light of the world, and the forty days for which it burns is a reminder of the time Jesus spent with his disciples before going to Heaven.

 VIDEO LINK

Watch the video on the Digital Zone to learn more about worship.

THINGS TO DO AND THINK ABOUT

1. Why is Easter so important to Christians?
2. What difference does Easter make to the actions of Christians?
3. In what ways is Easter connected to sacrifice and atonement?
4. Do you think that a Christian's beliefs about Easter would change their life?
5. What arguments could people make to say that Easter is no longer relevant?
6. Does it matter what kind of Resurrection Jesus had?

 **DON'T FORGET**

Easter celebrates the Resurrection of Jesus.

 ONLINE TEST

Test yourself on this topic at www.brightredbooks.net

CHRISTIANITY
COMMUNION

Christmas and Easter are the two main annual events in the Christian calendar but **communion** is another big event which takes place in most Christian churches (Quakers and the Salvation Army are two examples of churches that do not celebrate communion). In some churches communion is daily but in others it takes place weekly or several times a year.

THE IMPORTANCE OF COMMUNION

Communion is probably the most important act of worship in Christianity. It is based on an event in Jesus' life. That event was the last meal he had with his disciples when he gave them bread and wine. He told them that the bread represented his body and that the wine stood for his blood (which would be sacrificed for them the next day). Different churches have their own way of celebrating this meal, but the significance of it for each is similar.

This celebration can be called different things including:

- Eucharist – thanksgiving for Christ
- Holy Communion
- The Breaking of the Bread
- The Lord's Supper

The **communion elements** are symbolic. The bread stands for the **body of Jesus** which was to be broken the day after he had the Last Supper, and the wine **stands** for his blood which was to wash away the **sins** of humanity. Communion gives Christians the opportunity to remember the last night of Jesus' life and that he **sacrificed** himself for the sake of humanity.

Let's look at how communion is performed in three Christian denominations:

- Orthodox
- Roman Catholic
- Church of Scotland

The communion services of each of these three denominations have a similar order, actions and words to other services. There are Bible readings and **prayers**. Most of these will mention the Last Supper Jesus had with his disciples. The other **words** used are the words of the Nicene Creed, when Christians state what they believe. The table below shows the similarities and differences between communion services.

VIDEO LINK

Learn more about Holy Communion by watching the video on the Digital Zone.

contd

50

Christianity – Communion

	Church of Scotland	Roman Catholic	Orthodox
Bible	✓	✓	✓
Praise	✓	✓	✓
Nicene Creed recited	✓	✓	✓
Prayer	✓	✓	✓
Frequency	Three or four times a year	Daily	Daily
Participation	• Anyone who is baptised • Anyone who the Kirk Session is satisfied understands what it is about • Any child who the Kirk Session is satisfied understands what it is about	• Must have confessed any mortal sins • Must be a practising Catholic • Must be baptised	• Must be members • Must be baptised • Must have confessed sins recently • Must have gone through mental preparation, including the day before communion • Must be a practising Orthodox Christian
Presence of Jesus	• The bread and wine symbolise the body and blood of Jesus	• Bread and wine are kept in a tabernacle behind the altar • The priest asks the Holy Spirit to transform the bread and wine • The bread and wine are transformed to become the body and blood of Jesus • They may look the same but they have been transformed	• Bread and wine are brought into Church in the Great Procession • Bread and wine are taken to the altar at the front of the church which is behind decorated closed doors • The priest asks the Holy Spirit to transform the bread and wine • The bread and wine become the actual body and blood of Jesus
Distribution of the elements	• Minister repeats the words of Jesus and gives bread and wine to the church elders first • People are given bread and wine by church elders • Minister has communion at the same time as the people	• Priest repeats the words of Jesus and takes the bread and wine • People come to the front of the church and receive the bread and wine from the priest • Some churches only give the bread (which is actually a wafer)	• Priest repeats the words of Jesus • People go forward to receive bread and wine from the priest • Priest uses a communion spoon to give them the elements

DON'T FORGET

Different names are used for the Eucharist.

ONLINE TEST

Test yourself on this topic at www.brightredbooks.net

THINGS TO DO AND THINK ABOUT

Now you are going to explain different themes in Christian worship. So, for example with the first bullet point you have to find three worship activities that celebrate the life of Jesus and explain how each one celebrates his life. You do the same for each bullet point. This will help you analyse beliefs.

- Three worship activities that celebrate the life of Jesus.
- Three worship activities that involve learning.
- Five worship activities that might be sad.
- Three worship activities that might be happy.
- Three worship activities that are the most relevant today.
- Two worship activities that might cause debate.
- Two worship activities that show the importance of Jesus.
- Five worship activities that are community events.

CHRISTIANITY
LIVING THE LIFE

As we have already learned, one big part of being a Christian is the spiritual life and the worship that accompanies it. Another is living the life of a Christian, and this is achieved by following the example Jesus outlined in his teaching and demonstrated through his actions.

When Jesus taught about the Kingdom of God he portrayed a new world where love and care for others would be a priority. The Church takes this very seriously.

TYPES OF CHRISTIAN ACTION

There are various types of action that Christians take to carry out the work of the Church. Many Christians *donate* via collections at church services and through other avenues, and this money goes towards funding the work of the Church at home and abroad. It helps pay for staffing, transport costs, accommodation, supplies and training in each of the different areas where the Church works.

Prayer is another type of action that Christians take. They believe that through prayer God will make good things happen which will benefit those being prayed for.

Another form of action is *campaigning*. Christians are often involved in campaigning for various causes and against injustices. They may be involved in anti-nuclear or anti-racism or anti-abortion demonstrations, and protests against government or local council policy changes.

Christians may also give their *time*. This can be through taking part in voluntary activities run by the Church (or any type of local community or charity work. The work may not be linked to the Church but the reason for doing it is Christian). They want to give time their time to help those less fortunate than themselves in the same way that Jesus did.

Christians may also give their *talents*. Jesus taught Christians to share their talents. Some Christians work for the Church in education, in medicine, in caring and in counselling. They may work only for the Church or they may work in addition to their regular job.

Christianity – Living the Life

CARING

All churches are known for their caring activities. The Church of Scotland, through its Social Care Council, CrossReach, has specialist dementia care homes for older people, provides support and assistance to the homeless and people with learning difficulties, and also runs residential rehabilitation services for individuals with substance misuse problems.

Christians do not necessarily manage the care homes and support centres but they are run in line with Christian principles. Some congregation members volunteer to help in them and congregations help finance them with donations from weekly collections at church services.

Some churches provide care and shelter for the homeless. Homeless shelters are also run by the Salvation Army and by joint church ventures. Volunteers from local churches help out by serving food, providing warm clothes, and by showing compassion towards individuals who may feel disregarded by other parts of the community.

The church also supports individuals suffering from addictions. The objective is to free them from addiction and religious belief may help with that.

THINGS TO DO AND THINK ABOUT

Train of Thought

Below is a very basic map of the rail network in Scotland. Rather than having stations we have Christian beliefs and practices. What you have to do is to try to make different journeys across the map by making connections between the beliefs and practices. Some of the journeys are straightforward and the connections are fairly obvious, but others may require a bit more thinking. To get to each station you have to make the connection between your destination and your home station.

Try these journeys:

- Christianity Central to Heaven
- Prayer to Jesus
- Christianity Central to Messiah
- Judaism to Covenant
- Sacrifice to Judgement

Alternatively, get a blank map from your teacher and make up your own network, ensuring that there is a clear connection between each of the stations.

To finish with, write out your journeys like an exam answer.

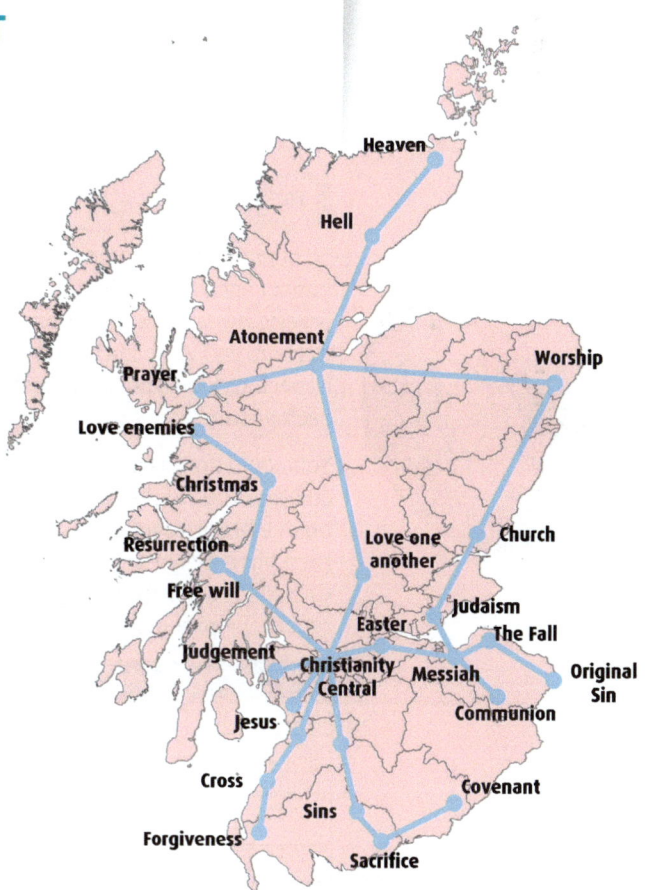

53

CHRISTIANITY
RMPS SKILLS

ACTIVITY: Connect Four

This activity is designed to get you making connections showing the importance of a belief. The minimum number of connections you have to make is four (hence the title Connect Four). You need to explain what the connection is in each case. Write in SIN in the circle at the bottom of the first column. Now try to connect three beliefs or practices to SIN. If you can connect more than three then that is great. Move on to the next column with another belief or practice.

When you have done this for a few beliefs and/or practices, write out answers explaining why they are so important.

ACTIVITY: Project

The examples over the last few pages show some of the ways in which Christians involve themselves in helping others. You now have the chance to explore this further. Choose any one of the activities carried out by Christians and explore the work done by a Christian organisation of your choice. At the end of this project you should re-read the section above then give your view of church involvement in the world.

ACTIVITY: The Impact-o-meter

To begin with divide one page into three columns with the headings Belief/Practice, Impact and Explanation. In the first column write down the Christian beliefs and practices that give Christians a feeling of security. Then explain your answer. Go on to Hope and write in the first column those things in Christianity that give a Christian hope. Carry on until you reach the bottom of the grid, providing an explanation for each answer.

You could do this exercise a different way and add in a Yes/No column after the Impact column. You would place a tick or a cross in the Yes/No column and would only focus on one belief/practice at a time. So, for example, you could write Jesus in the first line then put a tick or a cross in the Yes/No column indicating whether or not Jesus gives Christians security, then go on and explain the reason for your choice. You would then repeat the process for Jesus for each of the different impacts.

Belief/Practice	Impact	Explanation
Jesus	Security	Belief in Jesus might make people feel secure because...
Sin	Hope	
Worship	Belonging	
	Understanding	
	Responsibility	
	Coping	
	Guilt	
	Superiority	
	Delusion	
	Extreme	
	Superstitious	
	Experience	

Christianity – RMPS skills

IMPACT ON LIFESTYLE

 Impact Mosaic

1. Find some squared paper. Down the left-hand side of the page put the heading Belief or Practice (as shown below). Next, write the words along the row beside it. Then add the beliefs and practices you have studied into the column beneath it (as below).
2. Get some coloured felt-tip pens or pencils.
3. Work your way down the list on the left like this: Look at the first belief/practice in the top row (Nature of God). Ask yourself how big an impact this has on the lifestyle factor of Christians shown in each of the rows (for example, **Materialism**):
   Colour in the cell in RED if you think it has a big impact.
   Colour in the cell in ORANGE if you think it has an impact of some sort.
   Colour in the cell in GREEN if you think it has very little or no impact.
   Then go on to the impact of the Nature of God on Habits and colour in the cell accordingly.
4. Carry on down the list for the impact of the Nature of God on each lifestyle factor of Christians then move onto the second belief/practice in the top row (Humans in God's likeness).
5. Continue until you have completed the table.

Belief or Practice	Nature of God	Humans in God's likeness	Free will	Sin	Jesus as the Incarnation of God	Death and Resurrection of Jesus	Judgement	Heaven and Hell	Following Jesus' Teaching and Example	Worship
Materialism										
Habits										
Friends										
Stress										
Routines										
Self-denial										
Renunciation										
Statement										
Sacrifices										
Decision-making										
Integration										
Daily Living										

 ## THINGS TO DO AND THINK ABOUT

The next step is to make these into answers you could use in the exam. To do this, rewrite what you have put in the Impact-o-meter and the Impact mosaic and make each into a paragraph or two to give an ideal evaluation answer. It might look something like this:

> Religion has an effect on the daily lives of Christians. The greatest effect comes from beliefs about God because they will feel more secure and less alone in a universe where there is a God behind everything. Christians also believe in free will. Again, this could have an impact on their behaviour or actions because they are going to have choices and be held responsible for these choices by God. Their daily actions will also be affected because for some Christians, they will wish to worship God in small ways in their daily lives in their thoughts, words and deeds.

CHRISTIANITY
THE RELEVANCE OF CHRISTIANITY

So how do you know how relevant Christianity is today? Very often religion is seen as something that belongs to the past and no longer has relevance in a scientific world. It may be true that for some people it is irrelevant but for millions of people Christianity remains very relevant today. What is it that makes Christianity relevant? What is it that makes some people believe Christianity is no longer relevant?

It is too easy to say that religion is no longer relevant and it would be a poor exam answer that tried to argue that case. Whether you believe in Christianity or not, it is relevant. You may believe that the Church is an outdated institution with outdated ideas but again that does not mean to say it is not relevant. Something that has had the global impact of Christianity is a long way off from being irrelevant and unimportant.

- In a positive way Christianity has:
- Shaped the world we live in
- Contributed to the social, moral and cultural development of humanity
- Contributed to the progress of civilisation
- Changed the lives of countless millions of people

- But it is not all good. Christianity has had a negative impact on the world:
- Wars have been fought because of it
- People have lost their lives because they rejected it
- It abused its power
- It developed moral positions which were harmful to the innocent

Christianity is still something that its opponents 'go after'. You get humanists who want religion in general and Christianity in particular to have their influence reduced by not having automatic places on the committees of public bodies. Or you get individuals who go after Christian beliefs about God and the Universe and how mistaken Christians are. You could also have people who object to some Christian views on the death penalty, gender equality or euthanasia.

If individuals feel the need to go after Christianity then clearly it is still relevant. If it was irrelevant, nobody would bother with it. Furthermore, if individuals, whether for or against Christianity, feel the need to respond to its beliefs or practices, that also makes it relevant because, once again, if it was irrelevant, nobody would raise an eyebrow over anything that it said or did.

On a more personal level there are individuals who have gained a lot from their commitment to Christianity. It could be anything from the dramatic change that takes place in a serial killer or drug addict through to the company and comfort Christianity offers those who are lonely or confused. These things happen. These things are real.

Whether you believe Christianity is true or not the fact is that the individual sees it as being highly relevant to them.

That being said, there are those who see its relevance in a more negative way at a personal level. They may have been disillusioned by attitudes towards their sexuality or their doubts about some Christian teachings for example. They may have been hurt by the actions of other Christians or the pronouncements of the Church on issues like gay marriage, divorce, abortion or terrorism. Although the experience was negative it still remains relevant because it has influenced individuals and communities in the way they understand the world.

Christianity – The relevance of Christianity

ACTIVITY: Relevance of Christianity

In this activity, you should write a belief or practice in the first column (for example, sin). In the second column, you should state whether it is relevant or irrelevant, and then in the final column you should provide evidence to support your judgement.

Belief/Practice	Relevant/Irrelevant	Evidence
Sin	Irrelevant – it does not make much difference to the way people live	Sin isn't something people worry about today because they do not see life as a big test or that God judges them. This is an old and outdated belief.

ACTIVITY: World Cup of Relevance

We are going to have a knockout tournament. You can enter any beliefs or practices in it (although eight have already been suggested). The purpose is to get you thinking about relevance by pitching one belief or practice against another. You can play with friends if you like. Here's how to play:

1. Each match in the tournament involves two players. You should have a timer and allow one minute for each player's answer. A goal is scored for each answer. If no answer is given then play passes to the other player without a goal being scored.

2. Decide who will be the home player and who will be the away player. In each match the top belief/practice is taken by the home player, and the bottom belief/practice is taken by the away player. For instance, in the Sin versus Free will match, Sin is the home player because Sin is on top. The home player starts and gives one reason why Sin is relevant today. The away player then gives one reason why Sin is irrelevant today. Then the away player gives one reason why their belief or practice (in this case, Free will) is relevant today, and the home player says why that belief or practice (Free will) is irrelevant, and so on. Each player has three attempts. If it is a draw after three attempts each then it is sudden death until one player wins.

In the next round the same procedure is followed except this time it is four goes each, then five each in the final.

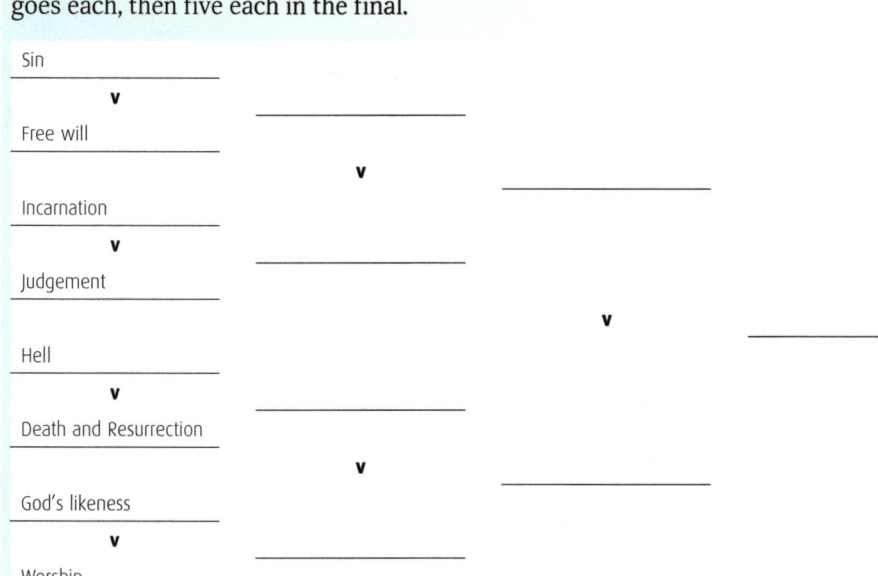

Morality and belief

TOOLKIT

MAKING MORAL DECISIONS

Deciding what is right and what is wrong is one of the toughest challenges human beings face. Below is what is behind the moral decisions that everyone makes. Few people stick to one ideal when they decide what is right and what is wrong. Instead, they base their decision on a number of factors.

CONSEQUENCES

One widely accepted piece of reasoning behind deciding what is right or wrong is considering the consequences. There are various calculations people make to measure consequences:

- The amount of suffering a decision will cause.
- The amount of happiness a decision will cause.
- Whether the consequences will uphold commonly held values.
- Whether or not the consequences will produce the best possible result.

Why use this approach?	What's the downside?
• No fixed rules • Flexible • Allows for circumstances • Promotes happiness • Makes people responsible	• Lack of rules • Consequences are unpredictable • Some things are the same regardless of the situation • Fails to promote the value of human life over happiness

DUTY

'Right and wrong should be decided by what your duty is…'

This is another way of approaching decision-making. Consequences should not play a part in moral decision-making. Here's what often plays a part:

- Some things are always wrong.
- Some things are always right.
- Do what is right, regardless of the consequences.
- Avoid what is wrong, regardless of the consequences.
- Fairness and justice.

Why do it?	Why not?
• Clear rules • Human life is valued • Some things are wrong in themselves • Clear-cut • Fair and just	• Too rigid • Too many exceptions to the rule • People's duties come into conflict • Circumstances need to be taken into account • Lack of evidence of absolute moral rules

AUTHORITY

In certain circumstances people in positions of authority tell us what is right and what is wrong. These people could be in the Houses of Parliament, where politicians debate and determine the laws of the land. It could also come from leaders of religious organisations who believe that God (or a similarly important figure in their religion) would recommend making the same decision. Or it could come from experts in

contd

Toolkit – Making moral decisions

a particular area who know a lot about the subject in question. This is summarised as decisions about right and wrong being made by state authorities, religious authorities and expert authorities. Between the three of them they advise us what is right and what is wrong. Authority might be:

A reliable guide for us because...	An unreliable guide for us because...
• State representatives are elected to do what the people want • The state's priority is to protect its people • The state will take advice • Experts know the issues inside out • Experts have no political or religious bias • Religious leaders are interested in the welfare of all • Religious teachings are clear • Religious leaders consult experts	• The state can get it wrong • The state can abuse its power • The state can make unjust laws • Experts may have vested interests • Experts can be wrong • Religion may make claims about God's will that are wrong • Religious teachings are out of date • Religion has its own agenda

RIGHTS

Another key part of moral decision-making comes from respecting an individual's rights. Since the end of the Second World War many countries have adopted the Universal Declaration of Human Rights. These are written down as articles and there are 30 of them. We don't need to know all of them for this course but here are some that have particular relevance:

- We are all born free and equal.
- Don't discriminate against anyone.
- We all have the right to life.
- Torture is forbidden.
- You have rights no matter where you are.
- We are equal before the law.
- No unfair imprisonment.
- We are innocent until proven guilty.
- We have a right to privacy.
- We have the right to believe in what we want.
- We have the right to say what we think.
- We have the right to social security.
- We all have the right to a good life.
- We have a duty to protect the rights and freedoms of other people.
- Nobody can take away our rights.

 **DON'T FORGET**

The Universal Declaration of Human Rights is agreed but not universally followed.

Look at these individually and you probably wouldn't argue with any of them. They seem to be fair and reasonable, and you'll find that many of the rules in your school are based on these rights. There are good things and not so good things about these.

Good	Not so good
• Establishes a baseline of rights for all • Guarantees rights • Cross-cultural • Promotes rights, freedom and responsibilities • Promotes the common good • Not harmful • Makes values absolute	• Presumes everyone has equal rights forever • Does not permit removal of rights • Does not respect different cultures and traditions • There can be conflicts between rights • Assumes values do not change • Potential harm results from some rights

 VIDEO LINK

Learn more about the Universal Declaration of Human Rights by watching the video at the Digital Zone.

 ONLINE TEST

Test yourself on morality and justice at www.brightredbooks.net

 THINGS TO DO AND THINK ABOUT

World Champion Right

In boxing, the champion takes on challengers. The winner of the match wins by a knockout or on points. Knockouts are clear defeats. Victories on points are often close fights. You are going to try to work out which is the Champion Right.

Choose a right. Match it against another right. Which one is more important? By a knockout or on points?

Either explain why it's a knockout or a victory on points. Repeat against other rights.

Morality and belief

MORALITY AND JUSTICE

CAUSES OF CRIME 1

The causes of crime are difficult to understand. There is disagreement between experts and other people. Your view of the causes of crime will affect your view of punishment, how we should respond to crime, and whether or not we should support **capital punishment**.

The causes of crime can be divided as follows:

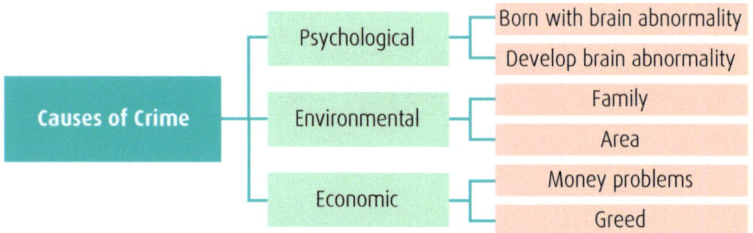

PSYCHOLOGICAL CAUSES OF CRIME

If a person is born with, or develops, a brain abnormality then they may have problems making judgements or with self-control. The moral issues include:

- Whether or not we should be concerned about the consequences of the actions of individuals with brain abnormalities since they only affect a few people.
- Whether or not the state has a duty to care for people with brain abnormalities no matter what they do.
- Whether or not the individual's human rights are being overlooked.

ENVIRONMENTAL CAUSES OF CRIME

If a person is born or grows up in a difficult family circumstance and/or neighbourhood, then they may have problems making judgements or with self-control. The moral issues include:

- Whether or not we should be concerned about the consequences (crimes) which arise from difficult family circumstances and/or neighbourhood.
- Whether or not it depends on how difficult things are for an individual.
- Whether or not society is to blame for not fulfilling its duty to support individuals born or growing up in difficult family circumstances and/or neighbourhood.

ECONOMIC CAUSES OF CRIME

If an individual is experiencing poverty or is greedy then they may have difficult choices to make and/or lack self-control. The moral issues include:

- Whether or not we should be concerned about the consequences (crimes) which arise from people experiencing poverty and/or being greedy.
- Whether or not it depends on what is causing the poverty and/or greed (no matter what crime is committed).
- Whether or not individuals know naturally that committing crimes is wrong.

One of the major concerns affecting each of these causes is that if it is agreed that they are causes over which people do not have any control, then why are we charging, sentencing and punishing them?

DON'T FORGET

The three main causes of crime are Psychological, Environmental and Economic.

Morality and Justice – Causes of crime 1

CAUSES OF CRIME: RELIGIOUS VIEWS

Buddhism

The Buddha's teaching on crime and punishment can be found in a part of the Sutta Pitaka called the Cakkavatti Sutta. The Buddha tells the story of a king who ruled by the Dhamma, but who then changed and stopped giving to those in poverty: as a consequence of this poverty became widespread, theft increased, violence increased, and killings increased.

Causes:

- Failure to follow the Dhamma = *Lack of virtues*
- Greed is the key cause = *Economic*
- Three poisons of greed, hatred and delusion lead to unskilful actions which lead to crime = *Psychological*

So Buddhism narrows it down to not having enough virtues to be a good person, to economic problems, hatred of others, and deluding yourself into thinking that the things you gain through crime are permanent, when in fact they are anicca, just like everything else. So we have a mix of causes.

Christianity

In biblical times, the causes of crime were not well understood. Cruelty, torture and the death penalty were common and there were very few prisons. Laws were considered to be from God and he gave humans:

- Free will, the ability to choose how we act – *Psychological*
- Laws to help humanity use their free will responsibly – *Obey authority*
- A natural inclination to do good or evil – *Natural*

So, from the Bible it appears that the causes of crime come from our free will, which was given to humans by God as a gift. The main cause of crime is to ignore the laws that God has given to use free will responsibly. These laws are forgotten about by societies and this leads to crime. This then is seen as humanity's fault.

Islam

The Qur'an and the **hadiths** tell us a lot about how Muhammad viewed the causes of crime. In these books there is a lot written about punishment, some of it very severe.

Allah gave:

- The ability to make choices – *Natural*
- Strict rules and expectations – *Obey authority*
- The ability to make the wrong choices – *Psychological*

Islam is clear that the choices are humanity's and that if it chooses to follow its animal nature and rebel against the rules of Allah then that is its decision.

VIDEO LINK
Head to the Digital Zone to watch a video on the causes of crime.

ONLINE TEST
Test yourself on morality and justice at www.brightredbooks.net

THINGS TO DO AND THINK ABOUT

1. From religious teaching on the causes of crime, find examples where religion seems to see environmental, economic and psychological causes of crime.
2. What additional causes of crime do religious people identify?
3. Based on their understanding of the causes of crime, how would you expect religious people to respond to crime?

MORALITY AND JUSTICE
CAUSES OF CRIME 2

What do others have to say about the causes of crime? You will see that there is little agreement.

THE EXPERTS

The Criminologists

'Criminals choose to commit crime because they believe crime pays.'
(Beccaria, seventeenth century)

'There is no simple answer to the question "What is crime?" and therefore no single answer to "What causes crime?" Different types of crime often have their own distinct causes.'
(Scottish Centre for Crime and Justice Research, http://www.sccjr.ac.uk/publications/)

'Young people have goals in life including popularity with peers, independence, financial security and good relations with parents. The inability to achieve any of these goals could cause crime.'
(Greenberg, Elliott, Huizinga, Ageton, twentieth century)

The Neuroscientists

'If we buy into the argument that for some people factors in their biology greatly raise the risk of them becoming offenders, can we justly turn a blind eye to that? Is it really the fault of the innocent baby whose mother smoked heavily in pregnancy that he went on to commit crimes? Or if he was battered from pillar to post, or even if he was born with an abnormally low resting heart rate, how harshly should we punish him? How much should we say he is responsible? There is, and increasingly will be, an argument that he is not fully responsible and therefore, when we come to think of punishment, should we be thinking of more benign institutions than prison?'

(Adrian Raine, 2013)

The Mayo Clinic studied people with **antisocial personality disorder**, a condition that many convicted criminals have. Those with the disorder 'do not care about right and wrong. They may often break the law and the infringe rights of others.'

(http://www.mayoclinic.org/diseases-conditions/antisocial-personality-disorder/more-about/in-depth/ssc-20199002)

contd

Morality and Justice – Causes of crime 2

The Sociologists

Social Learning Theory is the idea that children are influenced by the family, their peers and the media in relation to criminal behaviour. This idea is proposed by Sutherland and Bandura.

(http://www.psychlotron.org.uk/newResources/criminological/A2_AQB_crim_learningTheory.pdf)

'Let us make no mistake… crime… is a factor in public health, a key part of all societies… A healthy society requires both crime and punishment. Both are unavoidable; both are purposeful.' (Durkheim, nineteenth century)

THE COURTS

'A female murderer who randomly murdered three men was described by the judge as a "cruel, calculated, selfish and manipulative serial killer".'

'A drunk driver killed a vet and the judge had this to say: "You have shown no remorse for your actions – quite the contrary – your arrogance in giving evidence and in the social enquiry report is quite staggering."'

DON'T FORGET
There is agreement that crime has causes but there is no real consensus on what causes are the most important.

'A 51-year-old psychiatric nurse, the judge said, "I am sure you have seen a great many things working as a psychiatric nurse that are troubling. You are not the first and not the last person who works in that field to try to cope with some of the experiences you have seen, inappropriately by the misuse of alcohol."'

'A 39-year-old heroin addict who frequently shoplifted to feed her habit heard a judge say this about her, "It is desperate in a way. I recognise that this lady has a lot of problems and she needs a lot of help. But she has not got the heart, the gumption or the ability to take what the court offers."'

VIDEO LINK
Head to the Digital Zone to watch a clip on deviance.

'The Conservative Party, in their 2015 manifesto, promised tougher sentences for repeat offenders but also addiction and rehab support for them.'

THINGS TO DO AND THINK ABOUT

1. Make a to-do list of the things that society has to organise to tackle the causes of crime.
2. Make a wish list of the things that offenders might want to look for to stop their criminal behaviour.
3. Now, in relation to the causes of crime, imagine you are the First Minister of Scotland and you are campaigning for re-election. Complete this statement with a list of the things you will do if re-elected: 'I will tackle the causes of crime by…'

ONLINE TEST
Test yourself on morality and justice at www.brightredbooks.net

MORALITY AND JUSTICE

MORAL ISSUES

There are three main views on the causes of crime. Some will dismiss the causes, some will accept some causes and some will accept all causes. But what are the moral implications of these views and what do religious and non-religious people think of them?

DISMISS THE CAUSES OF CRIME

Issue	Consequences	Duty	Human Rights
Bad	• Injustice may be done to offenders • People wrongly punished • Crime not reduced	• Duty to care for the vulnerable – not done • Duty to prevent crime as well as protect people – not done • Duty to tackle society's ills – not done	• Right to be free from discrimination – denied • Right to not be wrongfully imprisoned – denied • Right to a decent standard of living where we can thrive – denied
Good	• No excuses accepted • Equal justice for all • Deters criminals	• Duty to protect the public – done • Duty to uphold law – done • Duty to punish offenders – done	• Right to be free and equal – upheld • Right to be treated equally before the law – upheld • Right to protect the freedom and rights of others – upheld

Religious views	
Agree	Disagree
Buddhism: lacks compassion, can't ignore the causes of crime. Christianity: lacks compassion, identifies the causes of crime. Islam: lacks compassion, helps to control causes of crime.	Buddhism: could be kamma payback. Christianity: crime is a choice, God has given us laws to obey. Islam: crime is a choice, God has given us laws to obey.
Non-religious views	
Agree	Disagree
Experts: unjust and unfair, crime is a consequence of something else, for instance, mental health problems, poverty, the environment. Courts: unjust and unfair, there are clear causes of crime in some cases. Politicians: unjust and unfair, crime has causes.	Experts: everyone knows right from wrong, these are just excuses for criminal behaviour. Courts: sometimes the cause is just pure evil or an evil person. Politicians: causes are just excuses for criminal behaviour.

DON'T FORGET

Religious people disagree with each other on the causes of crime and so do non-religious people.

VIDEO LINK

Learn more about the biological causes of crime by watching the video at the Digital Zone.

Morality and Justice – Moral issues

ACCEPT SOME CAUSES OF CRIME

Issue	Consequences	Duty	Human Rights
Bad	• Offenders treated fairly • Support can be put in place • Crime could be reduced	• Duty to care for the vulnerable – done • Duty to prevent crime as well as protect people – done • Duty to tackle society's ills – done	• Right to dignity – upheld • Right to not be wrongfully imprisoned – upheld • Right to proper social and health care – upheld
Good	• Some people get away with crimes • Justice becomes unequal • Criminals will play the system	• Duty to protect the public – not done • Duty to uphold law – not consistently done • Duty to punish offenders – not consistently done	• Right to feel safe – denied • Right to be treated equally before the law – denied • Right to protect the freedom and rights of others – denied

Religious views	
Agree	Disagree
Buddhism: shows some compassion, allows for rehabilitation of criminals. Christianity: shows some compassion, an opportunity to support criminals. Islam: shows compassion, helps criminals to put things right with themselves and their victims.	Buddhism: could be kamma payback. Christianity: crime is a choice, God has given us laws to obey. Islam: crime is a choice, God has given us laws to obey.

Non-religious views	
Agree	Disagree
Experts: unjust and unfair, crime is a consequence of something else, for instance, mental health problems, poverty, the environment; we can't choose acceptable causes. Courts: unjust and unfair, there are clear causes of crime in some cases; unclear about unacceptable causes of crime. Politicians: unjust and unfair, crime has causes.	Experts: everyone knows right from wrong, cause are just excuses for criminal behaviour. Courts: sometimes the cause is just pure evil or an evil person. Politicians: causes are just excuses for criminal behaviour.

ACCEPT ALL KNOWN CAUSES OF CRIME

Issue	Consequences	Duty	Human Rights
Bad	• Could change the criminal justice system • Greater understanding of the offender's behaviour • Fewer miscarriages of justice	• Duty to care for the vulnerable – done • Duty to prevent crime as well as protect people – done • Duty to tackle society's ills – done	• Right to dignity – upheld • Right to not be wrongfully imprisoned – upheld • Right to proper social and health care – upheld
Good	• Offenders get away with the crime • Justice is not being seen to be done • No deterrent effect	• Duty to protect the public – not done • Duty to uphold law – not done • Duty to punish offenders – not done	• Right to feel safe – denied • Right to be treated equally before the law – denied • Right to protect the freedom and rights of others – denied

Religious views	
Agree	Disagree
Buddhism: shows compassion, allows for rehabilitation. Christianity: shows compassion, an opportunity to support criminals. Islam: shows compassion, helps criminals to put things right with themselves and their victims.	Buddhism: could be kamma payback. Christianity: crime is a choice, God has given us laws to obey. Islam: crime is a choice, God has given us laws to obey.

Non-religious views	
Agree	Disagree
Experts: unjust and unfair, crime is a consequence of something else, for instance, mental health problems, poverty, the environment. Courts: unjust and unfair, there are clear causes of crime in some cases; risk of an imbalance in the justice system. Politicians: unjust and unfair, crime has causes.	Experts: everyone knows right from wrong, causes are just excuses for criminal behaviour. Courts: sometimes the cause is just pure evil or an evil person. Politicians: causes are just excuses for criminal behaviour; potential votes can be lost if a politician is perceived to be soft on criminals.

THINGS TO DO AND THINK ABOUT

Debates: Explain who would win the debate and why:
- Crime has no causes   v   Crime has many causes
- Justice that recognises causes   v   Justice that does not recognise causes
- Religious views on causes   v   Non-religious views on causes
- Duty to prevent crime   v   Duty to support the vulnerable

ONLINE TEST

Test yourself on morality and justice at www.brightredbooks.net

MORALITY AND JUSTICE
THE PURPOSES OF PUNISHMENT 1

The reasons why we think people commit crimes affects how we think they should be treated. We're going to look at two things together: the purposes of punishment and also some UK responses to crime. It is difficult to talk about one without taking the other into consideration.

COMMENTS ON CRIME AND PUNISHMENT

Plenty has been said about crime and punishment, as you can see.

The power to punish is not essentially different from that of curing or educating.
Focault (philosopher)

Punishment is not for revenge, but to lessen crime and reform the criminal.
Elizabeth Fry (prison reformer)

Let the punishment match the crime.
Cicero (philosopher)

Justice demands that courts should impose punishment befitting the crime so that the courts reflect public abhorrence of the crime.
Justices A.S. Anand and N.P. Singh (Indian judges)

Punishment is justice for the unjust.
Augustine of Hippo (theologian)

If he who breaks the law is not punished, he who obeys it is cheated. This, and this alone, is why lawbreakers ought to be punished...The aim of criminal law cannot be correction or deterrence; it can only be the maintenance of the legal order.
Thomas Szasz (psychologist)

No punishment has ever possessed enough power of deterrence to prevent the commission of crimes.
Hannah Arendt (philosopher)

The following can be said regarding punishment in general and UK responses to crime:

- There is an element of punishment in most sentences.
- The more serious the crime, the more people want **retribution**.
- The less serious the crime, or the younger the offender, the more people want there to be **rehabilitation**.
- People want to be protected from the most dangerous criminals.
- **Deterrence** usually involves tougher sentences and tougher prison regimes.
- The more democratic a country is, the more likely rehabilitation is likely to be important.
- There is confusion about how to deal with individuals who have **challenging issues** – punishment, treatment, **reformation**?

Morality and Justice – The purposes of punishment 1

PUNISHMENT PURPOSES

Protection
- Protect society
- Protect Offender

- **Consequence:** people feel safer, offender maybe feels safer, draws a line for acceptable behaviour, law upheld.
- **Duty:** state has a duty to protect people, state had a duty to deal with threats to society, state has a duty to uphold laws.
- **Rights:** rights and freedoms of individuals protected, right to feel safe is protected, right to quality of life is protected.
- **Authority:** the Law seeks to protect citizens, God expects leaders to protect individuals, experts recognise the need to be protected.

Deterrence
- Discourage others
- Discourage Repeat offence

- **Consequence:** makes an example of the offender, puts other people off, draws a line for acceptable behaviour.
- **Duty:** law-makers have a duty to deter people from crime, courts have a duty to reduce crime by punishments which deter.
- **Rights:** deters criminals from infringing our rights to property, freedom from discrimination and life.
- **Authority:** sets an example of how the State/God expects us to behave, public statement of expectations.

Retribution
- Payback
- Discourage others

- **Consequence:** the few suffer so the majority may benefit, may not commit crime again, victims feel justice is done.
- **Duty:** suffering can help people learn, suffering can be a deterrent as well, suffering sets an example of what to expect.
- **Rights:** upholds the rights to property, freedom from discrimination and life, payback time for those who ignore.
- **Authority:** state has to ensure that justice is *seen* to be done, religions have God using retribution as means of reform.

Reformation
- Retrain/treat
- Prevent re-offending

- **Consequence:** offender gets a second chance, cure the cause; remove the effect, less crime.
- **Duty:** there is a duty to help those in need, a duty to remove the causes of the problem, a duty to care for everyone.
- **Rights:** the right to proper health and social care is upheld, the right be treated humanely is upheld and the right to a good life too.
- **Authority:** God demands justice and reformation, the State has reformation as an aim for prison, State can protect and reform.

 **DON'T FORGET**

The causes of crime are often taken into account when sentencing people.

 VIDEO LINK

Learn more about the causes of crime by watching the video at the Digital Zone.

 ONLINE TEST

Test yourself on morality and justice at www.brightredbooks.net

 THINGS TO DO AND THINK ABOUT

1. Why should the causes of crime be a consideration in sentencing?
2. What might the consequences be of saying that the only cause of crime is that some people are just bad?
3. To what extent has the State a duty to tackle the causes of crime?
4. Why might some people argue that the causes of crime are just an excuse for bad people?
5. If you had to choose the most serious cause of crime, what would it be and why?

MORALITY AND JUSTICE
THE PURPOSES OF PUNISHMENT 2

We've looked at attitudes towards punishment held by religious and non-religious groups. Now we shall examine exactly what is being said by whom.

ONLINE TEST
Test yourself on morality and justice at www.brightredbooks.net

DON'T FORGET
The UK justice system (and many others) claim that reformation is their objective but the other three purposes of punishment each has a part to play.

VIDEO LINK
Explore the topic of justice further by watching the video at the Digital Zone.

DETERRENCE

Purpose of Punishment	Consequences	Duty	Human Rights
Deterrence	• Injustice may be done to offenders • Deterrence may not work • Making an example of someone is humiliating	• Duty to prevent crime – done • Duty to protect the public – done • Duty to remove offenders – done	• Right to not be humiliated – denied • Right to not be wrongfully imprisoned – denied • Right to a good life – denied
	• People feel safer • Tries to reduce offending • Helps protect society from potential offenders	• Duty to help the offender – not done • Duty to pay back the offender – not done • Duty to prevent crime – not done, still goes on	• Right of all to feel safe – upheld • Right to property – upheld • Right to protect the freedom and rights of others – upheld

Religious views	
Agree	Disagree
Buddhism, Christianity, Islam: follow the teachings of Buddha, Jesus and Muhummad and there will be a world without the need for deterrence.	Buddhism: kamma will get criminals in any case. Christianity: everyone is answerable to God in the end, we must carry out God's justice here. Islam: everyone is answerable to Allah in the end, we must carry out Allah's justice here.

Non-religious views	
Agree	Disagree
Experts: deterrence works in some cases. Courts: deterrence sends out a strong message. Politicians: deterrence sends out a strong message.	Experts: deterrence cannot be proven. Courts: justice needs to be seen to be done; justice promotes deterrence. Politicians: the public need protection, communities need to be safer.

PROTECTION

Purpose of Punishment	Consequences	Duty	Human Rights
Protection	• Injustice may be done to offenders • Society may not need protecting • Does not deter others	• Duty to protect public – done • Duty to protect offender – done • Duty to remove offenders – done	• Right to have rights – denied • Right to not be wrongfully imprisoned – denied • Right to a good life – denied
	• People feel safer • Problem is removed from society • Society needs protected from most criminals	• Duty to punish the offender – not done • Duty to pay back the offender – not done • Duty to deter others – not done	• Right of all to feel safe – upheld • Right to property – upheld • Right to protect the freedom and the rights of others – upheld

Religious views	
Agree	Disagree
Buddhism, Christianity, Islam: sometimes required but must have rehabilitation.	Buddhism: kamma will get criminals in any case. Christianity: everyone is answerable to God in the end, we must carry out God's justice here. Islam: everyone is answerable to Allah in the end, we must carry out Allah's justice here.

contd

Morality and Justice – The purposes of punishment 2

Non-religious views	
Agree	Disagree
Experts: protection is not always needed, the offender needs protection, too. Courts: we need to support offenders until they no longer are a threat. Politicians: we need to make society better by not putting people in prison; we need to understand what makes people offend.	Experts: everyone knows right from wrong, we need protecting from bad people. Courts: justice needs to be seen to be done; justice protects the innocent. Politicians: the public need protecting.

RETRIBUTION

Purpose of Punishment	Consequences	Duty	Human Rights
Retribution	• Injustice may be done to offenders • Retribution is not proven to work • Making an example of someone is humiliating	• Duty to prevent crime – done • Duty to protect the public – done • Duty to remove offenders – done	• Right to not be humiliated – denied • Right to have rights – denied • Right to a good life – denied
	• People feel safer • People feel justice is done • People feel the prisoner suffers for what he has done	• Duty to help the offender – not done • Duty to pay back the offender – not done • Duty to prevent crime – not done, still goes on	• Right of all to feel safe – upheld • Right to property – upheld • Right to protect the freedom and rights of others – upheld

Religious views	
Agree	Disagree
Buddhism: causes harm to others; bad kamma for those who do the harming, it lacks compassion. Christianity: lacks forgiveness; it is wrong to deliberately cause harm; love your enemies. Islam: lacks mercy; it is wrong not to offer rehabilitation.	Buddhism: kamma will get criminals in any case. Christianity: God permits revenge; the purpose of punishment is suffering. Islam: Allah permits revenge; Allah's laws are being broken so there must be a penalty.

Non-religious views	
Agree	Disagree
Experts: retribution only works with some, it tackles the act but not the cause of the act. Courts: retribution is not always the answer for similar crimes. Politicians: it can be cruel, and can deny individuals their rights.	Experts: it works if it is severe enough. Courts: justice needs to be seen to be done; justice promotes retribution. Politicians: the public need protection, and communities need to be safer.

REFORMATION

Purpose of Punishment	Consequences	Duty	Human Rights
Reformation	• Injustice may be done to victims • People may not feel safe • Might make it appear that crime pays	• Duty to prevent crime – not done • Duty to protect the public – not done • Duty to remove offenders – not done	• Right to not be humiliated – upheld • Right to have rights – upheld • Right to a good life – upheld
	• Offenders treated with respect • Long-term result could be less crime • Tackles the cause but not the effect	• Duty to help the offender – done • Duty to support the vulnerable – done • Duty to treat people equally – done	• Right of all to feel safe – denied • Right to property – threatened • Right to protect the freedom and rights of others – threatened

Religious views	
Agree	Disagree
Buddhism: could cause harm to others, bad kamma should not be rewarded, people need protection. Christianity: lacks justice, does not set an example, fails to act when God's law is broken. Islam: lacks justice, does not set an example, fails to act when Allah's law is broken.	Buddhism: compassionate and provides a chance to retrain offenders, which creates a good society. Christianity: most loving thing to do, it shows forgiveness, which creates a good society. Islam: creates a good society; Allah is just and merciful, we should be, too; gives a second chance.

Non-religious views	
Agree	Disagree
Experts: reformation only works with some, it fails to punish the crime. Courts: the role of courts is to sentence criminals, not reform people. Politicians: it is costly and unproven, with too high a re-offending rate; not a potential vote-winner.	Experts: it works if it is done properly; it treats offenders as humans, recognising that crime has causes. Courts: a recognition that for some offenders punishment is not appropriate. Politicians: need to recognise offenders' human rights, and need to invest more in rehabilitation programmes and early intervention.

MORALITY AND JUSTICE
RELIGIOUS VIEWS ON PUNISHMENT

Things become more complicated when you examine religious and non-religious views on the purposes of punishment. Basically, you can find support within any religion for each of the purposes of punishment. We will now summarise the views of Islam, Christianity and Buddhism.

ISLAM

In **Islam**, the aim is to promote human welfare and this is achieved by living according to the Qur'an. In doing so people will neither want nor need to commit crimes. Islamic justice tries to protect five things: life, **Allah**, reason, family and property. This is achieved through three forms of punishment: **prescribed**, **discretionary** and **retribution.**

Prescribed punishments

These are for crimes forbidden by Allah. He decides the punishment and no alternative is possible. Crimes that have prescribed punishments include theft, highway robbery, fornication outside marriage, making false accusations, drinking alcohol and apostasy.

Punishments are administered to protect and deter.

Discretionary punishments:

- Are given for infringing the rights of Allah.
- Are given for infringing the rights of individuals.
- Have no fixed penalties.
- Take into account the needs of society and changing attitudes.
- Aim to bring a benefit to society, to the criminal, and reduce the harm that has been caused.

Punishments are administered to protect, deter and rehabilitate.

Retribution

Although this means an eye for an eye, the victim, or the family of the victim, has the right to forgive. This is only in the case of deliberate killing or injury and where there is some benefit of doubt in favour of the accused.

Severe punishments are administered to provide retribution, protection and deterrence.

Islamic republics are countries that are governed by strict Islamic principles and tend to have less forgiving views on the causes of crime (for example, Saudi Arabia, Iran and Iraq).

Countries where Islam may be the religion of the majority, but are not run as Islamic republics, tend to be less severe in their applications of punishment (for example, Algeria).

Prison conditions in many Islamic countries are harsh because of poor staff training and a lack of finance to help build better prisons. A poor record on human rights in an Islamic country may be the fault of its government and not Islam.

CHRISTIANITY

Christianity's view of the causes of crime and purposes of punishment have varied considerably over time. Today, there are Christians who support tough punishments for criminals and reject the causes of crime as valid excuses for criminal behaviour, and there are other Christians who believe that criminals should be forgiven and supported through rehabilitation. A major challenge for Christians is to clarify the Bible's teachings on the causes of crime and purposes of punishment. Why is this a challenge? You can use different parts of the Bible to justify different viewpoints. This leads to disagreement about the causes of crime and purposes of punishment.

contd

Morality and Justice – Religious views on punishment

Bible teachings

Causes of crimes:

- Humanity sinning against God by breaking His laws.
- Humanity's natural tendency to do evil things.

The punishment:

- Must fit the crime.
- Must not be revengeful.
- Must deter.
- Must offer rehabilitation.

How do we know this?

'Do not seek revenge.' (from Leviticus in the Old Testament)

'If the guilty person deserves to be beaten [...] the judge must not impose more than forty lashes.' (from Deuteronomy in the Old Testament)

'...he shall make restitution from the best in his own field and in his own vineyard...' (from Exodus in the Old Testament)

'The penalty shall be life for life, eye for eye.' (from Leviticus in the Old Testament)

But then Jesus came along and said:

'But if anyone slaps you on the right cheek, turn to him the other also.'

'Love your enemy. Do good to those who hate you.' (from Matthew's Gospel)

As you can see there is a range of views held by Christians who can find support for those views from the Bible.

The Joint Faiths Advisory Board on Criminal Justice in Scotland represents the current views of many Scottish Christians on criminal justice. Its aims tell us a lot about their beliefs in relation to the causes of crime and their approach to punishment:

- To promote values of reconciliation, forgiveness and restoration, and to support initiatives that use **restorative justice** practices.
- To report on matters relating to the wellbeing of those who are in custody or under supervision within the Community Justice system.

> **DON'T FORGET**
>
> On the whole religions try to support prisoners in their rehabilitation.

> **VIDEO LINK**
>
> Watch the video at the Digital Zone to find out more about chaplaincy in prisons.

BUDDHISM

In Buddhism punishment serves the following purposes:

- To *restore* the community and the victim.
- To let kamma act on the criminal.
- To *deter* the offender committing future crimes.
- To *rehabilitate* the offender.

A thought from Buddhism

'Especially generate compassion for those whose ill deeds are horrible. Punishment should be carried out with compassion, not through hatred nor desire for wealth or for retribution, since retribution is another name for revenge; "revenge" implies the action is done with anger, and therefore would burden the executioner with hatred and its resultant poor karma.' (Nagarjuna, Buddhist scholar)

THINGS TO DO AND THINK ABOUT

There are themes running through religious responses to crime. See if you can find at least two of the following themes in what religions say about punishment:

COMPASSION   REVENGE   FORGIVENESS   DETERRENCE   REFORMATION

ONLINE TEST

Test yourself on morality and justice at www.brightredbooks.net

MORALITY AND JUSTICE
NON-RELIGIOUS VIEWS ON PUNISHMENT

THE ORGANISATIONS

UK Government

Purpose of prisons: in giving effect to sentences or orders of imprisonment or detention imposed by courts, prisons must aim to: (a) protect the public, (b) reform and rehabilitate offenders, (c) prepare prisoners for life outside prison, and (d) maintain an environment that is safe and secure.

(https://www.gov.uk/government/organisations/hm-prison-service)

Scottish Prison Service

- Belief: we believe that people can change.
- Respect: we have proper regard for individuals, their needs and their human rights.
- Integrity: we apply high ethical, moral and professional standards.
- Openness: we work with others to achieve the best outcomes.
- Courage: we have the courage to care regardless of circumstances.
- Humility: we cannot do this on our own, we recognise we can learn from others.

(http://www.sps.gov.uk/)

Federal Penitentiary Service, Russia

- Carry out criminal punishments.
- Control behaviour of convicts who have been given suspended sentences.
- Ensure the protection of rights, freedoms and legal interests of convicts and detainees.
- Ensure the safety of convicts within the walls of institutions and detention centres.
- Provide convicts and detainees with conditions of **incarceration** consistent with the rules of international law.
- Activity organizations for helping the convicted in social adaptation.

(http://fsin.su/)

Saudi Arabia Ministry of Justice

- Look after every prisoner.
- Before release prisoners must be helped to reintegrate into society.
- Provide access to education for prisoners.
- Breaking prison rules can result in solitary confinement, loss of privileges, or no more than ten lashes.
- Prisoners must not be abused.

(https://www.moj.gov.sa/En/Pages/default.aspx)

United Nations

The treatment of persons sentenced to imprisonment or a similar measure shall have as its purpose, so far as the length of the sentence permits, to establish in them the will to lead law-abiding and self-supporting lives after their release and to fit them to do so. The treatment shall be such as will encourage their self-respect and develop their sense of responsibility.

From the beginning of a prisoner's sentence consideration shall be given to his future after release and he shall be encouraged and assisted to maintain or establish such relations with persons or agencies outside the institution as may promote the best interests of his family and his own social rehabilitation.

(http://www.ohchr.org/EN/ProfessionalInterest/Pages/TreatmentOfPrisoners.aspx)

contd

Morality and Justice – Non-religious views on punishment

Thailand Ministry of Justice, Department of Corrections

Vision
- To become an efficient agency in keeping into custody and rehabilitating prisoners in order to return decent citizens to the community.

Mission
- Professionally keeping prisoners in custody.
- Rehabilitating prisoners efficiently.
- International standard achievement.
(http://www.correct.go.th/eng/index.html)

THE PRACTICE

United Kingdom

Prisons are currently failing to deliver their most basic duty, to ensure the safety of the people in their care. Record numbers of deaths, assaults and self-harm show a system struggling to cope. People are sent to prison and lose their liberty as punishment, not for punishment, and certainly not to lose their lives.
(UK Prison Reform Trust, http://www.prisonreformtrust.org.uk/)

Saudi Arabia

Reports from the UN praise the running of Saudi prisons. There is a focus on trying to retrain the offender and maintain contacts with his or her family. The US review of Saudi prisons said that local prisons might be overcrowded but that in general the health and welfare of offenders was very important. As regards punishment, in 2014 there was only one report of an amputation being carried out in Saudi Arabia; corporal punishment is often a last resort. The main **criticism** of Saudi Arabia is the strictness of the laws compared to European and American laws.

Thailand

The Worldwide Movement for Human Rights had this to say about Thailand's prisons:

The Thai Department of Corrections' motto, 'Caring Custody, Meaningful Rehabilitation, International Standard Achievement', could not be further from the reality of the Thai prison system. Thailand's prison conditions fail to meet international standards and to create an environment conducive to the rehabilitation of prisoners.

Sweden

The Council of Europe inspectors said in 2015 that Sweden's prisons were of a good-to-excellent standard. No reports of ill treatment. Plenty of meaningful work and a relaxed atmosphere in most prisons. The prison staff have to like all kinds of people. The use of prison in Sweden is a last resort.

Turkey

In 2015 the Council of Europe inspected a number of Turkish prisons. It was a mixed report. Some prisons were well run and had good accommodation and support whereas others had overcrowding, lack of activities, and reports of beatings in the form of kicks, slaps and punches. The police and prison officers in juvenile prisons were the worst offenders. Concerns were raised about the lack of health care, communication with the outside world and social care.

DON'T FORGET

Check over the Universal Declaration of Human Rights to see which ones are being protected.

VIDEO LINK

Find out more about this topic by watching the videos at the Digital Zone.

ONLINE TEST

Test yourself on morality and justice at www.brightredbooks.net

THINGS TO DO AND THINK ABOUT

Let's think of things in threes. Write them down:
- Three positive and three negative consequences of punishment.
- Three human rights upheld and three broken by punishment.
- Three duties achieved and three not achieved by punishing.

MORALITY AND JUSTICE

PURPOSES OF PUNISHMENT AND CAUSES OF CRIME

Trying to match the causes of crime with the purpose of punishment is complex in regard to the morality of punishment and the moral issues surrounding different causes of crimes. Instances of this complexity are outlined below.

MENTAL HEALTH ISSUES

- Deterrence?
- Retribution?
- Protection?
- Reformation?

If a person is mentally ill then you cannot deter them; you can't say: 'Stop being ill or else.' If a person is ill and their illness makes them dangerous then **maybe** the public and the offender need to be protected for safety reasons (not for punishment). If a person is ill what benefit does it serve in punishing them? It is like being punished for having the flu. It has to be reformation if a person is ill because then their **mental health issues** are being treated (not punished).

POVERTY

- Deterrence?
- Retribution?
- Protection?
- Reformation?

If a person is poor and is in financial difficulties then you can't say: 'Stop being poor or else.' Being poor is not something people choose to be: you can be **born into poverty** or it can occur during life. How can you deter people from being poor when the part of the country they stay in is also poor and unable to help them? Shouldn't the protection be from poverty, and not from those *in* poverty who commit crimes in a state of desperation? Is retribution or revenge going to remove an individual's poverty? What might remove their poverty is reformation, which should include **support** to help them overcome their financial difficulties.

DON'T FORGET

You need to remember that you are dealing with the moral (not the social) issues related to crime.

ENVIRONMENT

- Deterrence?
- Retribution?
- Protection?
- Reformation?

VIDEO LINK

Learn about rabbis looking after Jewish prisoners by watching the video at the Digital Zone.

You don't have any control over who your parents are. If they are a **bad influence** throughout your childhood then you cannot change them and have other parents bring you up. It's similar with environment, the area you live in. It could be an area where there is a lot of crime which may well affect you. Can we blame a child who suffers from poor parenting and/or is brought up in an area of significant **criminal activity** if they themselves commit a crime when they grow up? Shouldn't they be protected from inadequate parenting and a poor environment? Is retribution in these circumstances simply a case of punishing poor parenting and environment?

Morality and Justice – Purposes of punishment and causes of crime

THINGS TO DO AND THINK ABOUT

Working with the Issues

1. What's more important…
   (a) Reforming offenders or punishing offenders?
   (b) Preventing crime or deterring potential offenders?
   (c) Protecting the public or reforming offenders?
   (d) Deterring potential offenders or reforming offenders?

   Explain each answer with at least two reasons.

2. What's worse…
   (a) Religious views on deterrence or non-religious views of deterrence?
   (b) Religious views on protection or non-religious views of protection?
   (c) Religious views on retribution or non-religious views of retribution?
   (d) Religious views on reformation or non-religious views of reformation?

   Explain each answer with at least two reasons.

3. Try to work out three consequences for each statement:
   (a) All sentences involved only punishing the offender.
   (b) Christian teaching was put into practice with offenders.
   (c) Buddhist teaching was put into practice with offenders.
   (d) All causes of crime were proved to be true.
   (e) Human rights did not apply to offenders.

4. What's wrong with…
   (a) Having tough sentences?
   (b) Religions perhaps being against reformation?
   (c) Having difficult conditions in prisons?
   (d) Remembering the causes of a crime when sentencing an offender?
   (e) Having punishments fit the crime?

5. What would make everything better?
   (a) Causes of crime being scientifically proven.
   (b) All punishments being severe.
   (c) Protecting society as a top priority.
   (d) Deterring offenders as a top priority.
   (e) Religious views being adopted towards offenders.

Take your pick from these, or if you don't like any of these then make up your own, and explain your answer using strong arguments and evidence. After this exercise, you can do it again for 'What would make everything worse?'

ONLINE TEST

Test yourself on morality and justice at www.brightredbooks.net

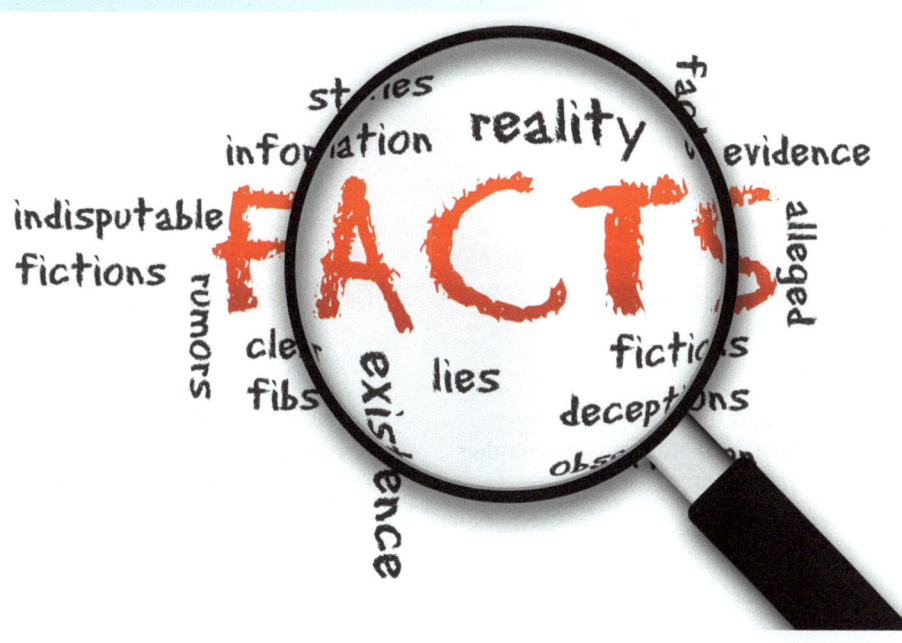

MORALITY AND JUSTICE

UK RESPONSES TO CRIME

THE RESPONSE OF GOVERNMENT

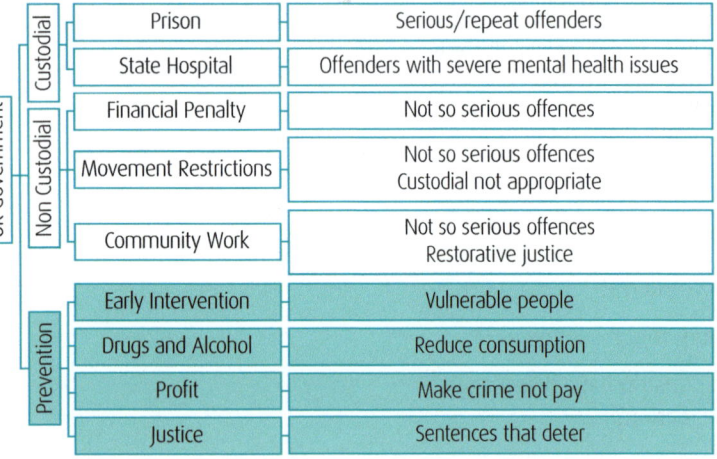

Note that in the exam both the UK and Scottish Governments come under the subject heading of UK responses to crime. The diagram opposite shows that the UK Government has three main options in responding to crime. These are **custodial (prison) sentences**, **non-custodial sentences** and, for many perhaps the most important, **crime prevention**.

In addition to the work of the UK Government, local councils provide a range of support through education and social work to support offenders and their families while they serve their sentences in prison and prepare for release. Local council social work departments and other agencies provide background reports on offenders enabling the courts to decide the best way of dealing with them. An offence which has been committed may often be a symptom relating to other events in their lives.

In crime prevention, investment is made in early intervention and education. Schools and social workers work together to identify individuals who are at risk early on in their lives, and may have family support programmes in place. There are also education programmes run by local councils and the police about substance misuse (legal and illegal) since drugs are the cause of a sizable amount of crime in the UK.

RESPONSES OF RELIGION AND CHARITY

Churches are involved in outreach programmes to offenders and potential offenders. The Roman Catholic Church and the Church of Scotland have been involved in the secure residential care of young people at risk or of young offenders. For example, the Good Shepherd Centre near Greenock has very close links with the Roman Catholic Church, and the Church of Scotland's Crossreach criminal justice programme supports offenders and potential offenders.

The charity Muslim Hands has built partnerships with male and female prison and probation services, youth groups and community organisations across the country, to address the concerns of Muslim prisoners and aid their rehabilitation upon release.

Much of the work done by churches and charities is similar to that arranged by local councils (indeed, local councils often utilise their services) and includes:

- Exploration of the causes of offending.
- Psychological support.
- Spiritual support.
- Learning support.
- Financial support.
- Addiction counselling.
- Careers advice.
- Intensive counselling.
- Housing advice.

One common objective is to support young people in difficult situations and help them:

- Start again.
- Avoid destructive behaviour.
- Cope with their situation.
- Avoid offending or re-offending.
- Prepare for work.
- Integrate socially.
- Develop a moral compass.

The motivations of these organisations include:

- Reforming the individual.
- Crime prevention.
- Follow the examples set by Jesus and Muhammad and other religious figures.
- Compassion for the disadvantaged.
- To show how living by Christian/Muslim principles can steer one away from offensive or criminal behaviour.

contd

Morality and Justice – UK responses to crime

EXAMPLE:

Angulimala is a UK Buddhist charity which supports prisoners. Its focus is on helping prisoners to cultivate the Five Precepts and the calmness that meditation can bring. Most of the Buddhists in prison are converts to Buddhism; statistics show that prisoners on long-term sentences are more likely to be attracted to Buddhism, possibly because it helps them find meaning to and a purpose in life to sustain them while locked away for a long period. The service is non-judgemental and covers both staff and prisoners.

Compassion comes through strongly in the work of Angulimala as does the aim of reformation. After prison contact is maintained (if so desired) while the ex-offender reintegrates into the community.

EXAMPLE:

SACRO is a Scottish community justice charity. One aspect of its work is to support offenders. The belief is that offending and its consequences are most effectively dealt with through an emphasis on community support (except where there is an overriding need to protect society).

SACRO organises restorative action, drug and alcohol misuse support, supervised bail (rather than putting people on remand), housing support, support for sex offenders and their families, mentoring, career advice, psychological support, counselling for those charged with racist or sectarian behaviour, early interventions and support for individuals with mental health illnesses who have committed offences.

SACRO offers around 30 different types of service across Scotland with the aims of keeping people out of prison, preventing re-offending, and helping the rehabilitation process by discussing areas of conflict with offenders so that they can be integrated back into the community once their sentences have been served.

ONLINE

Follow the link at www.brightredbooks.net to find out more about the story of Angulimala.

THINGS TO DO AND THINK ABOUT

Pick and Mix

The top line of boxes shows the various UK responses to crime. Below that is a random selection of statements which may or may not be applied to each of the responses. They are not in any order. You can do various things in this activity:

(a) You could match three statements with the responses and provide reasons for making those matches.
(b) You could try to make as long a chain of matches as you can between one response and statements without having any contradictions in it.
(c) You could see how many statements you can get to match a single response.

DON'T FORGET

You must be able to show why you can make the links.

Christian Responses	Government Responses	SACRO's Responses	Buddhist Responses
Do too little to make the offender suffer.	Reinforce our duties towards victim *and* offender.	Remove the bad consequences of offending.	Side too much with the offender.
Make society less safe.	Give the offender hope.	Try to tackle the causes of crime.	Show too much compassion.
Make individuals and victims better people.	Uphold the human rights of everyone.	Promote positive values.	Make society safer.
Have the benefit of the majority at the centre of what they do.	Have their duties to everyone at the centre of what they do.	Have human rights at the centre of everything they do.	Have the situation of individuals at the centre of everything they do.

MORALITY AND JUSTICE

THE DEATH PENALTY 1

In dealing with crime, the ultimate sanction is the death penalty or capital punishment. It was commonly used across the entire world until the nineteenth century, when countries with new democracies began to emerge and saw the death penalty as a barbaric means of oppression against their own citizens. Before this, the pain of execution (or any torture that went along with it) was part of the punishment. Its purpose was an act of retribution designed to deter others and to protect the law-makers and others. In the nineteenth century the focus of those using the death penalty was to find humane ways of carrying it out, to make it quick and painless. The feeling was that making an execution quick and painless was more morally acceptable. Let's explore what is happening in the world just now.

MORAL ISSUES

There are huge moral issues related to the death penalty. The concerns usually revolve around cruelty, miscarriages of justice, the value of life and human rights. These concerns are often raised. But think also of the consequences of using it, of the human rights that are denied, or the duties that are deserted, or the advice of experts in crime and morality, or how executing someone is going to make humans better people.

What (the methods)	Why (the reasons)	Where (the places)	Common features
Lethal injection	Murder	USA	Infrequent
Hanging	Drug offences	Africa	Global appeals against using it
Firing squad	Espionage	Asia	Long legal process
Head shot	Terrorism	Middle East	Long delays
Beheading	There are other reasons but, compared to those noted above, they do not happen frequently	50+ retentionist	Botched executions
Stoning (rare)		30+ retentionist, but rarely used	Miscarriage of justice
Gassing (rare)		100+ abolitionist	
Electrocution			

Potentially bad	Potentially good
Devalues life, denies human rights, pure revenge, cannot be undone	Problem removed, debt repaid, justice done, no re-offending, people safe

Consequences

These consequences raise moral issues. The decision to be reached is whether the consequences are so good or bad that the death penalty should or should not be used. But perhaps human rights are more important than consequences.

Potentially denied	Potentially upheld
Right to life denied, cruel and degrading treatment, torture, human rights removed	Offender did not respect the victim's human rights, kill someone and you lose your human rights

Human rights

Everyone is entitled to human rights. The death penalty has to involve removing some of them because the offender has not respected the rights of others. A decision is needed on whether the consequences of using the death penalty are more important than everyone's human rights being respected.

Potentially done	Potentially not done
Protect rights, life and dignity, care for offenders	Care for victims, protect society, deter others from crime, punish offenders

Duty

Duty can involve the idea that if something is right in every situation then it always right. The death penalty isn't always right because people who are innocent can and have been executed. It is our duty to protect life, but it is also our duty to ensure justice is done. Which leaves the question of whether our duty towards other people, victims and criminals is more important than the consequences of the death penalty and the human rights issues related to it. Or do we leave the decision about the death penalty to the State, religions and experts?

Potentially confusing	Potentially clear
Not a deterrent, should forgive, should reform, revenge is wrong	State/God says it is right, necessary to assert authority, shows strength

Authority

Who says that we should or should not use the death penalty? Experts can't agree on its effectiveness. Governments can't agree on whether it should be used or not. Religions and moral philosophers can't agree on whether it should be used or not. So should we bother with what they say at all? Should we listen to them before we think of the consequences, human rights and our duties? Or should we think about what would make humanity better?

RELIGIOUS VIEWS ON THE DEATH PENALTY

Christianity

- The Bible can support either point of view.
- Churches on the whole are against it.
- Churches want forgiveness and reformation.
- Life is sacred – so no death penalty.
- Because life is sacred – some argue the death penalty is needed to show it.
- The final judgement is God's so He decides what happens when the prisoner dies.
- We are agents for God's justice and have the right to carry out the death penalty on His behalf.
- The Bible commands against killing.
- God used killing to make points in the Bible.
- Jesus taught forgiveness.

Islam

- Qur'an and hadiths can support either point of view.
- Not as widely used in Muslim countries as some people think.
- Islam wants forgiveness and reformation.
- Life is sacred – so no death penalty in many Muslim countries.
- Because life is sacred – some Muslims say the death penalty is needed to show this.
- The final judgement is God's so He decides what happens when the prisoner dies.
- We are agents for God's justice and have the right to carry out the death penalty on His behalf.
- Some prefer to read the Qur'an and hadiths and argue that the death penalty is no longer required. Others say the truths in them are eternal.
- Muhammad taught compassion and mercy.

DON'T FORGET

Most Muslims countries have the death penalty but do not use it.

Buddhism

- The death penalty is used in some Buddhist countries.
- Buddhism teaches non-harm of living things.
- Buddhism teaches compassion and forgiveness.
- The Buddha disapproved of killing.
- The death penalty goes against the Five Precepts.
- There is no need for the death penalty because kamma will do its work.
- The Buddha responded to evil with skilful actions, the death penalty is unskilful.
- The death penalty creates bad kamma for all involved.

VIDEO LINK

Explore this topic further by watching the videos at the Digital Zone.

THINGS TO DO AND THINK ABOUT

Moral themes

1. Make a list of the religious arguments for and against the death penalty.
2. Make a list of the non-religious arguments for and against the death penalty.
3. Now try to work out what is behind these arguments by allocating moral themes to each one (they can have more than one moral theme). Place the letter of theme after each argument.

   Which ones seem to be concerned about the consequences of the death penalty?

   Which ones seem to be concerned about human rights in the debate about the death penalty?

   Which ones seem to be concerned about duties in the debate about the death penalty?

ONLINE TEST

Test yourself on morality and justice at www.brightredbooks.net

MORALITY AND JUSTICE

THE DEATH PENALTY 2

ARGUMENTS AGAINST THE DEATH PENALTY

Here are some non-religious views on the death penalty.

Reprieve

This charity was founded by a British citizen, Clive Stafford Smith. One part of its mission is to get rid of the death penalty and to support those facing the death penalty. Reprieve argues that cases involving the death penalty are often used by authoritarian governments, are flawed, and that accused individuals are poorly represented. In addition to this, many people on death row have significant unresolved personal and medical issues. Reprieve quotes Supreme Court findings that lethal injection is potentially excruciating, and they have successfully lobbied several drugs companies to stop selling their products to American states where they use lethal injection. Ironically, the drugs were designed to relieve pain and help the sick. Some American states are now experimenting with cocktails of drugs. Reprieve says that the death penalty denies many human rights and medical protocols and that it should be banned throughout the world.

United Nations

In 2014, the United Nations adopted a resolution for a continued moratorium (suspension) of the death penalty. The resolution wanted countries using it to suspend its use with a view to abolishing it. They reminded these countries that the death penalty is irreversible and that there is no conclusive evidence it is a deterrent. Suspending its use would help human rights and aid human progress. They called upon countries using the death penalty to reduce the number of capital crimes, to publish data about its use, to refrain from executing individuals under the age of 18, or those who have mental or intellectual disabilities or are pregnant. The United Nations views the death penalty as removing the right to life and being a cruel and degrading treatment.

European Union

The European Union policy on the death penalty reads: 'The European Union considers capital punishment to be a cruel and inhuman punishment, which fails to provide deterrence to criminal behaviour and represents an unacceptable denial of human dignity and integrity. Any **miscarriage of justice** – which is inevitable in any legal system – is irreversible.' It also has the abolition of the death penalty as a condition of membership and no member state has executed anyone since 1997.

Arab League of Nations

The Arab League of Nations developed their own variation of the Universal Declaration of Human Rights. It was based on the Cairo Declaration of Human Rights of 1990. The right to life was stated and there was a statement about being protected from losing your life without good reason. Only the most serious crimes should have the death penalty (as defined by Shari'ah laws) and there are restrictions on who can be given the death penalty as per the United Nations guidelines.

> Article 2 (a) Life is a God-given gift and the right to life is guaranteed to every human being. It is the duty of individuals, societies and states to protect this right from any violation, and it is prohibited to take away life except for a Shari'ah-prescribed reason. (b) It is forbidden to resort to such means as may result in the genocidal annihilation of mankind. (c) The preservation of human life throughout the term of time willed by God is a duty prescribed by Shari'ah. (d) Safety from bodily harm is a guaranteed right. It is the duty of the state to safeguard it, and it is prohibited to breach it without a Shari'ah-prescribed reason.
>
> Article 20 It is not permitted without legitimate reason to arrest an individual, or restrict his freedom, to exile or to punish him. It is not permitted to subject him to physical or psychological torture or to any form of humiliation, cruelty or indignity.
>
> **Cairo Declaration on Human Rights, 1990**

DON'T FORGET

Religious and non-religious views of the death penalty can be both for and against it.

ARGUMENTS FOR THE DEATH PENALTY

It is an easier task to find individuals who are for the death penalty, and they tend to be judges, lawyers, politicians and university experts. The following quotes outline the main themes of their positions.

contd

Morality and Justice – The Death Penalty 2

'Capital punishment may be morally required not for retributive reasons, but in order to prevent the taking of innocent lives…' (Cass R. Sunstein, PhD, Professor of Law)

'Indeed, other recent investigations, using a variety of samples and statistical methods, consistently demonstrate a strong link between executions and reduced murder rates… In short, capital punishment does, in fact, save lives.' (David B. Muhlhausen, US politician)

'I personally have always voted for the death penalty because I believe that people who go out prepared to take the lives of other people forfeit their own right to live.' (Margaret Thatcher)

'I would bring back capital punishment for serial murderers. It is not a crime of passion, it is clearly pre-meditated and cold-blooded. The reason why people are against the death penalty very often is because of the risk of getting it wrong. With serial murders, that is unlikely to happen.' (David Davis MP, Conservative)

'I will sign a strong, strong statement that will go out to the country, out to the world, that anybody killing a policeman, policewoman, police officer – death penalty.' (Donald Trump)

'Child and serial killers are never safe to be released back into society and quite frankly keeping them behind bars till they die is a waste of taxpayers' money. They forfeit any rights when they murder innocents.' (Godfrey Bloom MEP, UKIP)

'If you had the ultimate punishment for the murder of policemen and other heinous crimes, I am sure it would act as a deterrent. We must send a clear signal to people that crime doesn't pay. The punishment must fit the crime and yes, I do support capital punishment. For far too long the law has been on the side of the criminal. Law and order is breaking down in Britain and we must do something about it.' (Priti Patel MP, Conservative)

'I don't think you should support the death penalty to seek revenge. I don't think that's right. I think the reason to support the death penalty is because it saves other people's lives.' (George W. Bush, 43rd President of the United States)

'While the evidence tells me that the death penalty does little to deter crime, I believe there are some crimes—mass murder, the rape and murder of a child—so heinous, so beyond the pale, that the community is justified in expressing the full measure of its outrage by meting out the ultimate punishment.' (Barack Obama)

VIDEO LINK

Learn more about this topic by watching the videos at the Digital Zone.

THINGS TO DO AND THINK ABOUT

Word Clouds

A good way of building up a picture of views on issues is to create a word cloud. The more a word is used, the bigger it should be. Create one for the following:

- Religious views on the death penalty.
- Non-religious views on the death penalty.
- Pro-death penalty quotes.

ONLINE TEST

Test yourself on morality and justice at www.brightredbooks.net

MORALITY AND JUSTICE
WHOLE LIFE TERMS 1

THE ARGUMENT

So...

You have decided that the death penalty is cruel, is inhuman, violates human rights and is degrading. You have decided that life has a value and is sacred and has to be protected no matter what a person does or how horrible the crime. You have also made sure that in the unlikely event of the individual being proved innocent you have a sentence that can be reversed. You have sentenced the murderer to a **whole life term** in prison.

But...

Have you considered what a whole life term means? A whole life term means that the murderer can be sentenced to extreme numbers of years (one person in the USA has been given 161 life sentences, a woman in Thailand has a sentence of over 140 000 years), which means they will never be released. You have given the individual no hope of release. You have given the prisoner a life which (by any description) is not pleasant. You have given the individual no reason to reform or co-operate because nothing more can be done to him or her. You have subjected the prisoner to a cruel punishment, especially if they truly reform and are incapable of committing a crime again.

However...

The point is that the murderer has been removed from society and that makes society safer. Also, it means that people know that they will never be released and that will act as a deterrent; the sentence will also allow society to express its outrage over the crimes committed by the individual, and state that if you deny a person the right to live then you will forfeit your right to have a life.

But...

How can you argue that this is any better than being put to death? At least the death penalty is quick and final. Imagine knowing for your whole life that the walls of the prison are all you are ever going to see. How can you argue that a whole life term is doing anybody any good other than removing the risk of an irreversible sentence if a person has been wrongly convicted? How can you argue that the individual's life is worth living when they are stripped of much of their dignity? How can you argue that this promotes human rights or that whole life terms uphold the value and sanctity of life?

Therefore...

Whole life sentences create many complex moral issues which include:

- Governments say that prisons are for reform. Whole life sentences disregard any change that takes place in a person.

- Long periods of imprisonment are damaging and therefore cruel and inhumane.

- The death penalty involves prisoners dying quickly in prison, whole life terms involve prisoners dying in prison usually over a long period of time.

- If there is no prospect of release regardless of change in the individual, is that not inhuman and unfair in a justice system that is supposed to be fair?

- If there are whole life terms are we not then denying that human beings have an enormous capacity for **change**?

MORAL DEBATE

Key:
| Potentially good |
| Potentially bad |

Moral issue	Consequences	Duty	Human rights
With the death penalty a person is sentenced to die in prison. With whole life terms, a person is sentenced to die in prison.	Most people are protected so we feel safer.	The state has protected its citizens.	The individual's right to life is upheld.
	The individual takes a longer time to die with whole life terms.	The state is failing in its duty to spend taxes beneficially.	The individual is subject to cruel and inhuman treatment.
People need autonomy, Whole lifers have that reduced in prison.	The individual loses their freedom but keeps their life.	The prison fulfils its duty to punish.	The individual retains their right to life.
	The individual can still make choices.	The prison does not fulfil its duty to reform.	The individual loses many of their human rights.
The death penalty is final, people can move on. Whole lifers and their families do not have that.	Nobody will be left with the consequences of having been part of an execution.	The state has removed a threat to safety.	The human rights of the individual's family are not being upheld.
	There is no closure for anyone involved.	The victim's family may feel that justice has not been done.	In effect, the right to life is being denied.
Whole life terms do not fulfil the purpose of prison.	Purpose of prison is to protect and deter.	The prison's duty to reform can still be done with lifers.	The state's duty to protect the right to life of all citizens is upheld.
	Prisons are supposed to reform and prepare for release.	Prisons have a duty to give hope for a better future. Lifers cannot have this.	Everyone has a right to have hope – lifers are denied the hope of release.
Whole life terms are reversible. The death penalty isn't.	Mistakes are reversible.	The state has a duty to protect life and does it through whole life terms.	The right to life is upheld.
	The damage caused by whole life terms may not be reversible.	The state has not upheld its duty to give people dignity.	The right to a good quality of life is denied.
Whole life terms always create mental health issues for the prisoner.	This is what punishment is for.	The state has a duty to deter others, the mental pain may do the job.	The treatment the individual gets is no worse than their victim whose right to life was ignored.
	Mental illness can be like torture.	The state must not inflict any inhumane punishments.	The treatment in prison is cruel and inhumane.
The death penalty is an easy way out.	Quick, expensive and final.	If the state uses the death penalty, extreme caution is taken in every case.	The individual is given a quick, painless way out so their dignity is kept.
	Irreversible if the verdict was wrong, so speed is no advantage.	Mistakes are made regardless of the care taken.	Dying in front of an audience is degrading.
Some crimes can never be forgiven no matter what.	A line is drawn for all to see what is totally unacceptable.	The state has a duty to protect its citizens from dangerous people.	All human rights for individuals are protected.
	So some people are written off as beyond hope no matter how much they change.	The state has a duty to run a justice system that is fair – no parole means that the state is saying you will never be cured.	The human rights of the murderer are compromised.
The murderer never gave a thought or choice to their victim when they were killed.	Life tariff gives them time to think about it and suffer the guilt.	The state has a duty to protect its citizens from people who kill.	The murderer forfeits most of their rights by killing someone.
	The murderer could develop serious mental illness.	The state has a duty to treat the sick – maybe the murderer was sick.	Everyone should have the same basic rights regardless of what they have done.

DON'T FORGET
Whole life terms means that a person will never be released from prison.

VIDEO LINK
Learn more about this topic by watching the videos at the Digital Zone.

ONLINE TEST
Test yourself on morality and justice at www.brightredbooks.net

THINGS TO DO AND THINK ABOUT

1. Write down ten problems created by whole life terms.
2. Write down ten problems that are solved by whole life terms.

MORALITY AND JUSTICE
WHOLE LIFE TERMS 2

RELIGIOUS RESPONSES

Finding a clear religious response on the issue of whole life terms is difficult. The clearest statement in recent times has come from Pope Francis who said that keeping inmates imprisoned for life is 'a form of torture' and that all life sentences were 'a hidden death penalty' that should be abolished along with capital punishment. He added that, 'All Christians and people of good will are called today to struggle not only for abolition of the death penalty, whether legal or illegal, and in all its forms, but also to improve prison conditions, out of respect for the human dignity of persons deprived of their liberty.'

And that is about the clearest statement you will find. What you have to do to work out religious views is to look at what is said elsewhere about every other aspect of this topic and you will find that religious people are able to find support for both sides of the argument about whole life terms.

Buddhism: the cause of crime is greed and the Three Poisons. It can be cured by skilful actions and by following the Dhamma: the Buddha reformed a serial killer. Compassion and non-harm are central themes in Buddhist teaching.

Therefore, most probably against whole life terms.

Christianity: mixed views about the causes of crime but leaning towards not being entirely the criminal's fault. On punishment, it should be based on reform and forgiveness but there is also the view that humans are carrying out God's justice by punishing. On the whole in favour of rehabilitation and supporting prisoners' right to being treated humanely without cruelty. The Pope says that whole life terms are effectively a death penalty.

Therefore, no clear overall view but the Pope represents the biggest group of Christians so most probably against whole life terms.

Islam: Muslim countries do not have a strong history of lengthy imprisonment. Traditionally, punishments have avoided prison and opted instead for capital and corporal punishment, banishment and restorative justice. They believe God is just and merciful and they also believe that long-term imprisonment does not serve any great purpose.

Therefore, no clear overall view but probably more against than for on the grounds that prison systems have, historically, not been used extensively in Muslim countries. Most likely to feel that a whole life term is no better than the death penalty. At the time of Muhammad there were not really prisons as we know them, and whilst there are more in Muslim countries today, they do tend to be for shorter term sentences because the emphasis is on reformation and release. Whole life terms do not allow for people to change and to earn release and are therefore dishonest.

Morality and Justice – Whole life terms 2

NON-RELIGIOUS VIEWS

It is the same with non-religious views. There are as many which support whole life terms as do not. Those that do not support whole life terms prefer either the death penalty or whole life terms with the possibility (however remote) of release. The European Community has said that every whole-life-term prisoner should be entitled to parole if they have truly changed. They accept, though, that for some people the chance of getting parole is very slim. The point is that the European Community feels that it is cruel and inhumane to remove even the slightest hope of release.

Whole-life-termer Kenneth E. Hartman wrote this for *Counterpunch*:

> A traditional death sentence entails a comparatively short stay in prison, in specialized units and, almost always, in a private cell. People from all over the world, literally, will take up your cause and lobby on your behalf. A bevy of celebrities will champion your case in league with numerous well-funded national and international organizations. Your appeals are mandatory and subjected to the highest scrutiny. High-powered attorneys will volunteer to represent your interests. Assuming you lose all your appeals, you will die in a horrific medical procedure that lasts all of 15 or 20 minutes.
>
> Life without the possibility of parole, the other death penalty, has a radically different set of realities affixed to it. Because it really does mean life without parole, you will remain in prison until you die, however long that takes. You will serve your time in the most violent and repressive of prisons crammed into a cell (designed for one person) with whoever happens to be pushed in the door. No lawyers will volunteer to help you, and your appeals are neither mandatory nor subjected to any heightened scrutiny. You will not receive letters of encouragement and visits from supporters in this country, let alone from around the world. Those well-funded national and international organizations, fronted by familiar, famous faces, will not work to overturn your sentence. In fact, they will lobby against your interests.
>
> At some points, decades later, after living in atrocious conditions and growing old in prison (a fate worse than death, I assure you), you will die. It will not be under the watchful eyes of a worldwide audience of concerned activists. Rather, you will die alone in a nondescript, poorly staffed and managed, prison infirmary. Pain medication will be provided only begrudgingly, if at all, by medical staff who view you as their enemy.

DON'T FORGET
Whole life sentences are rare but there is a growing concern about them as a form of punishment.

VIDEO LINK
Watch the video on the Digital Zone for more on whole life sentences.

ONLINE TEST
Test yourself on morality and justice at www.brightredbooks.net

THINGS TO DO AND THINK ABOUT

On Balance

- Down one side of a page list all the arguments for the death penalty and on the other side of the page list all the arguments for whole life terms.
- Draw a line or lines between your first death penalty argument and those whole life term arguments that you think it is better than.
- Move on to the second argument and go through the same process.
- To finish… on balance, which approach has the stronger arguments – death penalty or whole life?
- You could repeat this process by doing the same kind of thing with arguments against the death penalty and against whole life terms.

Morality and belief

MORALITY AND MEDICINE

THE VALUE OF LIFE

We often hear phrases like 'life is sacred', 'every life is valued' and 'we must respect the right to life'. Few people would actually disagree with these phrases but in reality there are exceptions and not every life is regarded as sacred or valued. Species other than humans are used for food or clothing or entertainment and are, therefore, not treated as sacred or valued in the same way that human lives are.

So, what is clear is that **humans** have decided that a human life is more valuable than the life of any other species. However, in some circumstances, a human life can be taken, providing there are good reasons for doing so. Here is one way in which the value of human life is considered.

WHAT MAKES HUMAN LIFE VALUABLE?

The first step is to think about the **intrinsic and instrumental value** of things:

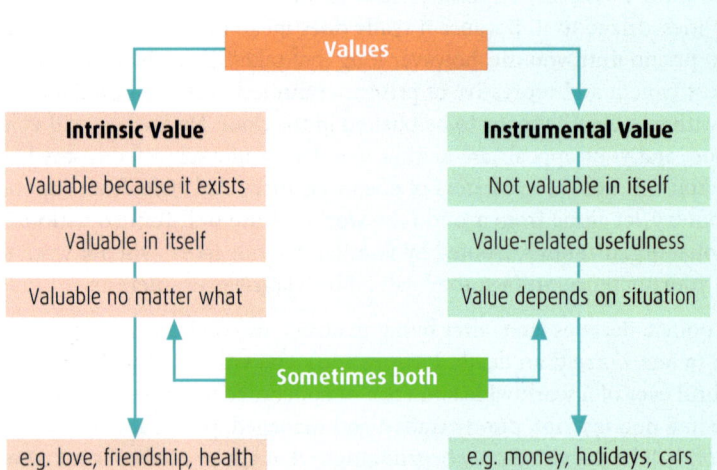

The debate is whether human life has intrinsic value, instrumental value, or a mixture of the two. This is summarised by these three questions:

- Does human life always matter? [intrinsic]
- Does human life matter depending on the situation? [mix]
- Does human life matter only when it is of some use? [instrumental]

Many people, both religious and non-religious, consider human life to have intrinsic value because humans have:

- A unique consciousness of themselves.
- A unique relationship between their body and mind.
- The ability to act through reason as well as instinct.
- The view that existence has a purpose.
- A sense of morality.
- The ability to form meaningful relationships.
- The ability to shape their own future.
- The ability to empathise and appreciate things.

contd

Morality and Medicine – The value of life

Religious groups speak of the **sanctity** of life. Sanctity means to be **holy**. To religious people, the sanctity of life can mean:

- Human life is not the property of humans to use as they like.
- Life is a gift from God to be used for higher purposes.
- Human life has been given so that humans may serve God.
- Humans were created in God's likeness.
- Human lifespan is decided by God, not humanity.
- God set humans apart from other creatures so they have a special status.
- Only humans can have a relationship with God.

If human life has intrinsic value, then…

- It must always be protected, no matter what
- Life is always seen as a good thing
- It can never be intentionally destroyed
- Taking a human life always has been and always will be wrong
- The intentional taking of a human life is a grave offence
- Every human life is equally valuable
- It must be respected

…but what if…

- You kill in self-defence?
- You put someone out of their suffering?
- You kill because other options were worse?
- You kill to punish for a crime or deter others?
- There is a war?
- The individual is a foetus?
- The quality of life is terrible?

…intrinsic value would change nothing.

However, if the value of life depended on…

- The usefulness of a person
- A person's skills
- The quality of life for a person
- The crime a person had done
- A person's awareness of the world
- The future value of the person to society
- The person being known to you

…then the value of life is instrumental.

DON'T FORGET

Most religious groups see life as having an intrinsic value.

VIDEO LINK

Learn more about intrinsic and instrumental value by watching the video at the Digital Zone.

ONLINE TEST

Test yourself on morality in medicine at www.brightredbooks.net

THINGS TO DO AND THINK ABOUT

1. Do we have a duty to give life an intrinsic value?
2. What might the consequences be if life is given an instrumental value?
3. Note down the human rights that you think we cannot do without. Which rights support the intrinsic value of life and which ones support the instrumental value of life?
4. Which would have the greater impact if enforced, intrinsic or instrumental value of life?

MORALITY AND MEDICINE

THE VALUE OF LIFE: RELIGIOUS AND NON-RELIGIOUS VIEWS

RELIGIOUS VIEWS ON THE SANCTITY OF LIFE

Below are two belief wheels. The top one covers what Eastern religions teach about the sanctity of life and the lower one covers what Western religions teach about it. At the centre of the wheel (the hub) is the belief, the spokes are the arguments used to support the belief, and the spaces between the spokes are the questions that are raised both about the belief and its support.

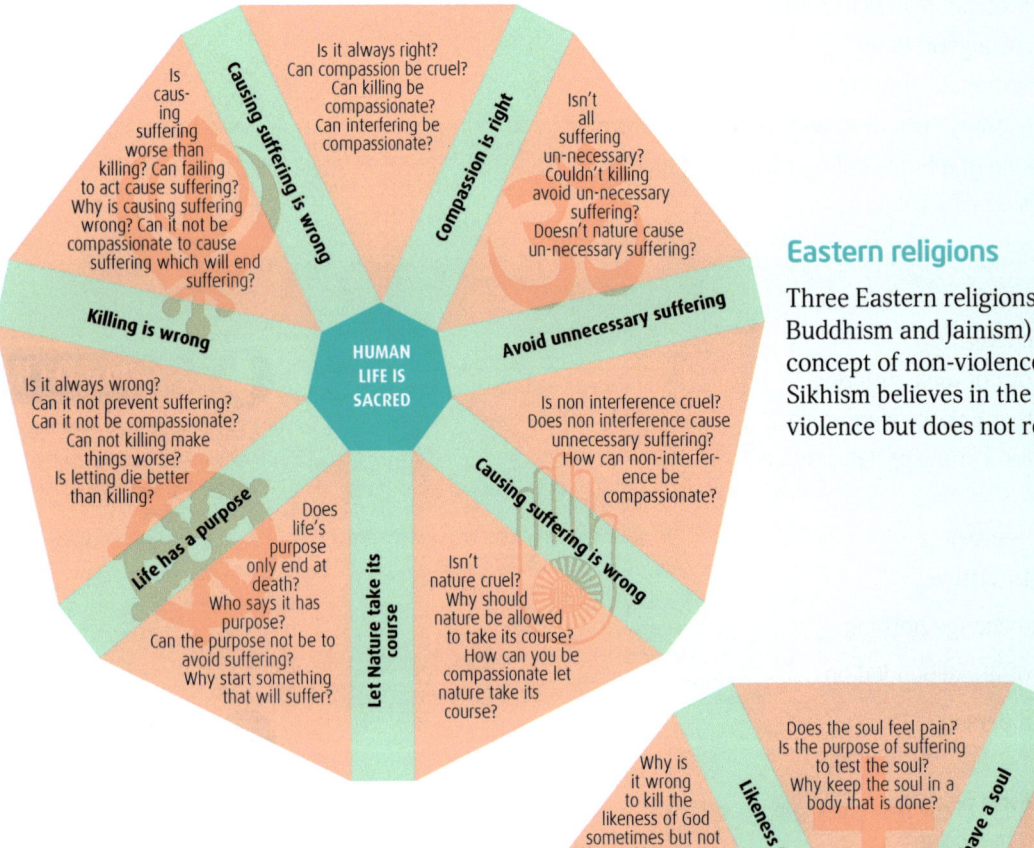

Eastern religions

Three Eastern religions (Hinduism, Buddhism and Jainism) all believe in the concept of non-violence (called ahimsa). Sikhism believes in the concept non-violence but does not refer to it as ahimsa.

Western religions

The approaches of the Western religions of Judaism, Christianity and Islam have a number of beliefs that are shared.

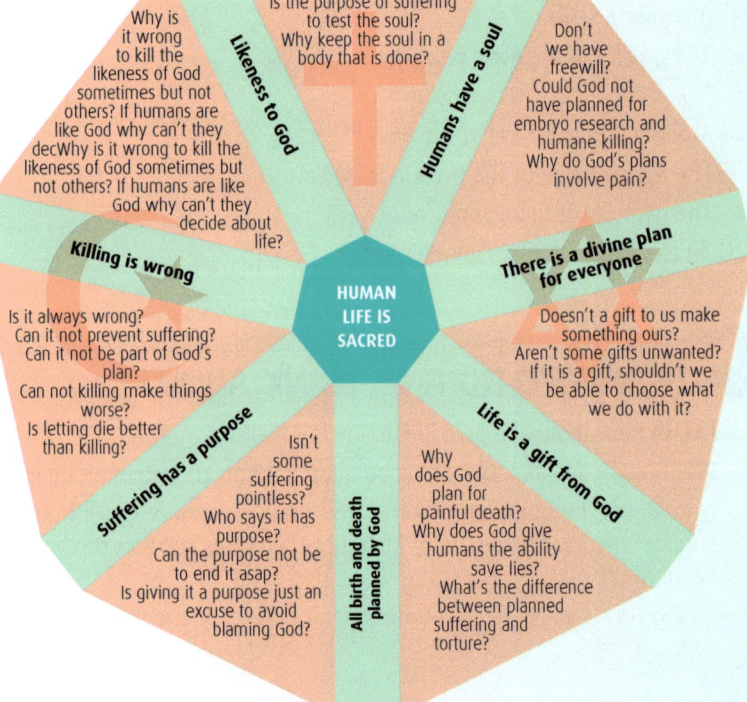

Morality and Medicine – The value of life: Religious and non-religious views

 **ACTIVITY:** Belief wheels

Look at the belief wheels on the previous page. When you give your answer to each question, always explain your choice.

1. What spoke from each one could be taken out and not weaken the belief?
2. What spoke could never be removed because it is vital to support the belief?
3. Choose the question in each spoke space that creates the biggest problem for the spoke.
4. Create a question which you think might blow the belief apart.

NON-RELIGIOUS VIEWS ON THE VALUE OF LIFE

Non-religious views on the value of life are different. Many moral philosophers have also expressed views on the issue. Two have been selected here.

	Pro-life organisations	Pro-choice organisations	Humanists	Philosophers	
				Glover	Kant
Human life has an intrinsic value	✓	✓	✓		✓
Everyone has the right to life	✓	✓	✓		✓
Vulnerable individuals need special protection	✓	✓	✓		✓
Every life is worthwhile from beginning to end	✓				✓
Everyone has the right to choose		✓	✓	✓	
Nobody should feel they have to make a decision one way or the other		✓	✓		
Every life is worthwhile from beginning to end provided the individual concerned considers it to be worthwhile		✓		✓	
It is intrinsically wrong to destroy a life that is worth living	✓	✓	✓	✓	✓
Some people have a life that is not a life worth living			✓	✓	
It is a basic human duty to protect the lives of innocent human beings	✓	✓	✓		✓
It is always wrong to actively or intentionally kill an innocent human being	✓				✓
Motives are very important, which means that it might be possible to kill an innocent human being if the intention was to relieve suffering and not kill (the **double effect**)	✓	✓	✓		✓

 VIDEO LINK

Learn more about views on the value of life by watching the video clips at www.brightredbooks.net

 DON'T FORGET

Non-religious groups do not necessarily believe the opposite of religious groups.

 THINGS TO DO AND THINK ABOUT

1. 'I am in favour of giving people a choice at the end of their life but I am pro-life for embryos.'

   Can you be in favour of one of these two things but against the other?
2. Is it always wrong to end the life of an innocent human being?
3. For you, what is a life worth living?
4. Is any life ever 'not worth living'?
5. Should there be a law allowing for lives that are not worth living to be ended?

89

MORALITY AND MEDICINE
MEDICAL ETHICS: RIGHTS AND CHOICES

Now we will look at the rights involved in medical ethics. To start with we will look at the United Nation's human rights that might apply to medical ethics.

UNIVERSAL DECLARATION OF HUMAN RIGHTS

There are many rights in the Declaration, but the ones noted below are the most relevant in medical ethics.

1. We Are All Born Free and Equal. We are all born free. We all have our own thoughts and ideas. We should all be treated in the same way.	**2. Don't Discriminate.** These rights belong to everybody, whatever our differences.	**3. The Right to Life.** We all have the right to life, and to live in freedom and safety.
5. No Torture. Nobody has any right to hurt us or to torture us.	**16. Marriage and Family.** Every grown-up has the right to marry and have a family if they want to.	**18. Freedom of Thought.** We all have the right to believe in what we want to believe.
19. Freedom of Expression. We all have the right to say and choose as we see fit.	**29. Responsibility.** We have a duty to protect the rights and freedoms of others.	**30. No One Can Take Away Your Human Rights.**

ONLINE

Learn more about the Universal Declaration of Human Rights at www.brightredbooks.net

Everyone involved in health and social care has certain responsibilities.

Medical staff	Individuals	Researchers	Carers
Autonomy: the right to choose must be respected.	An individual's health is their own responsibility.	Be aware of, and keep up to date with, all requirements relating to one's area of research.	Take responsibility for staying up to date with working practices.
Beneficence: non-harm and care are top priorities.	Is it the individual's responsibility to make their wishes known.	Research should only go ahead if the potential benefits outweigh any potential risks to the donors of the samples.	Establish and maintain the trust of service users.
Non-maleficence: avoid unnecessary harm.	It is the individual's responsibility to ensure that their family has protection in the event of their illness.	Patients should be informed when material left over following diagnosis or treatment might be used for research.	Respect the rights of service users provided their behaviour does not cause harm to themselves or others.
Justice: equal access to health and fair distribution of health resources.	It is the individual's responsibility to be involved in the health and welfare of family members.	Researchers should treat all personal and medical information relating to research participants as confidential.	Report any abuses of trust.

VIDEO LINK

Find out more about medical ethics by watching the video at www.brightredbooks.net

PERSONAL AUTONOMY (THE RIGHT TO CHOOSE)

A key issue in medical ethics is respecting the right to choose. This is also known as personal autonomy and it is about individuals being allowed to make their own choices in relation to reproductive and end-of-life decisions.

contd

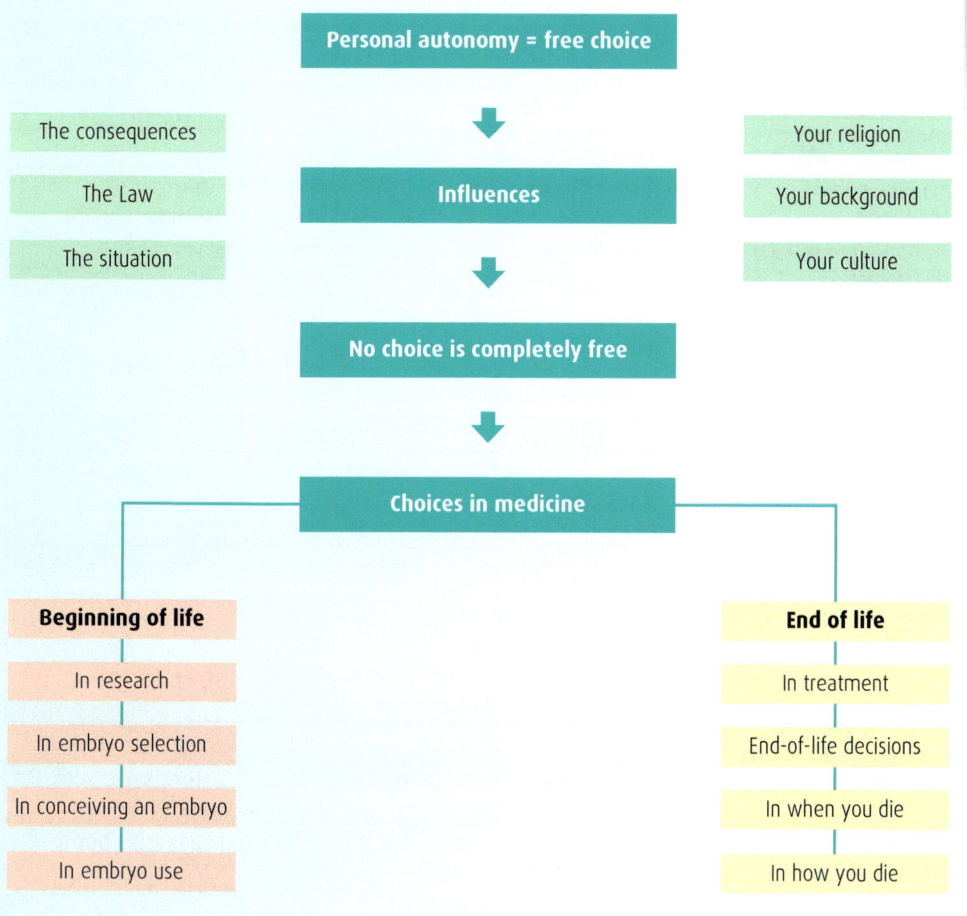

Morality and Medicine – Medical ethics: Rights and choices

```
                    Personal autonomy = free choice
                                  ↓
  The consequences                                          Your religion
  The Law                     Influences                    Your background
  The situation                                             Your culture
                                  ↓
                    No choice is completely free
                                  ↓
                         Choices in medicine
           ┌──────────────────────┴──────────────────────┐
     Beginning of life                               End of life
       In research                                   In treatment
       In embryo selection                           End-of-life decisions
       In conceiving an embryo                       In when you die
       In embryo use                                 In how you die
```

DON'T FORGET

Personal autonomy is the freedom to choose but some people argue that nobody has true personal autonomy.

THINGS TO DO AND THINK ABOUT

Would you rather:

- That scientists make their own decisions about embryo research or that there are laws to limit them?
- That couples had the option of selecting an embryo or that babies with disabilities were born?
- That everyone has the choice to conceive a child, or that children can only be conceived naturally?
- That people had the choice to die as they wish, or that they only die naturally?
- That people were euthanised or given high quality end-of-life care?
- That people had more freedom to choose, or that things should stay as they are?

Try writing bullet-point answers for each of these questions and you will see the issues about personal autonomy emerge.

ONLINE TEST

Test yourself on medical ethics at www.brightredbooks.net

MORALITY AND MEDICINE
THE MORALITY OF PERSONAL AUTONOMY

Viewpoint	Consequences of viewpoint	Duties related to viewpoint	Rights related to viewpoint
Life has an intrinsic value and should never be destroyed	• No innocent lives destroyed • Vulnerable protected • No grey areas – killing is wrong • Right to life protected	• Caring for the vulnerable – done • Protecting everyone – done • Preventing crime – done • Obeying the law – done	• Right to life – upheld • Rights of the vulnerable – upheld • Right to health care – upheld
	• Quality of life might be poor • Removes autonomy • Greater suffering possible	• Acting in patient's best interests – not done • Prevention of needless suffering – not done • Allowing free choice – not done	• Right to no degrading treatment – denied • Right to autonomy – denied • Protection of others' rights – denied

	Concerns about viewpoint	Agreement with viewpoint
Religious attitudes to this viewpoint	Eastern religions: lacks compassion, intrinsic value means people will suffer Western religions: lacks compassion, intrinsic value suggests God has willed the suffering	Eastern religions: life contains a spark of the Divine/energy, should be respected Western religions: life is a gift, should be treasured
Non-religious attitudes to this viewpoint	Pro-life: could cause more suffering Pro-choice: exposes everyone to the risk of being killed Philosophers: *Singer* – uncertainty about meaning of 'life worth living' **Kantian** – could cause more suffering	Pro-life: all life is protected Pro-choice: does not respect autonomy Philosophers: *Singer* – gives people choice, prevents unnecessary suffering *Kantian* – life is protected

Viewpoint	Consequences of viewpoint	Duties related to viewpoint	Rights related to viewpoint
Quality of life is more important than quantity of life	• Unnecessary suffering reduced • Circumstances taken into account • Autonomy respected • Scientific progress can be made • Money can be saved	• Acting in patient's best interests – done • Pain relief – done • Crime prevention – done • Autonomy respected – done	• Right to no degrading treatment – upheld • Right to autonomy – upheld • Protection of others' rights – upheld
	• Vulnerable at risk • **Slippery slope** risk • Risk of crime • Creates moral issues for medical staff	• Acting in patient's best interests – potentially not done • Prevention of killing – not done • Care of the vulnerable – not done	• Right to life – denied • Rights of the vulnerable – denied • Right to health care – denied

	Concerns about viewpoint	Agreement with viewpoint
Religious attitudes to this viewpoint	Eastern religions: lacks compassion, devalues people Western religions: lacks compassion, God's special creation is devalued	Eastern religions: life contains a spark of the Divine/energy, every life is worthy of respect and living Western religions: life is a gift, there is a Divine plan for every life
Non-religious attitudes to this viewpoint	Pro-life: everyone is put at risk Pro-choice: life's value is worth more than how useful it is Philosophers: *Singer* – uncertainty about what is meant by 'life worth living' *Kantian* – too many grey areas, morals have no grey areas	Pro-life: no grey areas, all life is protected Pro-choice: does not respect individual autonomy Philosophers: *Singer* – gives autonomy, prevents unnecessary suffering *Kantian* – life is protected

Viewpoint	Consequences of viewpoint	Duties related to viewpoint	Rights related to viewpoint
Intrinsic value of life depends on the situation	• Unnecessary suffering reduced • Circumstances taken into account • Autonomy respected • Scientific progress made • Money can be saved • Realistic because the value of life is not always a clear-cut issue	• Acting in patient's best interests – done • Pain relief – done • Crime prevention – done • Autonomy respected – done	• Right to no degrading treatment – upheld • Autonomy – upheld • Rights of others – upheld
	• Vulnerable at risk • The slippery slope • Risk of confusion • Moral issues for medical staff • Uncertainty – definition of a worthwhile life?	• Possibly not acting in patient's best interests • Crime prevention – not done • Duty to care for the vulnerable – not done	• Right to life – denied • Rights of the vulnerable – denied • Right to healthcare – denied

contd

Morality and Medicine – The morality of personal autonomy

	Concerns about viewpoint	Agreement with viewpoint
Religious attitudes to this viewpoint	Eastern religions: life has an unchangeable value Western religions: scripture is unclear on this, life is always sacred	Eastern religions: life contains a spark of the Divine/energy, every life is worthwhile Western religions: life is a gift, there is a Divine plan for every life
Non-religious attitudes to this viewpoint	Pro-life: everyone put at risk Pro-choice: some people just want to be told what to do and not have to weigh up the pros and cons Philosophers: *Singer* – uncertainty about meaning of worthwhile life *Kaniant* – too many grey areas, morals have no grey areas	Pro-life: all life is protected Pro-choice: prevents unnecessary suffering, protects human rights, meaningfully Philosophers: *Singer* – gives people choice and prevents unnecessary suffering *Kantian* – no grey areas, life is protected

Viewpoint	Consequences of viewpoint	Duties related to viewpoint	Rights related to viewpoint
Personal autonomy must always be respected	• Rights of thought and conscience protected • Autonomy • Gives people more freedom • Prevents people from being forced into decisions • Could reduce suffering • Could save money	• Act in patients' best interests – done • Duty to relieve pain – done • Duty to prevent greater evils – done • Duty to respect individual choice – done	• Right to no degrading treatment – upheld • Right to make autonomy – upheld • Right to die – upheld
	• Vulnerable at risk • Difficult to apply any laws • Could lead to unnecessary deaths • Risk that the right to life comes second to the right to choose	• Act in patient's best interests – not done • Duty to prevent needless killing – not done • Duty to care for the vulnerable – not done	• Right to life – denied • Rights of the vulnerable – denied • Right to health care – denied • Protection of others' rights – denied

	Concerns about viewpoint	Agreement with viewpoint
Religious attitudes to this viewpoint	Eastern religions: personal autonomy may be overtaken by the effects of kamma, so choice may not be that useful anyway Western religions: personal desires must always come after God's will	Eastern religions: individuals are empowered through personal autonomy to do good kamma, providing personal autonomy follows the law and improves kamma then it should be respected Western religions: God has given humans free will so that should be respected, God gives guidance on how to use one's personal autonomy
Non-religious attitudes to this viewpoint	Pro-life: too many grey areas in personal autonomy, everyone put at risk Pro-choice: people need the confidence that their choice is the right one, free choice might mean too many choices Philosophers: *Singer* – decisions are not just about oneself, they involve the entire community *Kantian* – humans cannot be trusted to always make the right choice, personal choice cannot be more important than the rule of absolute morals	Pro-life: informed choice should be respected but not as much as life Pro-choice: reinforces the right to choose Philosophers: *Singer* – gives people choice and prevents unnecessary suffering *Kantian* – it is always right to protect innocent life. It is not always right to let people choose

THINGS TO DO AND THINK ABOUT

Debates: explain who would win the debate and why:

Life has an intrinsic value v Life has an instrumental value

Personal autonomy must be respected first v Laws must be respected first

All lives should be valued v Lives worth living should be valued

Protect the right to life v Protect the right to die

DON'T FORGET

Moral issues arise from the consequences of an action, human rights and the duties we are expected to carry out.

VIDEO LINK

Watch the video on **utilitarianism** at the Digital Zone.

ONLINE TEST

Test yourself on medical ethics at www.brightredbooks.net

MORALITY AND MEDICINE

THE STATUS AND USES OF THE HUMAN EMBRYO

There is a debate about the status of the human **embryo**. There are three views:
- An embryo is a non-person.
- An embryo is a potential person.
- An embryo is a person.

Before looking at these three views more closely it is important to consider these facts about the embryo:
- The human embryo is created by two humans.
- The human embryo will only ever be human.
- It is highly unlikely that the embryo will feel pain in the first 14 days.
- Embryos usually contain the necessary parts for them to develop into humans.
- The DNA of every embryo is unique.
- The embryo has no sensations, no self-awareness, no reasoning or capability to communicate.

STATUS OF THE EMBRYO

VIEWPOINTS		An embryo is a non-person	An embryo is a potential person	An embryo is a person
	Experts	Philosopher Peter Singer argues that: 'When it becomes a being capable of feeling pleasure or pain is unclear, but if it can feel these two things then it has moral rights and it would therefore be morally right to do things to it like ensuring its right to live is protected.'	Professor Stephen Wilkinson from Lancaster University argues that: 'If an embryo is potentially human then it does not mean that it has full human rights. Just because someone will become a pensioner in five years (they are a potential pensioner), it does not mean that they have the rights of the pensioner now. It works the same way for an embryo: potentially human does not mean actually human.'	Dr. Alfred M. Bongioanni, Professor of Pediatrics and Obstetrics, University of Pennsylvania suggests that: 'I submit that human life is present throughout this entire sequence from conception to adulthood, and that any interruption at any point throughout this time constitutes a termination of human life...'
	Organisations	**The Human Fertilisation and Embryology Authority (HFEA)** permits research on embryos for up to 15 days, after which they must be destroyed. Organisations such as Marie Stopes and the British Pregnancy Advisory Service provide information about accessing abortion services.	The British Medical Association (BMA) argues that the rights of embryos increase the more they develop. There are no facts in relation to when life begins. Interference with an embryo raises more serious issues as the pregnancy progresses.	The Pro-life Alliance argues that: 'Medical textbooks recognise fertilisation, when a sperm fuses with an ovum, as the start of a new life. This single cell is a whole human being, not a part of the father or mother, whether it is created in a woman's body or on a laboratory slide.' (https://prolife.org.uk/wp-content/uploads/pdfs/Embryo_abuse.pdf)
	Religions	The Roman Catholic Church would reject this because its view is that the embryo is a human from the moment of conception. The Church of Scotland say a human embryo is more than just a bundle of cells. Buddhism, like Christianity, does not agree that embryos are non-persons. The energy of a deceased person is passed on to a new life which begins at conception.	The Church of Scotland has some support for this recognising that embryos cannot just be created for research and that those used should be spares from IVF.	Pope John Paul II wrote in Evangelium Vitae: '... the mere probability that a human person is involved would suffice to justify an absolutely clear prohibition of any intervention aimed at killing a human embryo'. In other words, whilst it cannot be proved for sure that the embryo is human we have to give it the benefit of the doubt.

Morality and Medicine – The status and uses of the human embryo

USES OF THE EMBRYO

The next thing to consider is how embryos are used. There are three main uses:

- For **reproduction** – fertility/PGD
- For **research** – sourcing/stem cells
- For **therapeutic** uses – sourcing/cloning

The chart below gives you a summary of how they are used.

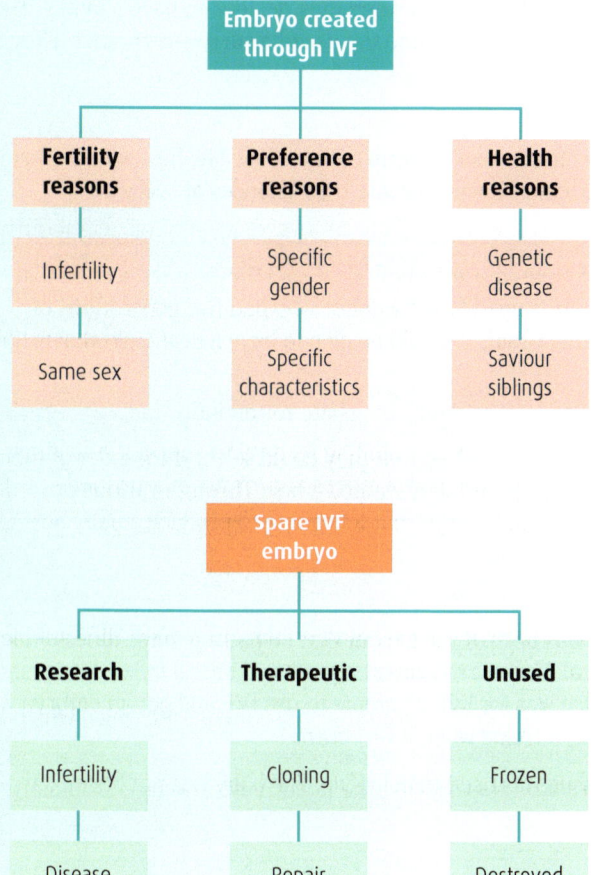

DON'T FORGET

In the UK, embryos are not created purely for research purposes.

ONLINE

Find out more about human **embryo research** by watching the video on the Digital Zone.

ONLINE TEST

Test yourself on medical ethics at www.brightredbooks.net

THINGS TO DO AND THINK ABOUT

1. What is a human?
2. What is a person?
3. What is the difference between a human and a person?
4. Is an embryo a human or a person or both or neither?

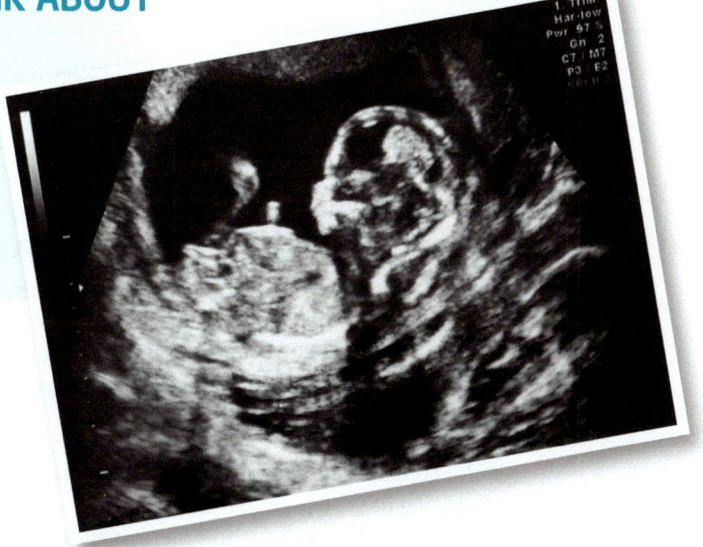

MORALITY AND MEDICINE
THE ISSUES RAISED BY USING EMBRYOS

CASE STUDIES

The best way to understand the issues raised by using embryos is to look at a variety of case studies.

The same-sex family
Gordon and Mark were married for three years when they decided to have a family. The only way this could be done was through IVF and the use of a surrogate mother. They are now the proud parents of a girl.

Childless
Sharon and Jack cannot have children. Jack's sperm count is low. The best way for them to have children is through IVF because it will increase their chances of success.

Disability preferred
In 2002, an American lesbian couple who were both deaf said they wanted a child that would be like themselves. They managed to get a donor who had five generations of deafness in his family One of them said, 'It would be nice to have a deaf child that is the same as us.'

Gender choice
A British couple went to a clinic in the USA so that they could select the gender of their baby. The family had a history of girls and they wanted a boy. Through various procedures they were eventually able to select an embryo that was going to produce a baby boy. They paid more than £15,000 for the procedure.

Saviour siblings
Kyle just wasn't right when he was born. It turned out that he had a genetic illness which was serious and potentially fatal. Various treatments were tried but all failed. Bone marrow was needed and the best chance was for Kyle's parents to use IVF and get an embryo which would probably produce the right tissue when it was born.

The baby was born and the tissue was used to help Kyle. The baby was not harmed in the process.

Down's syndrome
Irene and Peter were warned by doctors that there was a high risk their children would have Down's syndrome. They decided against PGD because they felt that they wanted to conceive naturally and take the risk. Their parents felt that this was selfish and irresponsible and that they should have PGD to ensure that their future children had the best possible chance in life.

Choices
Cystic fibrosis can be a life-limiting disease which affects the lungs. Nicola and Barry were anxious about cystic fibrosis when they were planning a family so they arranged a test. It was discovered that there was a high risk that any child they conceived would inherit the condition. They decided on PGD so that they could avoid the consequences of having a child with cystic fibrosis.

Stem cell research
Stem cells allow researchers to explore different things that stem cells can do: they can produce unlimited copies of themselves which allows research to take place. Researchers can use the information from stem cells to understand diseases better, offer better medicine, and find cures and better treatments for illness.

Therapeutic cloning
No copies of humans have been made but therapeutic cloning is possible. Therapeutic cloning has the potential to understand diseases better, reduce the need and waiting time for transplants, offer better medicines, and find cures and better treatments for illness.

Morality and Medicine – The issues raised by using embryos

There are moral issues raised by each of these cases and they can be divided into five categories:

Value of life	Interference with nature	The right to have a family	A disease- and disability-free world	Personal autonomy
Is the destruction of an embryo killing a human being?	Should science be bending the rules of nature?	Should anyone be allowed to have a family no matter their age or sexual orientation?	Is removing inherited disease always a good thing?	Is there a limit to personal autonomy in relation to embryos?
Is it right that you can get a baby to order without having sex?	Should humans be allowed to 'play God' with embryos?	How much choice should parents have about the children they conceive?	Is it morally wrong to use embryos to benefit humanity?	Is there a point where the right to choose stops?
Even if an embryo is human, is its life sacred?	Should nature be allowed to take its course?	Should science be allowed to create families for those that can't have them naturally?	Do humans have a responsibility to create babies that are healthy?	Are decisions about embryos up to the couple that created them and nobody else?
Should embryos be created purely for research?	If science can interfere with nature in other situations, why not with embryos?	Is it always up to parents to decide why they want to have children?	If humans can remove disability and disease with embryo research then why not?	Why is it anyone's business what a couple decide about their embryos?

THINGS TO DO AND THINK ABOUT

There are viewpoints on embryos from different groups that can be applied to each of these case studies.

Argument	Religious	Non-religious
Children to be conceived only by natural means.	RC	PL
God wishes families to have a male and female partner.	RC	
Creating life in a laboratory is taking over God's role.	RC	PL
IVF involves the destruction of embryos.	RC/Budd/CoS	PL
Method of producing sperm is immoral.	RC	
Surrogacy is unnatural.	RC	PL
Fertility clinics sell hope to the desperate.		PL
Embryos may not feel pain, neither do people under anaesthetic so no pain is a poor argument for using them.		PL
You should not harm living things.	Budd	
Wrong to make a profit out of the despair of infertile couples.	CoS	PL
Embryo selection is a form of eugenics.	RC/Budd	PL/DR
Embryo-screening is discrimination against the disabled.	CoS	PL/DR
Children should be conceived for their own sake and not for the sake of someone else.	RC/CoS	PL
There are alternatives to embryo research that should be developed and used.	RC	PL
Embryo-screening is available to those who have a high risk of passing on genetic disease.	CoS	HFEA
PGD prevents illness and disability.	CoS/Budd	HFEA
Everyone has the right to have a family regardless of gender or sexual orientation.		PC/LGBT
If we have the technology to prevent suffering we have a responsibility to use it.		PC
Embryos feel no pain and have nothing other than potential.		PC
Researching embryos could remove the suffering of others.	CoS/Budd	HFEA/PC
Choosing the gender of a baby isn't harming anyone.		PC
IVF is strictly controlled.	CoS/Budd	HFEA
Rules about sperm, eggs, saviour siblings, surrogacy and research are clear and enforced.	CoS/Budd	HFEA
Fertility clinics and surrogates give everyone the hope of having a family.		PC/LGBT
If it is possible to have a choice then why not, the embryos belong to the parents.		PC
There is a huge difference between a potential Olympic athlete and an actual Olympic athlete. Same with a potential human life in an embryo and an actual baby.		PC
It is time to get rid of the false status given to an embryo.		PC
Slippery slopes often don't happen. It is just panic mongering to say that it is a danger.		PC

DON'T FORGET

It is sometimes a good idea to concentrate on four or five issues and know them really well.

Key:
RC=Roman Catholic
CoS=Church of Scotland
Budd=Buddhism
PL=Pro-life groups
DR=Disability Rights groups
HFEA=human fertilisation and embryo authority
LGBT=LGBT groups
PC=pro-choice groups

VIDEO LINK

Explore this topic further by watching the video at the Digital Zone.

ONLINE TEST

Test yourself on medical ethics at www.brightredbooks.net

MORALITY AND MEDICINE

THINKING ABOUT EMBRYO USE

ACTIVITY: Consequence, Duty, Human Rights, Religion

1. Go back and read over the general information on how people make moral decisions.
2. Now look over the issues that have been covered in this topic.
3. Go through each one of the issues raised and decide what it seems to be concerned about: the consequences, doing one's duty, protecting human rights or doing what your religion tells you.
4. Write the aspects of each issue into the boxes you feel they fit into.

Issue	Consequences	Duties	Human rights	Religious beliefs
Fertility use				
Preference use				
Health use				
Experimental use				
Therapeutic cloning				
Destruction				

ACTIVITY: Working with the issues

1. What's more important...
   a. Protecting embryos or preventing disease?
   b. Giving people freedom of choice or protecting embryos?
   c. Using IVF to help childless couples or using IVF to cure disease?
   d. The right to life of an embryo or the duty to prevent suffering?

2. What causes more problems?
   a. Religious views of the sanctity of life or non-religious views of the value of life?
   b. Religious views of the beginning of life or non-religious views of the beginning of life?
   c. Religious views of embryo research or non-religious views of embryo research?
   d. Religious views of PGD or non-religious views of PGD?

3. Try to work out three consequences for each statement.
   a. No rules for embryo research.
   b. Compulsory embryo-screening.
   c. A complete ban on embryo research.
   d. Defining life as beginning at birth.
   e. Giving the right to a have a disease-free embryo.

4. What's wrong with...
   a. Wanting to have a baby with a disability?
   b. Screening out embryos with inherited serious illnesses?
   c. Saying that life does not begin at conception?
   d. Therapeutic cloning if it helps cure diseases?
   e. Using IVF for same sex couples?

5. What would make everything better?
   a. Treating every embryo as human from conception.
   b. Permitting any kind of embryo research.
   c. Making people pay for fertility treatment themselves.
   d. Deliberately destroying defective embryos.
   e. Taking a religious view on issues arising from embryos.
   f. Society getting rid of the idea of the embryo being life.

Make your choice, or if you don't like any of these then make up your own explaining your answer using arguments and evidence. You can do this exercise again by changing it to 'What would make everything worse?'

ACTIVITY: On balance

- Down one side of a page list all the arguments for embryo research and on the other side of the page list all the arguments against embryo research.
- Draw a line or lines between your embryo research argument and those arguments that you think it is better than.

contd

Morality and Medicine – Thinking about embryo use

- Move on to the second argument and go through the same process.
- To finish... on balance, which approach has the stronger arguments – research or no research?
- You could repeat this process by doing the same with:

The embryo is human against the embryo is not human.
People should have a choice of embryo against there should be no choice.
PGD is discrimination against PGD is a fair treatment of the embryo.

ACTIVITY: World Cup of Arguments

Here we have a tournament. You can have any beliefs in this. The purpose is to get you thinking about issues by pitching one view against another. Here's how it works:

1. You should have a timer and allow one minute for each answer. If no answer is given then the answer is passed over to the other player.
2. Decide who is going first in the **Infertility** reasons versus **Saviour siblings** match. Let's say Infertility reasons goes first. It is the home player because it is on top. The home player gives one supporting reason for the view. The away player then gives one reason why the view cannot be supported. The process is reversed and the away player has a go. Each player has three attempts each. If it is a draw after three attempts each then it is sudden death until one player wins.

In the next round the same procedure is followed except this time it is four goes each, then five each in the final.

```
Infertility reasons
        v                    _____
Saviour siblings
                                        v           _____
PGD reasons
        v                    _____
Characteristics reasons
                                                                v        _____
Gender-preference
reasons
        v                    _____
No embryos created
                                        v           _____
Therapeutic cloning
        v                    _____
Research reasons
```

ACTIVITY: Impact graph

This activity is designed to get you making a judgement about the impact of some of the issues in the debate about the use of embryos. The judgement you are making is about how big the impact is going to be. When something has a big impact on an issue it means that:

- It can be applied to most situations.
- It is related to other points in the debate.
- To miss it out is to miss the point of the argument.
- People have plenty to say about it.

Here are the key issues that run through the debate about the use of embryos:

- The intrinsic value of human life.
- The right to life.
- When life begins.
- The duties of people and professionals.
- The right to have a family.
- The right to choose.
- Playing God.

Here's how to do this activity:

1. Select one of the issues from the list above.

2. Decide on the impact it has on the debate about the use of embryos, on a scale of 1 to 10, and fill in the graph with a bar for each issue.
3. Support your judgement with reasons.
4. Explain your graph to someone who should question you.

Alternatively, you could look at the beliefs of a religious person and complete the same exercise making a judgement on the impact of these issues on their arguments in the debate about embryo use.

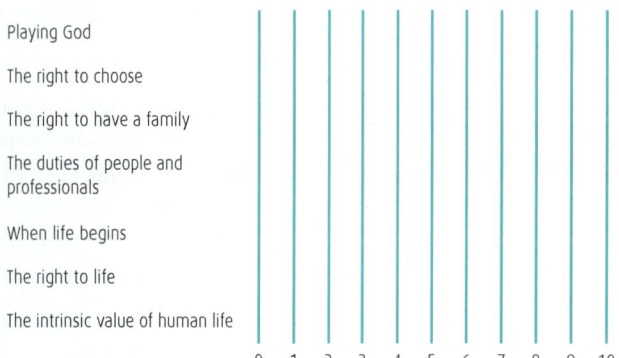

99

MORALITY AND MEDICINE
END-OF-LIFE DECISIONS

End-of-life decisions are not just about switching off life-support machines or the right to die. They are also about what care individuals want at the end of their lives.

WHAT IS AVAILABLE?

In Scotland and the rest of the UK, **euthanasia** is illegal. However, there are avenues open to individuals with the mental capacity to make decisions about their future when preparing for the worst:

- **Advance directive**: a document giving instructions of what to do if a person wishes to die if they are in a certain condition. Considerations:
  o can be done if you have capacity
  o probably legally binding
  o must be related to treatment for current condition.
- **DNACPR**: a document which instructs medical staff not to attempt resuscitation in certain circumstances. Considerations:
  o it is a legal document
  o can be signed by a relative where a patient has incapacity.
- **Refuse treatment**: when written or verbal permission has to be given for medical treatment. This can be refused. Considerations:
  o can be done if you have capacity
  o must be respected even if it means death.
- **Power of Attorney**: a legal document signed when a person has capacity giving other permission to make decisions. Considerations:
  o can be done if you have capacity
  o usually means family can make health and welfare decisions if you can't.

These are decisions that can be taken ahead of your death, each of which will give people control over what happens to them in certain circumstances. This happens mostly before end-of-life care begins.

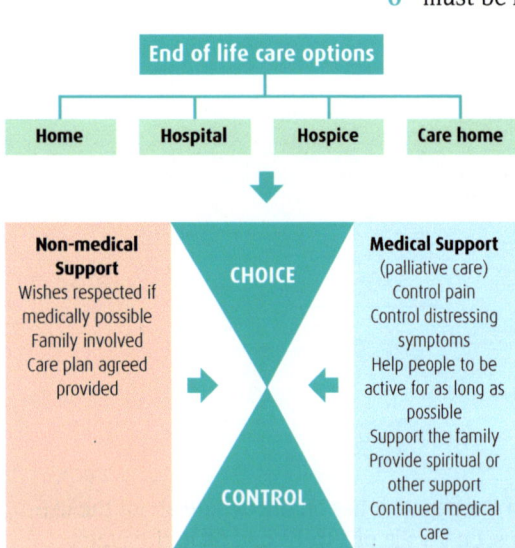

PALLIATIVE CARE

Palliative care is good care for those whose health is in permanent decline or those whose lives are coming to an end. Palliative care has made significant progress in the last thirty years and there are now professionals who specialise in it. Today, palliative care is offered in the last days, weeks, months or years of an individual's life. Everyone has the right to say what type of care they want and where they would like to die. Looking after the family is also part of end-of-life care practice.

There are three main types of palliative care:

- **Generalist** – Social and health care for those whose health is deteriorating. Provided in homes, care homes and hospitals.
- **Specialist** – Specialist care in hospices, palliative care units or an acute hospital who has complex, 24/7 palliative care needs.
- **End of life** – For patients who have started the process of dying regardless of other palliative care they have been getting.

The World Health Organisation (WHO) has identified what it expects providers of palliative care to offer:

'Palliative care is an approach that improves the quality of life of patients and their families facing the problems associated with life-threatening illness, through the

DON'T FORGET
Palliative Care is not purely end-of-life care.

contd

prevention and relief of suffering by means of early identification and impeccable assessment and treatment of pain and other problems, physical, psychosocial and spiritual.'

In Scotland there are three groups of providers:

- **NHS**/local authority
- Private sector
- Voluntary sector

Providers in each of these sectors can be inspected without notice by the Care Inspectorate who publish reports and have the power to close down facilities which do not meet minimum standards of care. So, in theory at least, palliative care will have a minimum standard.

Most palliative care is provided by care homes. In Scotland in 2016 there were just over 1100 care homes, three-quarters of which were privately run, providing care for more than 40,000, half of whom were suffering from the life-limiting disease, dementia. Over 70% of these patients died in the care home. The average length of stay was about three years. Most deaths were the result of Alzheimer's disease or vascular dementia. In 2016, the average weekly cost of a care home place was £650, but it can be anything upwards of £550.

In Scotland, there are twenty Specialist Palliative Care and End of Life Care units. Most of these are **hospices** which are funded by charities. Hospices provide a range of services and support patients in a number of ways. A lot of the work performed by hospices is done in the homes of patients. Approximately 55,000 people die each year in Scotland and some experts believe that three-quarters of them did not have the palliative care they required. The Scottish Government has made a commitment to fund 50% of the running costs of hospices although in 2016 the contribution was 39%.

(https://www.hospiceuk.org/docs/default-source/What-We-Offer/publications-documents-and-files/hospiceuk_ theroleofhospicecareinscotland_september2016. pdf?sfvrsn=2)

THINGS TO DO AND THINK ABOUT

When you read about any type of palliative care it sounds very caring and person centred. However, there are some arguments related to it:

Argument	Religious	Non-religious
We should ration pointless care at the end of life.		Gen
If people want to buy palliative care then they should be allowed to.		Gen
Private health care is run for profit, so private palliative care should be, too.		Gen
Palliative care just puts off the inevitable.		Gen
Money is tight so it is only right that those that can afford it pay for it.		Gen
The priority in medicine should be curing, not tending the dying.		Gen
Hospices do not help medical progress because they are there only to let people die well, not to defeat disease.		Gen
Money spent on palliative care is money that could have been spent on research.		Gen
Palliative care is just another way of saying 'we have given up'.		Gen
Palliative care makes patients who want to die feel like they are doing something wrong.		Gen
If euthanasia is legalised then there won't be any need for expensive palliative care.		Gen
Relief of all pain is sometimes impossible so palliative care for some people is a burden.		Gen
Everyone is entitled to the death that they desire if that can be arranged.		Gen
Humans are made in God's image and therefore human life is a gift and it is holy.	CoS/RC/Jud	
All lives are to be treated with respect whether at the beginning or end of it.	CoS/RC/Jud	BMA/ NCPC/WHO
The dying person is not to be viewed in isolation, many people including society, family and physicians are involved in discussions about their future care.	CoS/RC/Jud	BMA/NCPC/WHO
The death itself should not be the focus, rather it should be the time leading up to the death to achieve the best quality of life possible.		
Pain management is better understood now and no longer a strong reason for ending a person's life.		BMA/NCPC/WHO
A person's religious and spiritual life should be explored to give them strength and comfort as they face death.	CoS/RC/Jud	BMA/NCPC/WHO
End of life does not mean end of choice.		NCPC
Palliative care needs to be universally available.		BMA/NCPC/WHO
Everyone should be able to die well.	CoS/RC/Jud	BMA/NCPC/WHO
Palliative care removes the need for euthanasia.		NCPC

ONLINE

Find out more about the issues on the Digital Zone.

Key:
CoS=Church of Scotland
RC=Roman Catholic
Jud=Judaism
Gen=General non religious argument
BMA=British Medical Association
WHO=World Health Organisation
NCPC=National Council for Palliative Care

VIDEO LINK

Learn more about palliative care by watching the video at the Digital Zone.

ONLINE TEST

Test yourself on medical ethics at www.brightredbooks.net

MORALITY AND MEDICINE
PALLIATIVE CARE: CASE STUDIES

CASE STUDIES

Let's have a look at some case studies relating to Palliative Care.

Case studies		
Profit	**Charity**	**Last wish**
Rose had lived in a care home. It was costing her £800 per week. She took ill and was in hospital for three months. During this time the Care Home company reduced her fee by £200 per week. They said: 'We still have wages to pay and at the end of the day we are a business not a charity and we must make a profit.'	Margaret had cancer and spent the last two weeks of her life in a hospice. Her death was peaceful and she died with her family around her. Both she and her family were wonderfully supported by the hospice in her final few months. The hospice is a charity and Margaret paid nothing.	Eilidh lived on a Scottish island. She was 44 when she died. She had palliative care in her final months. She wanted to die at home. She was told that this was not possible because she needed specialist palliative care. She asked if she could be taken care of in a hospice but the nearest hospice was only a day hospice and had no spare beds. The last thing she wanted was to die in a hospital far away from her family. Sadly, she died in a hospital in Glasgow.
Means testing	**The will to live**	**Advance Directive**
Robert has dementia and requires social care because he is no longer able to look after himself. Dementia has caused his situation. Because he has savings and his own house he has to pay for most of his care. There are other people in the care home with dementia who had no savings and lived in a council house. They get the same care for free. It is paid for by the Government.	George was diagnosed with motor neurone disease three years ago. Its progression has made it look like he has got no more than six months to live. He has read all about palliative care and found it helpful but he does not want to go on. He feels everything is settled and he is happy to go before it gets any worse. He sees absolutely no point in going on.	Gemma has manic depression. She has tried to commit suicide three times but each time she has been saved. The doctor says she is of sound mind and can complete an Advance Directive, which she does. In it, she leaves clear instructions that she does not wish any medical treatment no matter what condition she is in at some future date. A month later she drinks poison. She can be saved by the doctors without too much difficulty but the next step for medical staff is awkward.

HARD QUESTIONS

The Cost of Palliative Care	The Purpose of Palliative Care	Equality and Fairness in Palliative Care	Responsibility for Palliative Care	Personal Autonomy
Should all palliative care be free?	Does palliative care have any useful purpose?	Should any distinction be made between illnesses requiring palliative care?	Who is responsible for providing palliative care?	Should people have the choice between palliative care and euthanasia?
Is palliative care a waste of scarce resources?	Does palliative care provide hope where there is none?	Why shouldn't those who can afford it pay for their care?	Does the state have any choice but to underfund palliative care?	Should palliative care be forced on people if they don't want it?
Is there anything wrong with making a profit out of palliative care?	Does palliative care do away with the need for euthanasia?	Should there be a time limit on palliative care?	Should everyone not take out insurance in case they need palliative care?	Should palliative care be a duty or a choice?

 **ACTIVITY** Worst Case Scenario

In this exercise, look at the case studies and work out what the consequences would be for an individual's duties, human rights and religious beliefs. You will need a big sheet of paper for this exercise.

Issue	What problems would it cause for people's duties?	What human rights would be denied?	What religious beliefs would be ignored?
No right to Palliative Care			
No equality in care			
Last wish not granted			
Means testing for care			
Loss of the will to live ignored			
Advance Directive ignored			

Morality and Medicine – Palliative care: Case studies

 ACTIVITY: Best Case Scenario

In this exercise, look at the case studies and work out what the consequences would be for an individual's duties, human rights and religious beliefs. You will need a big sheet of paper for this exercise.

Issue	How would this help people fulfil their duties?	What human rights would be supported?	What religious beliefs would be respected?
Universal right to Palliative Care			
Equal access to care			
Last wish granted			
No means testing for care			
Loss of the will to live respected			
Advance Directive accepted			

 **DON'T FORGET**

The quality of palliative care in the UK depends very much on your postcode.

 ONLINE

Explore this topic further by watching the film at the Digital Zone.

 THINGS TO DO AND THINK ABOUT

Debate Tennis

1. This works best with teams of three but it can be done with teams of two.
2. One person starts. They are the server. The server chooses one of the statements below and the team decides whether to be for the statement or against the statement. The teams then make up their arguments for or against the statement.
   a. Palliative care respects the right to life.
   b. Palliative care respects personal autonomy.
   c. End-of-life care should be free for all.
   d. People should pay for their own end-of-life care.
   e. Palliative care should be a priority.
   f. Palliative care is a waste of money.
   g. People should just be allowed euthanasia.
   h. Palliative care does not really act in anyone's interests.
   i. Life is not sacred.
   j. Life can lose its value when there is pain and suffering.
3. The server starts by giving one argument in favour of the statement.
4. The person opposite them on the other side gives a counter-argument.
5. The person next to the server gives another counter-argument and so on until one side cannot produce an argument.
6. Whichever side wins the argument gets to choose the next statement, and the exercise is done again. First to five points wins.

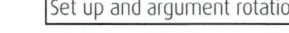 **ONLINE TEST**

Test yourself on medical ethics at www.brightredbooks.net

Set up and argument rotation

Server

103

MORALITY AND MEDICINE
ASSISTED DYING

TYPES OF SUICIDE

There is disagreement over whether assisted dying is a type of suicide. Groups supporting assisted dying insist that assisted dying and assisted suicide are two different things. Assisted dying is helping a person who is terminally ill to die; assisted suicide is helping a person who is not terminally ill to die. However, the UK Government, the Scottish Government and the European Association for Palliative Care do not make any distinction between assisted dying and assisted suicide.

There are three main types of suicide, self-inflicted, **assisted suicide** and **physician-assisted suicide (PAS)**. The differences between each type of suicide are:

- **self-inflicted** – no others are involved; no help is given from anyone else
- **assisted** – others help; no doctors are involved
- **physician-assisted** – others help; doctors do it.

In the UK today, assisted suicide and PAS are illegal. Suicide involves the belief that you have independently made the choice to take your own life, with or without the help of others. Some people see it as the ultimate freedom, it is a personal choice and one that should be respected. However, it is not as simple as that.

Our interest here is specifically in suicide whose purpose is pain relief in one way or another. The cause is related to the physical and mental health of the individual. Usually something has happened that has made their life physically and/or mentally intolerable, so that the best option for them is to end their life.

This brings us to the moral issues related to the right to suicide. We shall focus on two religious and two moral issues. For these we will examine assisted suicide and PAS.

The debate is about the moral issues relating to our right to kill ourselves, and it can be seen here:

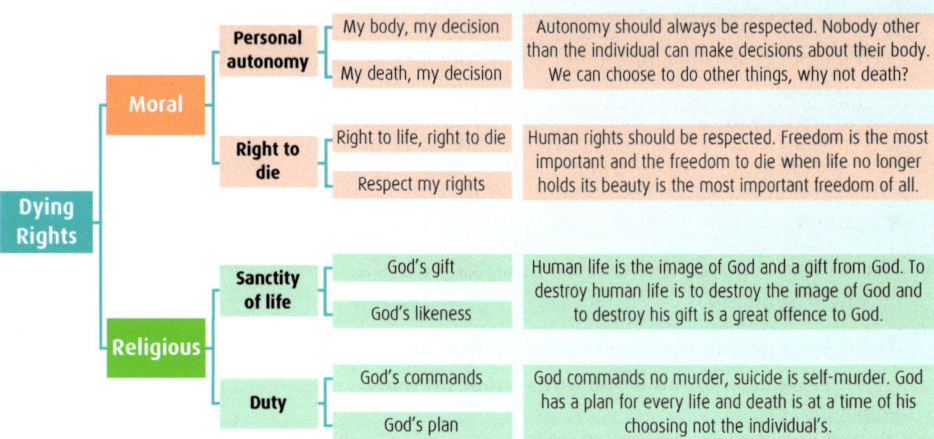

In addition to this are our rights as human beings. We all like to think that we have control over most of the things that happen to us in our lives. The Universal Declaration of Human Rights makes it clear that we have personal autonomy, and that when it comes to our life and death the statements given in the table on p105 may reflect the different views people have on certain aspects of this.

Morality and Medicine – Assisted dying

THINGS TO DO AND THINK ABOUT

Look at the table and write down: My life; My death; My choices.

- Copy the 'is a gift' from the My Life column next to the My Life title you have written.
- Choose one statement from the My Death column which ties in with the 'is a gift' statement.
- Choose one statement from the My Choices column which ties in with the My Death statement you chose and the 'is a gift' statement you wrote down.
- Explain the connections.
- Repeat the exercise starting off with any statement from any column and then match up the other two columns with it.

My life...	My death...	My choices...
Is a gift	Is my business alone	Should be mine alone
Is a gift from God	Is my family's business	Should involve the family
Is not a gift	Is God's business	Should involve God
Belongs to me	Should happen when I want (if possible)	Should be respected regardless
Belongs to my family	Should happen naturally	Should be respected if there is no harm
Belongs to God	Should happen when it is in my best interests	Should be respected if they are legal
Belongs to nobody	Should happen when God says	Should be respected if they are my religion

Traffic Lights

People often think of circumstances when it would be right for them to have the choice to die. Choices are not made in isolation. They have an impact on different people and groups of people. Look at the grid below of circumstances that are sometimes given by those who argue that we should have the right to deliberately take our own lives. You are going to colour code them based on whether or not the circumstances are OK for different people. You can rate them by using the colour code below.

- Red: never OK
- Orange: OK sometimes
- Green: always OK

I should have the right to die when...

	For the individual	For the family	For medical staff	For society in general	For religion
I am tired of living					
my physical suffering is intolerable					
my mental suffering is intolerable					
my physical and mental suffering is intolerable					
I have no hope of recovery					
I am in a persistent vegetative state					
further treatment delays my death					
I have lost my awareness of who I am					
I am no longer able to communicate with others					
I am no longer able to feel pleasure or pain					
I have left written instructions about it					
I have made my feelings clear to the family					
I have made my feelings clear to medical staff					
I am terminally ill					
I am terminally ill and within six months of my death					
Further treatment would be pointless					
I feel I am ready					
I feel God wants me to die					
I feel my family and I are ready					
I have freely given my consent to die					

There are no right or wrong answers. Compare your grid with others in class and explain your choices where you have different colours.

DON'T FORGET

There is no right to die stated in the Universal Declaration of Human Rights.

VIDEO LINK

Consider more viewpoints by watching the video at the Digital Zone.

ONLINE TEST

Test yourself on medical ethics at www.brightredbooks.net

MORALITY AND MEDICINE
ASSISTED DYING LAW

	Assisted suicide – illegal
	14 years in prison
	Helping relatives to go voluntarily abroad to die in a clinic – no prosecution
	No assisted suicide
	Assisted suicide is treated as murder or culpable homicide

THE LAW IN THE UK

In the UK today there are regional variations in the quality of and approach to end-of-life care for individuals, because of where they stay, or because of their family circumstances or physical condition, it might not be possible to offer everyone exactly the same options. One thing is clear though: euthanasia, assisted suicide and PAS are illegal in each of the countries that form the UK.

THE OPTIONS

In the UK, there are three main approaches to suffering and end-of-life care:

Palliative care, which we have already discussed.

Non-treatment decisions (NTD) are made when medical treatment is withheld or withdrawn because there is no medical benefit to the patient, or at the patient's request.

Palliative sedation occurs when medicines are given to relieve pain and suffering by making the patient unconscious.

In a number of these cases the patient will eventually die directly due to their condition, or due to something related to their condition. There are people who want more than these three options because they feel that the patient should have more options about what is going to happen to them. The additional options they want are:

Euthanasia, when a physician (or another person) deliberately kills a patient by giving them fatal doses of medication at their request.

Assisted suicide, when a person deliberately helps another person to end his or her life at their request.

Assisted dying, when a person deliberately helps a terminally ill patient to end his or her life at their request.

PAS, when a physician deliberately helps a person end their life by providing drugs for the patient to take themselves at their request.

AROUND THE WORLD

In 2017, assisted suicide was legal in Canada, Germany, Japan, Switzerland, and in the USA states of California, Colorado, Montana, Oregon, Washington and Vermont.

In general, the law states that the person:

- Must be suffering intolerable pain which is permanent.
- Must have a terminal disease and be in its later stages.
- Must make persistent requests (to die).
- Must be asked to make sure they weren't put under any pressure.
- Must be checked to confirm that they are in the right state of mind.
- Must be euthanised by a qualified person.
- Must give their consent.
- Must have their request carefully checked by different experts.
- Must ensure that any motive to help them is to end their suffering.
- Must be over the age of 16 or have parental consent.

contd

Morality and Medicine – Assisted dying law

In most countries in the world, physicians are not prosecuted when they withhold treatment from a patient which results in their death (rather than continued suffering). Physicians are not prosecuted when medication is given to relieve the patient's suffering, but a side effect of the medication is that it will hasten their death. This is known as the principle of double effect and it all hinges on the motive of the person who is giving the drug.

In countries where euthanasia or assisted dying (suicide) is available, an average of around 1.5% of all deaths are a result of euthanasia or assisted dying (suicide).

DON'T FORGET

Active euthanasia involves direct killing. **Passive euthanasia** involves allowing a person to die.

PERSONAL AUTONOMY AND END-OF-LIFE DECISIONS

End-of-life decisions are very difficult. They force you to imagine a time in the future when you are in a very bad way, and to decide what you would want to happen to you. Picturing yourself in a very bad way is very difficult to do, and you have no way of knowing for sure what the right decision would be. But, if you want control over what happens to you, and you want your decisions respected, then you have to make sure that those close to you know what they are. There are good reasons for both telling and not telling people what your wishes are:

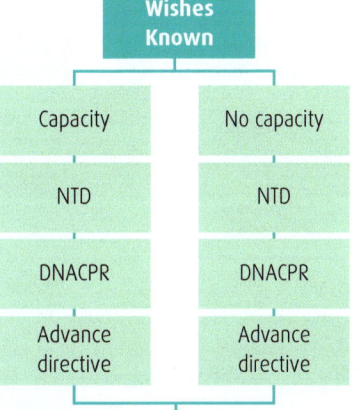

If a patient's wishes are known decision making is easier. If they have capacity then, if they wish, they may discuss them with family and physicians before making a decision. If wishes are known but the patient no longer has capacity to make decisions then their previously stated decisions will be respected and the appropriate course of action taken.

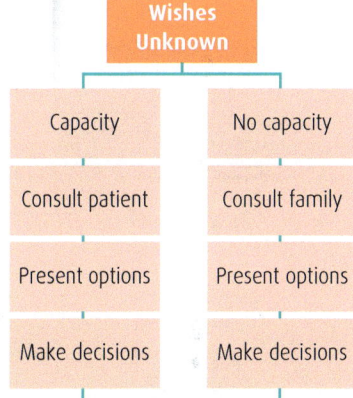

If a patient's wishes are unknown and they have capacity then they should be fully involved in decisions about their future medical care and have the options clearly explained to them. If they do not have capacity this is a discussion that will be had with the people closest to the patient who will usually try to make decisions that the patient would have made anyway.

THINGS TO DO AND THINK ABOUT

The moral issues here centre on consequences and duty.

Brainstorm the good and bad consequences of making your end-of-life wishes known to those close to you.

1. Rate the consequences as serious, fairly serious and not serious.
2. Are the consequences such that you should let people know your wishes?

   Now think of duty. Let's think of our duties to tell the truth and to protect our loved ones from harm.
3. Make a list of the ways in which our duty to tell the truth and our duty to protect our loved ones from harm might come into conflict if we were (a) to make our end-of-life wishes known, and (b) to not have any end-of-life wishes.
4. Is it more important in end-of-life decisions to tell the truth or protect loved ones from harm?
5. Does everyone have a duty to make their end-of-life wishes known?

The more you tell people about your wishes the more your personal autonomy can be respected. This personal autonomy does not extend to leaving instructions to anyone or asking anyone to end your life. That is illegal in the UK. You can ask as much as you like but nobody is allowed to help you out.

VIDEO LINK

Consider the topic of euthanasia in more depth by watching the video at the Digital Zone.

ONLINE TEST

Test yourself on medical ethics at www.brightredbooks.net

MORALITY AND MEDICINE
DYING CHOICES

The key point about dying in the euthanasia debate is that it is voluntary. That is, the person has made the choice when they have had the capacity to make that choice. The free and voluntary choice to die is carried out in various ways around the world (but not in the UK). The flowcharts below give an idea of how the process of euthanasia can generally occur and the moral issues arising from them.

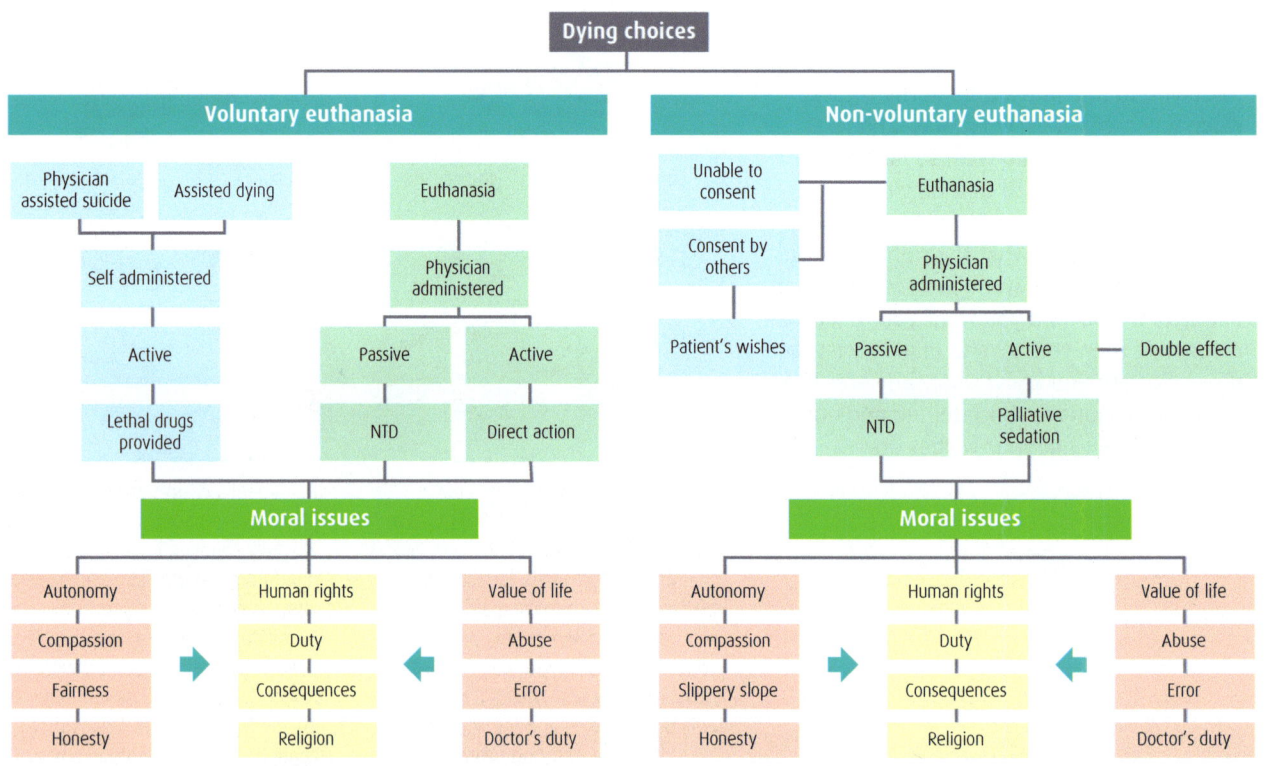

INTERPRETING THE FLOWCHART

- Dying choices can be voluntary or non-voluntary and this is described as euthanasia. **Voluntary euthanasia** is when the individual asks to die and is provided with drugs to do this. **Non-voluntary euthanasia** is when the individual is unable to give consent to anything and the decision is made for them by doctors and families.

- In Physician-Assisted Suicide (PAS) the individual takes an overdose of a drug which has been provided by somebody else. The individual has to take the lethal dose themselves.

- In assisted dying it can be anybody who provides the drugs. The individual will take the drugs themselves. This is active and direct action where the aim is to assist the individual to die.

- Palliative sedation occurs when patients are put into a deep sleep in their final days or weeks which results in their death, most often from some kind of infection.

- Euthanasia occurs when a physician ends the life of an individual. This can happen in three ways:

    o The passive approach is when the family agree to a NTD. Treatment is withdrawn or withheld because it will not bring any medical benefit to the patient.

    o The active approach is when the physician gives the patient a drug which will end their life. In the UK this is illegal.

    o Double effect aims to relieve the pain of the patient and not to end their life. The relief of pain will bring the patient's death forward.

DON'T FORGET

Double effect is usually the way religious people justify shortening a patient's life.

Morality and Medicine – Dying choices

THINGS TO DO AND THINK ABOUT

1. This activity is designed to make you think through the issues and the reasons behind them. Give examples to explain:

IF... THEN...		BECAUSE
IF people have the right to die THEN it changes a doctor's job	BECAUSE	Doctors are trained to preserve and save lives not end them
	BECAUSE	There might be a breakdown of trust between the doctor and the patient
IF people have the right to choose THEN they should be allowed to choose to die	BECAUSE	
	BECAUSE	
IF life is valuable from beginning to end THEN it should be protected from beginning to end	BECAUSE	
	BECAUSE	
IF people have the right to die THEN there won't necessarily be a slippery slope to wanting more rights about dying	BECAUSE	
	BECAUSE	
IF people are suffering terribly THEN they should be allowed to die on request	BECAUSE	
	BECAUSE	
IF people are not terminally ill but still suffering THEN they should be allowed to die on request	BECAUSE	
	BECAUSE	
IF letting die is worse than killing THEN assisted dying should be made legal	BECAUSE	
	BECAUSE	
IF our human rights are important THEN we should be given the right to die	BECAUSE	
	BECAUSE	
IF doctors make errors THEN it can never be right to give them the power to end the lives of others	BECAUSE	
	BECAUSE	
IF people make their end-of-life wishes known THEN end of life decisions are much easier	BECAUSE	
	BECAUSE	
IF everyone can get good quality palliative care THEN there is no need for assisted dying, assisted suicide or euthanasia	BECAUSE	
	BECAUSE	

2. **A New Right**

Imagine that the United Nations has decided to add a new right to the United Nations Declaration of Human Rights. The right to life is expressed like this:

The Right to Life. We all have the right to life, and to live in freedom and safety.

The United Nations has decided that we now have the right to die. How would you complete the statement?

The Right to Die.

You need to check a few things after completing the statement on the right:

- Are any rights contradicted by your statement?
- Are there any circumstances where the right would not apply?
- Does the right affect any other people in a bad way?

If it does then you'll need to go back and reword it.

VIDEO LINK

Find out more about double effect at the Digital Zone.

ONLINE TEST

Test yourself on medical ethics at www.brightredbooks.net

MORALITY AND MEDICINE
THE EUTHANASIA DEBATE

VIEWPOINTS

The table below gives a summary of different views of euthanasia.

RELIGIOUS VIEWS ON EUTHANASIA	Roman Catholic	Protestant	Islam	Buddhism
All forms of euthanasia are unacceptable	✓	✓	✓	✓
Voluntary euthanasia is acceptable in some cases				
Non-voluntary euthanasia is acceptable in some cases				
Everyone has the right not to be killed	✓	✓	✓	✓
Everyone has a special duty to protect the vulnerable	✓	✓	✓	✓
Life is sacred	✓	✓	✓	✓
Suffering has value and purpose	✓	✓	✓	✓
God determines your length of life	✓	✓	✓	
Double effect is acceptable	✓	✓	✓	✓
Futile treatment may be withheld or stopped	✓	✓	✓	✓
Life is a gift from God	✓	✓	✓	
Human life is not the property of humans	✓	✓	✓	
Society has a responsibility to look after the dying	✓	✓	✓	✓
To request your own death is unnatural	✓	✓	✓	

NON-RELIGIOUS VIEWS ON EUTHANASIA	Care Not Killing	BMA	Dignity in Dying	My Death, My Choice
All forms of euthanasia are unacceptable	✓	✓		
Voluntary euthanasia is acceptable in some cases			✓	✓
Non-voluntary euthanasia is acceptable in some cases			✓	✓
Everyone has the right not to be killed	✓	✓	✓	✓
Everyone has a special duty to protect the vulnerable	✓	✓	✓	✓
Life is valuable	✓	✓	✓	✓
There must be limits to human freedom even in a democracy	✓			
Hard cases make bad laws	✓			
Double effect is acceptable	✓	✓	✓	✓
Futile treatment may be withheld or stopped	✓	✓	✓	✓
There will be a slippery slope	✓	✓		
Very few dying people request euthanasia or travel abroad for it	✓	✓		
Society has a responsibility to look after the dying	✓	✓	✓	✓
The aim of medicine is to improve life, not shorten it		✓		
Terminally ill people with six months left should have the choice			✓	
The dying person should take the drugs themselves			✓	✓
People with incurable diseases and intolerable suffering should be given the choice				✓
Medical staff should not be involved	✓	✓	✓	
The patient should be in control of their death			✓	✓
Thorough checks on the person's mental health should take place			✓	✓

ACTIVITY: Order of merit

1. Look at the rights below. Explain which one should come first.
   Right to life   *Right to die*

2. Look at the rights below. Explain which one should be first and which one should be last.
   Right to life   *Right to die*   *Right not to be killed*

3. Look at the rights below. Explain which one should be first, second and third.
   Right to life   *Right not to be killed*
   Right to die   *Right to choose*

contd

Morality and Medicine – The euthanasia debate

4. Look at the rights below. Explain which ones should be the top two and which ones should be the bottom two.

   Right to life   Right not to be killed   Freedom of thought
   Right to die   Right to choose   and belief

 **Mix and match**

Look at the table showing religious and non-religious views on euthanasia.

1. Write down the points that seem to agree with each other on the value of life.
2. Write down the points that are about human rights.
3. Write down the points that seem to be concerned about the consequences.
4. Write down the points where all the viewpoints seem to agree.
5. Write down the points that seem to be concerned with the effect on doctors.
6. Write down the points that are hardest to argue against.

 Scruples

Read each statement and decide on your answer which should either be YES or NO or IT DEPENDS.

1. Everyone should have the right to assisted dying.
2. Assisted dying should only be allowed if a person gives their consent.
3. Everyone should have an Advance Directive.
4. Voluntary euthanasia should be legalised.
5. End-of-life care should be free.
6. Killing is no worse than letting die.
7. Only terminally ill people should be given assisted dying.
8. Human life has a special value and should not be destroyed by doctors.
9. Religion has plenty to offer in the debate about euthanasia.
10. Less should be spent on nuclear weapons and more spent on end-of-life care.

After each answer you should explain your choice.

 DON'T FORGET

Always give at least two reasons for your answer.

 ONLINE

Explore this topic further by watching the video at the Digital Zone.

 THINGS TO DO AND THINK ABOUT

Black, White and Grey

When a viewpoint is described as being black or white it means that there is no middle ground. So in a situation when something is either right or wrong, it can't sometimes be right and sometimes be wrong. Morality issues are neither right nor wrong. Usually there are grey areas which make it difficult to say that one or other side is right. In this task you are going to try to work out the grey areas between two viewpoints. You can do this by making up a situation that shows the answer is not clear-cut or by asking a What If... question.

 ONLINE TEST

Test yourself on medical ethics at www.brightredbooks.net

Black	Grey Areas	White
Everyone has the right to life		Everyone has the right to die
Palliative care is the best end-of-life treatment		Assisted dying is the best end of life treatment
Voluntary euthanasia should be legalised in the UK		The law in the UK is fine as it stands
Everyone should have free care until the end of their lives		The care you get should be based on your ability to pay
Human life is valuable		Human life can get to a point where it is no longer valuable
It is my body therefore it is my choice		The state should have the final say in your end-of-life choices

Religious and philosophical questions

TOOLKIT

RPQ BASICS 1

INTRODUCTION

There are two chapters in this book concerning religious and philosophical questions (RPQs). The two topics are Origins and the Existence of God. These two topics use some of the same knowledge and ideas. This toolkit contains this information and you should refer back to it as required.

PRINCIPLE OF SUFFICIENT REASON

If something has no explanation because there isn't one then we call this a *brute fact*. The opposite of a brute fact is the *Principle of Sufficient Reason* which states that there is an explanation for everything that exists even if we don't know it. So, in responding to questions about origins and the existence of God answers range from those who believe the answer is a brute fact to those who believe that there is an answer somewhere.

Some people say:	NO. We will never know because there is no answer.
	NO. We will never know because it is beyond our understanding.
Other people say:	YES. Everything has a purpose and an explanation.
	YES. Science will be able to explain everything one day.
Some disagree:	PARTLY. Most things have an explanation but some do not.
	PARTLY. God knows everything. We partly understand His Universe.

DON'T FORGET

Brute Fact – no explanation. Principle of Sufficient Reason – everything has an explanation.

HUMAN REASONING

Whether there is an answer to everything or not humans need to think. Reasoning is about the way we think. Humans use different thinking techniques to help them understand the world. There are different types of knowledge. The two main types of knowledge are:

- **a priori**: knowledge that is independent of experience
- **a posteriori**: knowledge based on experience, with a bit of reason thrown in.

But religious people argue that there is another type of knowledge:

- **belief**: knowledge based on experience, reason and *revelation* which has come from God in one way or another.

SCIENTIFIC METHOD

Science introduces us to another type of human reasoning. It is known as the **scientific method**, and contains these steps:

1. *Observation:* to watch what's happening.
2. *Hypothesis:* to explain why you think it is happening.
3. *Experiment:* to test your explanation.
4. *Verification:* to get other people to check your explanation.
5. *Falsification:* the idea that your explanation is correct until a better explanation comes along.

DEDUCTIVE, INDUCTIVE AND ABDUCTIVE REASONING

There are more types of reasoning humans use. Deductive reasoning is when you make a statement about something then find examples to show the statement is true. Inductive reasoning works the other way round, this is when you observe different examples of something and then go on to make a statement explaining them. The third kind of thinking is abductive, which is when you have incomplete evidence and base your conclusions on the most likely evidence.

> **DON'T FORGET**
>
> Human reasoning takes many forms but no form of reasoning is perfect. They all have their faults.

BIG BANG THEORY AND THE THEORY OF EVOLUTION

Equipped with these kinds of thinking techniques humanity attempted to explain the origins of the universe and of humanity itself. There are two scientific theories that have had a major impact on religious belief. One of these theories relates to the beginning of the Universe and is called the **Big Bang theory**. The other one relates to the development of life and is called the Theory of **Evolution**.

Both of these theories are regarded as facts by the scientific community although there is agreement that each one contains gaps and contradictions. Scientists are continually learning more about the beginning of the Universe and the development of life.

BIG BANG THEORY

Here is how the Big Bang theory works:

- **Empty universe:** before the Universe there was no space and no time. Absolutely nothing was there, not even empty space.
- **Singularity:** from a tiny point the Universe expanded and heated up very quickly. Everything that is in the universe today was compressed into this tiny hot point 13.5 billion years ago.
- **Explosion:** the expansion resulted in an explosion which marked the beginning of the universe.
- **Gas:** out of the explosion came gases which flew in all directions into the new space.
- **Clusters:** eventually the gases reacted with each other and formed into clusters which would eventually become stars, galaxies and planets.

> **DON'T FORGET**
>
> The Big Bang theory is viewed as incomplete by scientists.

EVIDENCE:
- Galaxy distribution is uneven across the universe like there was an explosion.
- Red shift of galaxies – rushing apart like there's been an explosion.
- Microwave Background Radiation – heat from explosion.
- Primordial Elements – the right amount of gases are present today for there to be a Big Bang.

THINGS TO DO AND THINK ABOUT

1. Make a list of questions that do not seem to have an answer.
2. 'Things that exist must have an explanation.' Do you agree?
3. Is it possible to know anything without experiencing it?
4. List in order the three most reliable sources of evidence, and the three least reliable sources of evidence.
5. What evidence do you feel is missing to make the Big Bang theory 100% complete?
6. Is it reasonable to believe in something that cannot be proved 100%?

TOOLKIT
RPQ BASICS 2

THEORY OF EVOLUTION

Here is how the theory of evolution works:

- **Variation:** individuals in a species have many variations – some are unique and some are inherited.
- **Genes:** inherited variations come from the parent of the species and are found in genes.
- **Adaptation:** individuals that are most able to adapt to the environment are most likely to survive and breed and pass their traits on to their offspring.
- **Extinction:** individuals that are poorly adapted are less likely to survive and breed and will eventually die out.
- **Mutation:** tiny changes build up over billions of years and often lead to the development of new species altogether.

DON'T FORGET

The Theory of Evolution is not viewed as complete by scientists.

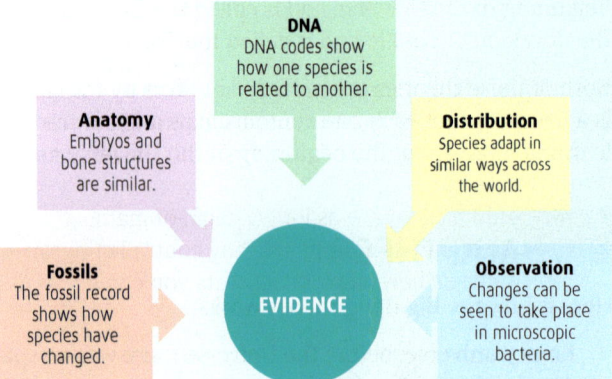

ANTHROPIC PRINCIPLE

A belief that is closely linked to the theory of evolution is the **Anthropic Principle**. It can be used both to prove the existence of God and to prove that God is responsible for the origins of human life. The basic idea is that the universe was set up in such a way as to produce intelligent life. It is not unusual for people who believe in the anthropic principle to speak of the Goldilocks Zone. It is the area surrounding a star where conditions are right for life to develop. Any variation to these conditions and it would not be right. The Goldilocks Zone is related to the Anthropic Principle as shown below:

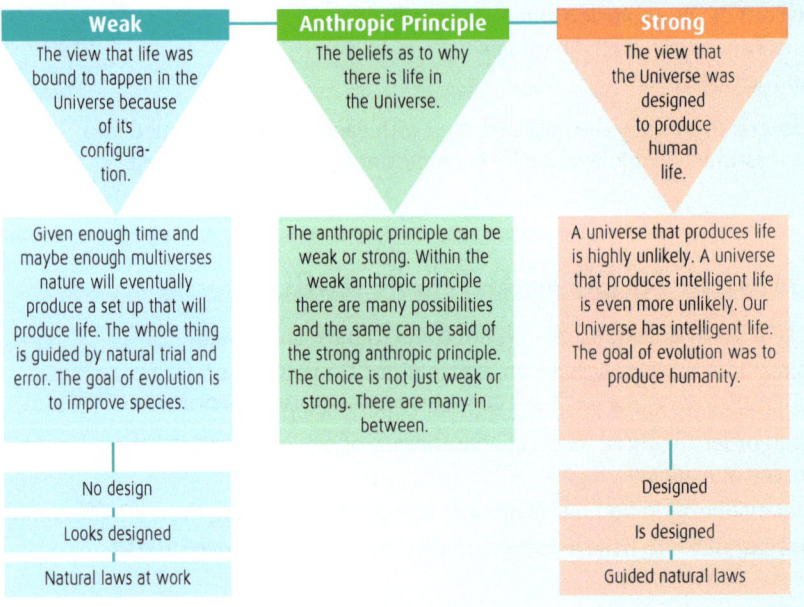

PHILOSOPHY OF RELIGION

Philosophy, like science, can be seen as being based on reason. It contributes two arguments that are traditionally used to prove the existence of God, the **cosmological** and **teleological** arguments (**First Cause** and **Design**).

COSMOLOGICAL ARGUMENT

The person most associated with the cosmological argument was the thirteenth century Christian scholar, **Thomas Aquinas**. He based his argument on his observations of the Universe.

Nature of the Universe		
Everything changes or moves and is changed or moved by something else.	Everything is caused and is caused by something else.	Beings are contingent. They depend on other beings to exist but no being needs to exist.

So, Aquinas had to show that		
There must be something that moves and changes things.	There must be something that is the cause of all causes.	There must be something that is not contingent and needs to exist because without it nothing else could exist.

So, he worked it out like this		
Nothing can move or change by itself.	Everything is caused by something else.	Every being that exists is contingent.
If everything is moving or changing then it needs something to start the moving or changing off.	Nothing can be the cause of itself.	Not every being can be contingent.
There isn't an infinite chain of movers or changers. There is a first mover that is not moved or changed by anything.	There isn't an infinite chain of causes. There is a first cause that is uncaused and the cause of all other causes.	There isn't an infinite chain of contingent beings. There is a non-contingent being whose existence is necessary.
The first mover is God.	**The first cause is God.**	**The necessary being is God.**

Thomas Aquinas made certain assumptions. An assumption is a belief that is thought to be true without actually having any proof for it. Aquinas makes three assumptions in his cosmological argument:

Aquina's assumptions		
Human knowledge of natural laws.	Infinite chains are impossible.	God is the only explanation.

And the problems are ... ?		
Humans do not know all the laws of nature.	Humans do not know that infinite chains are impossible.	There does not need to be an explanation.
Humans have only experienced a tiny part of the Universe.	Humans do not know whether or not there is a thing called infinity.	The explanation need not be God.

DON'T FORGET

Aquinas' Cosmological Argument is an *a posteriori* argument based on experience.

THINGS TO DO AND THINK ABOUT

1. What evidence do you feel is missing to make the theory of evolution 100% proven?
2. Is it reasonable to believe in something that cannot be 100% proved?
3. Make up a mind map which shows how the cosmological argument works.
4. Which one of Aquinas' assumptions do you disagree with the most?
5. Which problem do you think is the biggest for the cosmological argument?

TOOLKIT
RPQ BASICS 3

THE TELEOLOGICAL ARGUMENT

Thomas Aquinas is also associated with the Teleological or Design Argument, as is the nineteenth century philosopher, **William Paley**. Aquinas and Paley believed that on observing how the Universe worked you could see that it had been designed. This design was evidence that God existed. More recently, Michael Behe has developed a version of the Design Argument based on his idea of irreducible complexity, which is explained below.

DON'T FORGET

The Teleological or Design Argument is *a posteriori* argument (based on experience).

Nature of the Universe		
Aquinas	**Paley**	**Behe**
Everything has an order and works towards some purpose.	The Universe displays a high level of complexity.	The Universe contains interlinked and interdependent parts.
So, they had to show that		
The order and purpose in the Universe is not the result of chance.	Complexity can only be explained by design.	Interlinking and interdependence can only be explained by design.
So, they worked it out like this		
There is an order and purpose in the Universe.	Objects made by humans are the product of intelligent design.	There are biological forms which cannot operate unless all parts are present.
Order and purpose are a result of intelligence not chance.	The Universe is like objects made by humans and is the product of intelligent design on a bigger scale.	This means that some things in nature are irreducibly complex.
Therefore, nature is guided by an intelligent designer.	There is probably a designer who is vastly powerful and intelligent.	There is probably a designer who has designed irreducibly complex biological forms for the benefit of the Universe.
The designer is God.	**The designer is God.**	**The designer is God.**

They worked with some assumptions:

The assumptions		
The Universe is complex and orderly.	Order is the result of design.	God is the only explanation.
And the problems are...?		
Natural suffering and moral evil do not suggest order.	We have never seen a universe being built so we cannot infer that it is designed.	There does not need to be an explanation.
The Universe might just look as if it is ordered and designed but in fact it is not.	Humans do not know whether or not there is a thing called infinity.	The explanation need not be one god, it could be a team.

DON'T FORGET

Religious faith is based on both faith and reason.

DON'T FORGET

Religious people often use faith and reason to support their belief in the GCT (based on experience).

RELIGIOUS FAITH

Religious people have beliefs. These are based partly on reason but mainly on faith which is the belief that something is true that you cannot prove. In addition to this they believe in revelation which is that God communicates with them either through nature which is general revelation or through special actions which is special revelation.

GOD

Inevitably, when discussing the **origins of life** there is going to be some discussion of God. The best-known concept of God is the **God of Classical Theism (GCT)**. Many of the features of this God are common to the God that Jews, Christians and Muslims believe in, although the concept was formalised by Christian theologians. There are some crucial differences to how the God of each of these religions is understood in regard to different matters. For simplicity we will refer to the Christian GCT. This is how the GCT is viewed:

The GCT is a spiritual being and has no physical body. He is eternal and has always existed. He is personal which means that He wants to have a relationship with intelligent beings like humans.

God created the Universe out of nothing. He knows everything that can be known and has the power to do anything that can be done.

God is immanent and deeply involved in the world by manipulating events in history but at the same He is transcendent and does not depend on the world.

God is good and hates evil. He is also all loving and forgiving. Because He is good, He is also just. This means that He is fair in all His dealings with humanity.

And humanity knows God is like this because God has revealed Himself to humanity in various ways.

God reveals Himself in three main ways. He reveals Himself in:

- the scripture
- in nature
- in history
- through individuals.

TESTING THE ANSWERS

When you study your topic option for the RPQs, it will be put through six tests to see how well the answers stand up to various criticisms. These tests are shown below.

1. Facts

- Are the facts 'facts'?
- Have the facts been twisted?

2. Intuitive

- Is the viewpoint so obvious that there is no need to check it?
- Is it just common sense?

3. Experience

- Does the answer match our experience of the Universe?

4. Experts

- Do experts in the field agree?

5. Consistency

- Does the answer hang together well?
- Does the answer have contradictions?

6. Alternatives

- Is it the best possible answer?
- Is it the most likely answer?
- Are the alternatives any better?

THINGS TO DO AND THINK ABOUT

1. Make up a mind map which shows how the design argument works.
2. Which one of the assumptions do you disagree with the most?
3. Which problem do you think is the biggest problem for the teleological argument?
4. Make up a mind map which shows how the cosmological argument works.
5. What do you think might be the problems people have if they have faith without reason?
6. Is religious belief always wrong?
7. What beliefs link together well?
8. What beliefs contradict each other?
9. If there is a God, is it really possible to know anything more about Him than He exists?

Religious and philosophical questions

ORIGINS

ORIGINS OF THE UNIVERSE: THE DEBATE

IS THERE AN ANSWER TO THE QUESTION?

First, let's think about whether or not there is an answer to the question of how the Universe and life began. For many religious and non-religious groups these things have an explanation:

Reason for believing there are explanations	Reason for believing there might not be explanations	The current position
The Universe is set up in such a way that we can study it and explain it (intelligible).	Just because some of the Universe is intelligible it does not mean that everything has an explanation.	Both science and religion believe there are explanations about the origins of the Universe and the origins of life. It may be the case that we will never find the answers, but just because we can't doesn't mean that they don't exist.
Our instincts tell us that if the origins of things in the Universe can be explained then the whole thing can be explained.	Our instincts are not 100% reliable.	
Our reasoning tells us that if the origins of things in the Universe can be explained then the whole thing can be explained.	Just because it is true that some parts of the Universe have an explanation, it doesn't mean that is true of the whole Universe.	
The alternative of no explanation makes no sense.	We have convinced ourselves that the Universe has an explanation because the alternative is so unpleasant: a pointless Universe without a purpose or reason for existing.	

ANSWERS TO THE QUESTION

Questioning the origins of the Universe means thinking about how the Universe got started. It is a puzzle. It is a puzzle because, at one time, it was not here, none of it. Then suddenly, it was. Or was it? The fact that the Universe exists needs explaining.

There are different answers to the question of the origins of the Universe and they include:

1. There is no answer.
2. It was the Big Bang.
3. The Universe has always been here.
4. God made the Universe using the Big Bang.
5. God made the Universe exactly as it says in the scripture.

People may hold one of these views then something may happen (for example, a news item), which means they switch to a different viewpoint. This is normal.

Let's test these answers.

Origins – Origins of the Universe: The debate

ANSWER 1: THERE IS NO ANSWER

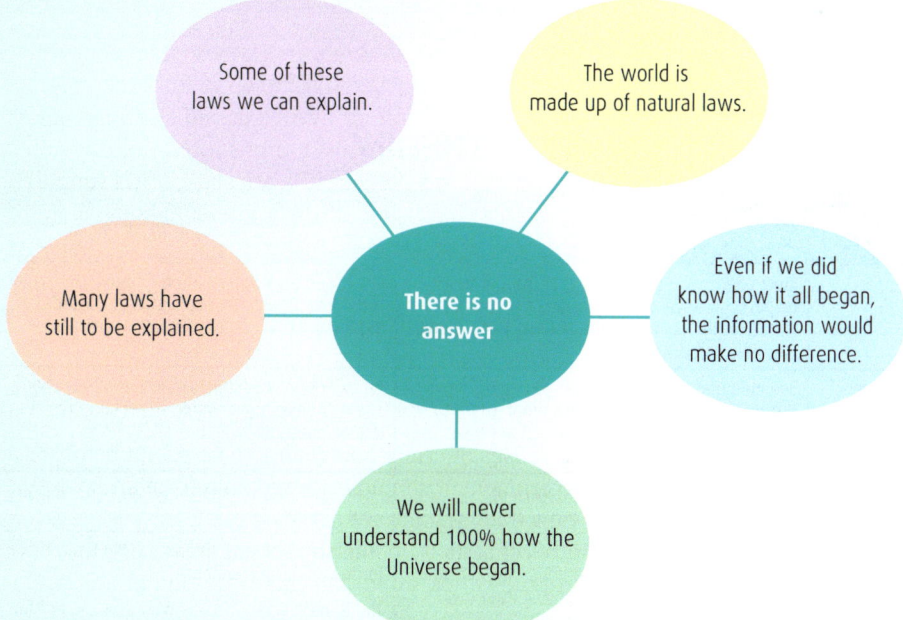

	"There is no answer."	
	Agree	**Disagree**
Factual	The only facts are things that are 100% provable. We cannot know everything about the universe and even if we could it is a fact that it won't make any difference to how we live.	It is based on the facts we have: we don't necessarily know all the laws that govern the Universe and, even although we understand some of the laws, there may still be others to discover and understand.
Intuitive	It is based on intuition. We confuse our hope of explanation with intuition. We convince ourselves of explanations because they give the universe purpose and that is a nice thought. However, if we take away the hope then the answer stands because it describes things as they really are.	No, it is not based on intuition or common sense. They tell us that the universe has been set up in such a way that it has explanations even if we do not know them yet.
Experienced	Our experience is based on what we can observe and since we cannot observe universes being made then there is no answer that we are able to give.	The universe is intelligible, that is we can make sense of it because there are answers. An answer must exist, because everything must be capable of an explanation since we have discovered more and more things throughout history.
Supported	Some **atheist** philosophers accept that there are some things which may never have an explanation. These are brute facts. We like to think there is an explanation but there is none.	The fact that science looks for answers means that there is a point and that the search for answers is worthwhile. Furthermore, religious people and philosophers have already provided answers: that God made the Universe and all its governing laws.
Consistent	This viewpoint is consistent because it does not seek answers where they do not exist or cannot be known.	It is not a consistent answer because it does not match experience. Humans continually search for explanations, even when they do not know if there is an answer.
Best	It is the best answer because it does not waste time speculating on things we don't know and it prevents humans inventing stuff to fill in gaps in their knowledge.	Not the best answer simply because it refuses to take part in the debate. Not taking part in the debate contributes nothing to it.

 DON'T FORGET

The Principle of Sufficient Reason says that there is an explanation for everything.

 VIDEO LINK

Learn more by watching the clip at the Digital Zone.

 ONLINE TEST

Test yourself on origins of the universe at www.brightredbooks.net

THINGS TO DO AND THINK ABOUT

1. What is the biggest weakness in this viewpoint?
2. What is the biggest strength in this viewpoint?
3. Overall, explain whether you think this viewpoint is weak or strong.

ORIGINS

ORIGINS OF THE UNIVERSE: BIG BANG OR INFINITE?

ANSWER 2: THE BIG BANG THEORY

	The Big Bang started the Universe.	
	Agree	**Disagree**
Factual	Most scientists would agree that the Universe began with a massive explosion. Although the whole picture is incomplete, the Big Bang theory is widely accepted.	It is based on scientific interpretation, not actual facts. And it does not explain what caused the Big Bang.
Intuitive	The idea that the Universe had to begin somewhere is intuitive, and also that it is governed by laws that we may not yet have discovered and/or understand.	An explosion is destructive and results in chaos, and it is unlikely we would expect it to result in a Universe we can live in.
Experienced	It is based on scientists' experiences of observation, research and investigation.	None of us were there. Universes don't appear from nowhere.
Supported	Most scientists state that the Universe began with a massive explosion. Although the whole picture is incomplete, the Big Bang theory, or Standard Model, is widely accepted. Many religious groups accept the Big Bang Theory. Pope Francis said: 'The Big Bang, which is today argued as the origin of the world, does not contradict the divine act of creation; rather, it requires it.' Similarly, in Islam there is no problem with the Big Bang; indeed, some Muslim scholars argue that descriptions of it can be found in the Qur'an. However, some religious groups who accept the Big Bang Theory have a concern that it does not mention God as the creator of the Universe. They want God to be given a direct involvement, almost in the same way a parent creates a child.	Scientists adjust and amend the Big Bang Theory to make it fit the evidence. There are religious groups who don't accept the Big Bang, for instance Christians who believe that every word of the Bible is literally true; because the Big Bang is not mentioned in the Bible, it cannot be true. Another reason some religious groups reject the Big Bang is that it removes God from creation; this contradicts scriptures which state God is the creator of the Universe.
Consistent	To the extent that the Big Bang Theory is incomplete. So long as scientists conduct research and make new discoveries then the theory will remain a work in progress.	Scientists twist the evidence to fit into the Big Bang theory; they are obliged to do this because admitting they were wrong would put them in a difficult position.
Best	For most scientists and some religious groups it is, although the religious groups will state that God used the Big Bang to create the Universe.	Some religious groups maintain the belief that the answer to the origins of the Universe can only be found in scripture.

DON'T FORGET

Many religious groups believe the Big Bang was God's way of creating the Universe.

ANSWER 3: THE UNIVERSE HAS ALWAYS BEEN HERE

	The Universe has always been here.	
	Agree	**Disagree**
Factual	It depends on what you call a 'fact'. There is factual evidence and theories come from them and there is sufficient factual and theoretical evidence around to consider an infinite universe as a possibility.	This answer is not based on fact. It is based on interpretations of fact and theory. It is full of 'might be' and 'possible'. These words do not point to facts.
Intuitive	If you have a view of the Universe being an eternal cycle of rebirth as Hindus believe, then your viewpoint is based on your intuition.	No, this is not intuition. Our instincts tell us it has a beginning. It is un-natural to think that it has been there forever because it leaves so many questions unanswered.
Experienced	Our experience is that natural things die and regenerate in different forms. Everything has a life time. It could be the same with the universe, that once it dies it just recycles itself.	We have never seen a universe being created or destroyed so we cannot really tell what is or isn't recycled.
Supported	Physicists like Stephen Hawking and Alan Guth wonder if there could be many universes existing at the one time. This is called the **multiverse**. Some scientists propose an **oscillating universe** in which the Universe goes through cycles of birth, death and rebirth. This is sometimes called the Big Bang, Big Bounce and Big Crunch. Hinduism supports the idea that the Universe works in cycles, just like the oscillating universe.	**Monotheistic** religions reject an eternal universe because that means the Universe was never created; God creating the Universe is an integral part of their faith; the Universe and God are seen as separate things.
Consistent	This answer is consistent because it relies on science for its data. It does not introduce supernatural beings to explain things. The evidence can support the idea just as much as it can support the Big Bang.	No, it is inconsistent. It goes against our experience of a universe of beginnings and endings. It goes against the ideas of actual and potential infinity and the truth is that an eternal universe contradicts the evidence that we have at the moment.
Best	Yes it is. It removes the need to bring in some supernatural being to explain the beginning of the Universe. The idea is no less believable than any of the other ideas.	No, there is widespread acceptance of the Big Bang theory.

DON'T FORGET

A monotheistic religion is one where there is one God who is distinct from the Universe.

VIDEO LINK

Find out more about steady state theory by watching the clip at the Digital Zone.

ONLINE TEST

Test yourself on this topic at www.brightredbooks.net

THINGS TO DO AND THINK ABOUT

1. Which answer can be justified more: Answer 1, Answer 2 or Answer 3?
2. What's more important in this debate: that it is based on fact or that it is supported by experts?
3. What would you see as the strongest point against this answer?
4. Would an eternal universe remove the need for belief in God?
5. What would you see as the strongest point against this answer?

ORIGINS

ORIGINS OF THE UNIVERSE: GOD DID IT 1

ANSWER 4: GOD MADE THE UNIVERSE USING THE BIG BANG

	God made the Universe using the Big Bang.	
	Agree	**Disagree**
Factual	It is based on facts. The universe has a beginning. Things that have beginnings need to be started. God is the most likely explanation.	Just because something had to start the Universe it doesn't mean it was God of classical theism.
Intuitive	If our intuition tells us that something far greater than the Universe is the explanation for the Universe. This could be God.	Intuition surely tells us that the universe was formed through natural means rather than some supernatural being which is not intuitive at all. That is superstitious.
Experienced	Our experience tells us that things do not create themselves. The creation of the Universe could be similar. The Big Bang may well have been the reason but what was the trigger? This could be God.	We do not have any experience of universes being created so we cannot know what it is like. This is even more so the case with idea of a god creating the universe.
Supported	Religious groups take two approaches: they use either science or scripture as evidence that God made the Universe using the Big Bang. Pope Francis I: 'When we read about **Creation** in **Genesis**, we run the risk of imagining God was a magician, with a magic wand able to do everything. But that is not so... The Big Bang, which today we hold to be the origin of the world, does not contradict the intervention of the divine creator but, rather, requires it.' Some religious groups believe in **scientific foreknowledge**. They believe **scripture** contains messages relating to modern science. For example, in Isaiah 42 in the Bible it says: 'This is what the Lord says – He who created the heavens and stretched them out,' which is understood by some Christians to mean the expansion after the Big Bang. Some **Muslims** suggest that **singularity** is mentioned in the Qur'an: 'Have those who disbelieved not considered that the heavens and the earth were a joined entity, then We separated them, and made from water every living thing?' Philosophers take a different approach. The cosmological argument (see the RPQ *Toolkit* on page 115) proposes that there is no such thing as **actual infinity** and that God is the Uncaused First Cause.	Religious experts tend to reject the idea of scientific foreknowledge. Science doesn't investigate religious claims about the origins of the Universe or the Big Bang: Stephen Hawking is satisfied that God had nothing to do with the beginning of the Universe: Because there is a law such as gravity, the universe can and will create itself from nothing, [...] spontaneous creation is the reason there is something rather than nothing, why the universe exists, why we exist... It is not necessary to invoke God to light the blue touch paper and set the universe going. Hawking and Mlodinov, *The Grand Design.* There is no reason why a **supernatural being** like God should be the First Cause.

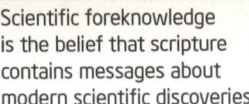

DON'T FORGET

Scientific foreknowledge is the belief that scripture contains messages about modern scientific discoveries.

contd

Origins – Origins of the Universe: God did it 1

	God made the Universe using the Big Bang.	
	Agree	**Disagree**
Consistent	It is consistent because it uses science and religion. Science on its own has the contradiction of who started it and religion on its own has the contradiction of how it started. It combines the science and religion to make it all make sense.	It is not consistent because it tries to combine two areas of human thinking that are completely unalike: science and religion.
Best	Are any of the alternatives more believable? Is believing that the Big Bang happened for no reason more ridiculous than stating it was God's doing? For religious groups it is the best possible answer because it means that God had a clear role in creation. Through his **omniscience** and **omnipotence** he knew exactly how to create a Universe capable of supporting life.	No, it means claiming things are true when we don't know if they are. This involves plugging gaps in our knowledge with God: this is called **God of the Gaps**. When something cannot be satisfactorily explained then God becomes the explanation.

VIDEO LINK

Watch the video at the Digital Zone to explore viewpoints.

ONLINE TEST

Test yourself on this topic at www.brightredbooks.net

THINGS TO DO AND THINK ABOUT

1. Five questions are listed below. Which one would be the hardest to answer and why?

    a) Can you give two facts that support this answer?

    b) Can you give one thing from your experience that would support this answer?

    c) Can you give two reasons why God would want to make a Universe using the Big Bang?

    d) Can you give two reasons why the First Cause of the Universe has to be God?

    e) Can you give two reasons why it makes sense to believe that God used the Big Bang?

2. Is believing that the Big Bang just happened for no reason at all any more unreasonable than saying it was God?

3. Is believing that the Universe just popped into existence out of nothing any more unreasonable than saying that God made it using the Big Bang?

4. If God did not make the Big Bang, then why are the other explanations more reasonable?

ORIGINS OF THE UNIVERSE: GOD DID IT 2

ANSWER 5: GOD MADE THE UNIVERSE EXACTLY AS IT SAYS IN THE SCRIPTURES

An explanation of how religious people approach understanding their sacred scriptures is needed first.

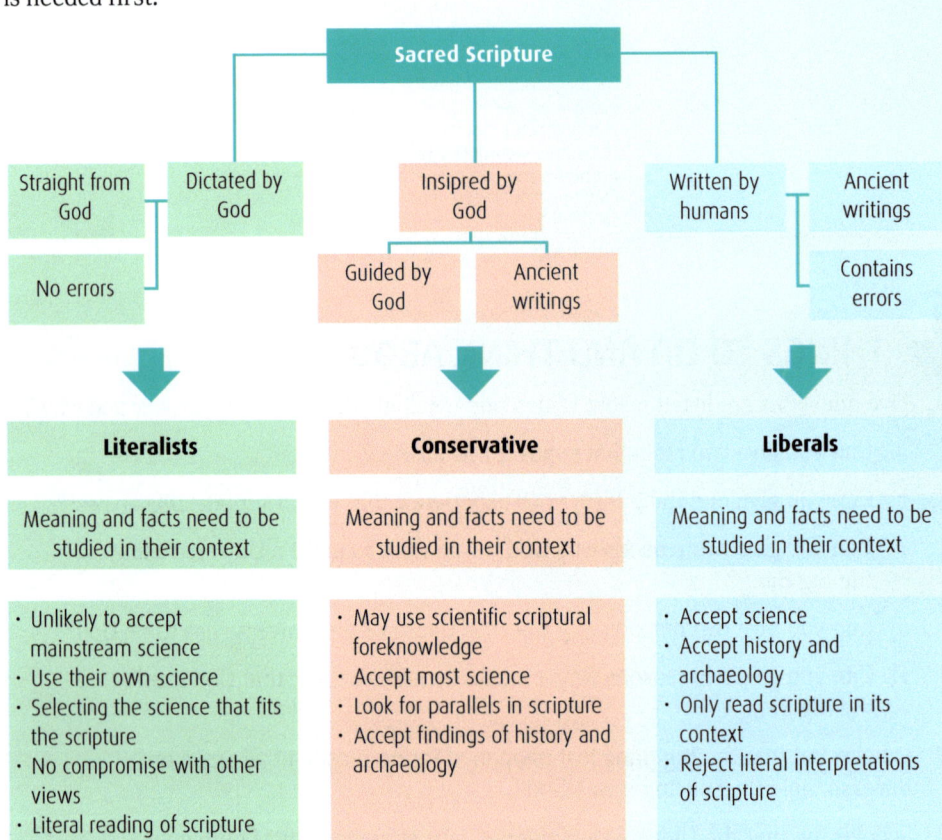

	Agree	Disagree
	God made the Universe exactly as it says in the scriptures.	
Factual	For **literalists**, they are dealing with facts about the origin of the Universe in their sacred scripture. For **conservatives**, they are dealing mainly with ancient myths or understandings of Creation which has some similarities.	For **liberals**, creation stories are myths and they tell us more about the world the writers lived in than how God made the Universe. For historians and archaeologists, creation stories are myths that were passed on orally before being written down. They are myths from a variety of cultures. For scientists, creation stories are myths that have nothing to offer in terms of explanations for the Universe.
Intuitive	If you accept that God spoke directly to people and told them how He created the world, it will be clear that this is how He did it.	Most people's intuition is that creation stories are myths. They may have meaning which can be taken seriously, but their content is not factual.

contd

Origins – Origins of the Universe: God did it 2

	God made the Universe exactly as it says in the scriptures.	
	Agree	**Disagree**
Experienced	Some literalists might argue that in their experience their sacred scriptures have been shown to be true and can therefore be trusted.	In our experience, we do not issue commands and make things suddenly appear out of nowhere as seems to be suggested by religious scripture.
Supported	**Creation Science** is used by some Christian literalists to support their claims about the Bible and to reject conventional science. This viewpoint is supported by literalists because God is in control of the Universe from the moment prior to its creation. This makes the creating the Universe a deliberate act rather than the result of a random explosion. It states God has complete authority over the creation and existence of the Universe.	Creation Science is not supported by the vast majority of scientists: their claims are dismissed because they do not follow established scientific methods to draw their conclusions. Some religious groups criticise literalist interpretations of scripture because they don't believe they should be read in that way. Indeed, Pope Francis suggested that to treat religious books as literal truths is actually an abuse of them.
Consistent	Creationists use quotes from scientific journals to support the scriptures. Using scientific information out of context in this way can reassure believers who may be worried about any contradictions arising from the **counter-argument** made by scientists.	There are inconsistencies in the Bible; for example, light is created before the Sun. Creationists claim the Earth is 6000–10,000 years old. The evidence suggests it is much older than that.
Best	The Bible is not open to interpretation. It says that God made the Earth in six days and that is exactly what it means. Scientists cannot even agree on the age of the Earth but the Bible is clear.	Definitely not the best answer because it goes against established scientific research. Its claims are based on books from the pre-scientific age.

DON'T FORGET

Creationists usually have a literal understanding of their sacred scripture. Most religious people are NOT creationist.

VIDEO LINK

Watch the clip at the Digital Zone to explore viewpoints on this topic.

ONLINE TEST

Test yourself on this topic at www.brightredbooks.net

THINGS TO DO AND THINK ABOUT

1. Find a creationist story and explain three problems with taking it literally.

2. Suppose you are up against a creationist whose answer to your criticisms of their beliefs is always: 'That is not what it says in the holy book.' What three points would you make against this line of thinking?

3. Suppose you believed that science was wrong and your sacred book was right. What evidence would be the best to use to prove this?

ORIGINS

ORIGINS OF LIFE: THE DEBATE 1

Human beings are the most incredible life form on Earth. Our origins of life need to be explained and understood. There are different answers to the question and they include:

1. There is no answer.
2. The theory of evolution explains how life began.
3. God used evolution to create life.
4. God created life exactly as it says in the scriptures.

ANSWER 1: THERE IS NO ANSWER

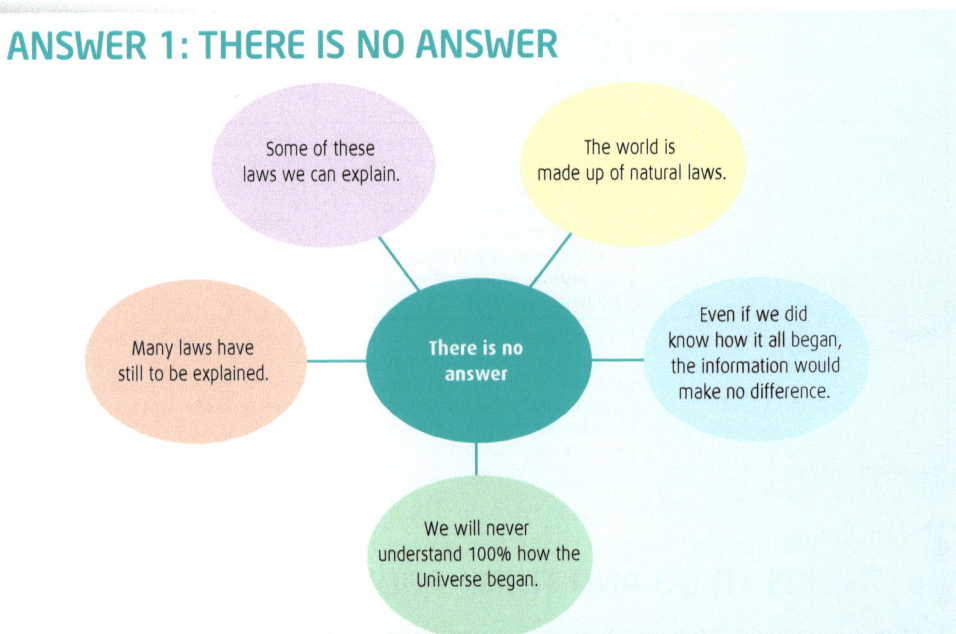

	There is no answer.	
	Agree	**Disagree**
Factual	It is based on the facts we have: we don't necessarily know all the facts about the origins of life, and there may still be more to uncover and understand.	We do not know if we will ever know all the facts governing the origins of life, or what difference knowing how life began will make to us.
Intuitive	It could be said that our instincts tell us that the universe is full of opposites, so it would make sense to say that just as many things do have an explanation, it is just as likely that there could be many things without any explanation; the ultimate origin of life is one of these things.	To say that there is no answer goes against our intuition. The universe is intelligible, which means that we can make sense of it to an extent. It surely makes sense to say that if one part of it is intelligible then the whole is intelligible.
Experienced	Experience is built on how people **want** to see the world not how the world really is. People therefore want to see an explanation for life. If that view is valid, so is the other view when people want to see a world where there are things without explanation.	This view is not based on experience. There is evidence and theory which has been produced through research. We can observe things like evolution taking place, this is experience.
Supported	Some atheist philosophers accept that there are some things which may never have an explanation. These are brute facts.	Scientists continue to investigate because they believe that there are explanations for the origins of life. Religious groups believe that there is already an explanation, that God was responsible for the origins of life.
Consistent	The answer works well because it does not attempt to fill in gaps of information with guesswork.	The answer just doesn't add up. To say there is no ultimate answer is basically not coming to the debating table. It closes off any discussion and humanity sees a purpose in getting answers.
Best	It sticks to the evidence and does not rely on faith and guesswork.	This is a poor answer because it goes against human instinct to search for answers and it ignores things like experience and evidence.

ANSWER 2: THE THEORY OF EVOLUTION EXPLAINS HOW LIFE BEGAN

	The origins of life can be explained by the theory of evolution.	
	Agree	**Disagree**
Factual	Evolution is based on an interpretation of factual evidence. That does not mean to say that the theory is complete but evolution is currently the best explanation for the origins of life.	Paul Broun, when a United States Senator in 2012, said this of evolution: 'There's a lot of scientific data that I found out as a scientist that actually show that this is really a young Earth. I believe that the Earth is about 9000 years old. I believe that it was created in six days as we know them. That's what the Bible says.'
Intuitive	It is counter-intuitive to us initially but once studied, most of us gain an understanding of how the theory of evolution works. Magic is no longer magic when you know how the tricks are done.	Kirk Johnson of the Smithsonian Institute said: 'It was an amazing discovery that we're all related, but it was not obvious. It's not obvious that I'm related to a strawberry.'
Experienced	Our experience limits us to small-scale perspectives. However, if we study and understand how one species evolves then we can use that experience to see how other species change over time.	We have not actually seen one species evolve because this is a process lasting millions of years. This means some people question evolution's validity as the reason for the origins of life.
Supported	Refer to the RPQ *Toolkit* on page 114 to see why scientists and religious groups believe evolution to be true. Jerry Coyne, in his book, *Why Evolution is True*, had this to say: 'Evolution gives us the true account of our origins, replacing the myths that satisfied us for thousands of years.' Most religious people still believe that ultimately God is the origin of human life. Nobel Physics prize-winner, Charles Townes, combined evolution and religion when he said: '…the Bible's description of creation occurring over a week's time is just an analogy, as I see it.'	Ken Ham despairs of other Christians who accept evolution: 'Today many laypeople, ministers, and Christian educators are powerless in their presentation of the gospel. They have rejected Genesis, the foundation of biblical doctrine. They have believed the twentieth century origins myth – evolution.'
Consistent	There are examples in evolution theory that do not make sense: for instance, useless organs in human beings. No scientist claims that the theory of evolution is complete or to fully understand everything that has been discovered so far.	What science does not explain is how the mechanism of evolution came about. The laws of nature could not evolve as they went along, they had to be complete from the start for the Universe to be able to work, evolution included.
Best	With the evidence available just now, it is the best possible answer. No other scientific, philosophical or religious explanation of the origins of life comes close to having this amount of evidence to support it.	No, because it does not explain the origins of life. It only explains the process of change. How can we believe that life in the Universe evolved from gases into intelligent beings capable of asking how they came to exist? It is implausible for this to have happened by nature alone.

DON'T FORGET

There are many theories of evolution.

THINGS TO DO AND THINK ABOUT

1. Why do some people think that evolution matters?
2. If you were a religious person would evolution destroy your beliefs?
3. Does the fact that evolutionary theory has got some things wrong mean that the whole idea is flawed?
4. Is evolution a bigger threat to belief in God than the Big Bang Theory?
5. In what ways could evolution be used to support belief in God?

VIDEO LINK

Learn more about evolution by watching the video at the Digital Zone.

ONLINE TEST

Test yourself on this topic at www.brightredbooks.net

ORIGINS

ORIGINS OF LIFE: THE DEBATE 2

ANSWER 3: GOD USED EVOLUTION TO CREATE LIFE

	God used evolution to create human life.	
	Agree	**Disagree**
Factual	Astronomer Paul Davies said, 'According to the standard models of particle physics and cosmology there are thirty-something adjustable quantities needed to describe the physical world. Simple calculations then suggest that meddling with some of them, even by a tiny amount, would prove lethal, wrecking any hope that life could emerge in the universe.' Davies doesn't think God is behind it all but the importance of the Goldilocks Zone is intriguing.	Some scientists, including Stephen Hawking and Richard Dawkins, suggest that we live in a multiverse. There are many universes each with its own set of natural laws and only a few of them are set up in such a way that they can produce and support life.
Intuitive	It is intuitive to look at something complex (for example, an eye) and think that it required intelligent design to create it.	Nature can be beautiful and inspiring but it can also be ugly and harsh. If evolution was indeed God's method, then He created a cruel and pitiless set of natural laws that let the weak die, and allows grotesque and painful **mutations** to develop.
Experienced	William Paley compared the workings of the Universe to a watch. He concluded that because a watch is highly complex and needs a designer, and the Universe is more complex than a watch then it is most likely that the Universe has a designer. So, our experience suggests an intelligent designer could have designed evolution.	**David Hume** said that you can't compare natural things to human-made objects. He suggested that you could just as easily compare the Universe to a house proving that a team of gods made the Universe since houses require teams of people. Furthermore, he said that we had been conditioned to think that the Universe had a design.
Supported	Freeman Dyson says, 'The more I examine the Universe, and the details of its architecture, the more evidence I find that the Universe in some sense must have known we were coming.' Freeman Dyson, *Disturbing the Universe*. New York: Harper and Row, 1979. Christian Physicist, Karl Gilberson, who supports evolution argued that, 'A common sense interpretation of the facts suggests that a super-intellect has monkeyed with physics, as well as with chemistry and biology, and that there are no blind forces worth speaking about in nature.' Michael Behe accepts evolution and rejects a literal interpretation of the Bible: 'For the record, I have no reason to doubt that the universe is the billions of years old that physicists say it is. Further, I find the idea of common descent (that all organisms share a common ancestor) fairly convincing, and have no particular reason to doubt it.' *Darwin's Black Box*, Michael Behe, 1996 The key point is that God is deeply involved in creating life and directing it in such a way that it produces a being that is capable of having a relationship with God.	Richard Dawkins sees no role for God in evolution at all: 'Darwinian natural selection can produce an uncanny illusion of design. An engineer would be hard put to decide whether a bird or a plane was the more aerodynamically elegant. So powerful is the illusion of design, it took humanity until the mid-nineteenth century to realise that it is an illusion.' *New Scientist* Paul Davies rules God out as well: 'If there is an ultimate meaning to existence, as I believe is the case, the answer is to be found within nature, not beyond it. The universe might indeed be a fix, but if so, it has fixed itself.' *The Guardian* The online religion and spirituality magazine, Patheos, states: 'Evolution does not say God exists; neither does it say God does not exist. Such a question simply cannot be considered by science. It is, instead, one for theology or philosophy. What evolution *does* do is provide a consistent scientific explanation for the development of life that does not require direct divine intervention – it does not require miracles, but neither does it forbid them.' *Patheos*

DON'T FORGET

Paley's Watch Analogy supports the idea that the Universe was designed.

ONLINE

Follow the links to the sources here at www.brightredbooks.net

contd

Origins – Origins of life: The debate 2

	God used evolution to create human life.	
	Agree	**Disagree**
Consistent	Evolution as a natural law is cruel and wasteful. The weak die and it allows fatal and painful defects. This does not support the idea of a God who is all good and all powerful. There is a problem called the Inconsistent Triad which says that evil exists. If God is all good then he will want rid of evil. If he is all powerful then he can get rid of evil. But evil exists, so either he is not all powerful or not all good, or perhaps does not even exist.	Mathematician Amir Aczel had this to say: 'The incredible fine-tuning of the Universe presents the most powerful argument for the existence of an immanent creative entity we may well call God. Lacking convincing scientific evidence to the contrary, such a power may be necessary.' *Time* Creationist Ken Ham argues that, 'Even trillions of years wouldn't be enough time to produce the simplest cell... Add all that up [the stuff you need for evolution] and you're left with an inescapable conclusion: there must be a powerful and super-wise Creator. With such a Creator, you no longer need billions of years. He could create everything in much less time – say six days. According to the Bible, this Creator – God – did exactly that.' Ham rejects evolution so for him, there is no contradiction. God made the world, as told in the Bible.
Best	There is no clear and agreed explanation of where evolution came from. There is no explanation for humanity's unique consciousness and intelligence. It is easier to believe that the life that evolved from formless gases was guided by something like God than being the product of random chance.	It cannot be the best answer if it is simply filling in the gaps that we do not understand. As yet, there is no explanation for how the laws arose. Bringing in a supernatural being whose existence cannot be proved or tested does not solve the problem. In fact, it sets human thinking back.

ONLINE TEST

Test yourself on this topic at www.brightredbooks.net

THINGS TO DO AND THINK ABOUT

Looks at the statements below and state whether you agree, disagree or are 50-50. Explain your choice.

1. Life appeared as a result of chance.
2. The Universe was set up to produce intelligent life.
3. The Universe was set up to produce human life.
4. Evolution needed to be guided to produce human life.
5. God guides evolution.
6. God started evolution and then let it take its own course.
7. It is easier to believe that evolution is purely natural than God is behind it.
8. There are no better alternative explanations for evolution than God being behind it.
9. Even if God did exist, he would not have used evolution to produce life.
10. The Goldilocks Zone cannot be a coincidence.

ORIGINS

ORIGINS OF LIFE: THE DEBATE 3

ANSWER 4: GOD CREATED LIFE EXACTLY AS IT SAYS IN THE SCRIPTURES

Some background information first. The Jewish and Christian creation stories in Genesis are the same. They contain the following features:

- Two different creation stories.
- The stories are together in one book of the Bible.
- God created from nothing.
- He created over six days.
- He created space and environmental elements first.
- He created creatures next.
- He created humans last.

The Muslim description of creation can be found in the Qur'an. It has the following features:

- Ideas about creation are found in many different parts of the Qur'an; they are not all in the one place.
- Allah created over six periods of time.
- No order of creation is specified.
- Allah created things in Heaven, things on Earth and things between Earth and Heaven.
- Life emerged from the water.
- Allah waited until conditions were right for the creation of humans whom he created separately from animals.

Hindu creation myths are rather complicated because there are several. The general features of them are:

- There is no single creation story in any single sacred book.
- The Universe is either a part of God, made by a number of gods, hatched from a cosmic egg or the work of a mysterious creator.
- As for humans, gods made them and the worlds they live in, or **humans are made from individual parts of God's body to form the caste system.**
- No periods of time are specified.

Some religious groups take creation stories literally, some a mix of literal and symbolic and some purely symbolic. It would be true to say that the majority of religious people do not take their creation stories literally.

	God created life exactly as it says in the scriptures.	
	Agree	**Disagree**
Factual	For religious people who believe that their sacred book is 100% true it most certainly is. They use science and their sacred book to support their views but the science they use is often very carefully selected to tie in with their scriptures and would not be considered to be science by other scientists.	It is not based on facts. Quite the opposite in fact. The use of information about evolution is selective. They focus on what is wrong and not what is right. People supporting this idea cherry-pick the problems, ignore the strengths, and twist scientific facts to suit their beliefs.

contd

	God created life exactly as it says in the scriptures.	
	Agree	**Disagree**
Intuitive	If you believe, as literalists do, that sacred books are inspired or written by God and contain no errors then you would think it is common sense to accept everything in them as 100% true.	If you were given a 2000-year-old medical textbook, would you trust it? Probably not. Would there be any difference if you were given a book about how life came about that was over 1000 years old? Probably not. Our instincts would tell us that any book of that age would not be able to give explanations such as we have today.
Experienced	It is possible. The groupings of created things in the Qur'an and the Bible have some similarities with science.	For others, both in science and in religion, it is proof that the ancient people who wrote these texts were using insights made by the many remarkable thinkers who lived and taught in the ancient world. They would argue that these same similarities can be found in other sacred books, cultures and intellectual works.
Supported	John UpChurch writing on the Answers in Genesis website put it like this: '...We believe the Bible is God's perfect Word. It records the true history of the Universe as revealed to us by the one who saw everything happen.' The Creation Research Institute is very clear that the Bible is right: 'All things in the universe were created and made by God in the six literal days of the Creation Week. The creation record is factual, historical... thus all theories of origins or development that involve evolution in any form are false.'	Denis Alexander warns against treating the Bible as a science book: 'Christians should not abuse the Bible by trying to treat it as a scientific textbook, when scientific writing as we understand it now did not even get going until thousands of years after the early chapters of Genesis were written.' Pope Francis agreed when he spoke at a meeting on the issue: 'When we read about Creation in Genesis, we run the risk of imagining God was a magician, with a magic wand able to do everything. But that is not so.' Professor Francesca Stavrakopolou, who is an atheist and expert on the Bible, warned: 'I don't think you can use the Bible as a reliable historical source.' The Christian Intelligent Design movement was founded by Philip E. Johnson, who said, 'To put things on a more rational basis, the first thing that has to be done is to get the Bible out of the discussion [about creation].'
Consistent	There are no contradictions if you believe that your sacred scripture is 100% true and 100% from God. There might appear to be contradictions but these are the result of human misunderstandings and ignorance, not because the contradictions are real.	This viewpoint is full of contradictions. It goes against current scientific thinking and evidence. It goes against established methods used to study sacred scripture. It treats sacred scripture as literal truth and takes it completely out of its historical and cultural context. It interprets evidence from science and literary studies in a way that few qualified people would interpret it.
Best	It is the best answer because it is based on the truth of sacred scripture, say many literalists. Evolution does not match up with a Divine loving God. The world is in decay because of our sin, it is not evolving. It started off perfect and is on a downward spiral. Some literalists believe that far from evolving and improving, the world is in a state of final decay.	Absolutely not, say many religious people and scientists. This viewpoint belongs to more ignorant times. For some religious people God has given humanity the tools to understand the processes of nature and these tools have allowed the discovery of evolution. For non-religious people, this viewpoint is the opposite of what any reasonable minded person would think.

ONLINE

Go to the Digital Zone to check the sources to these viewpoints.

ONLINE

Read Alexander's full viewpoint at www.brightredbooks.net

ONLINE

Follow the link to the Answers in Genesis website at www.brightredbooks.net

DON'T FORGET

Creationism is a minority view among religious people.

ONLINE TEST

Test yourself on this topic at www.brightredbooks.net

THINGS TO DO AND THINK ABOUT

1. 'It no longer makes any sense to believe what scripture says about creation.' Do you agree?
2. Why do some people insist that scripture is true?
3. Does it really matter how humans got here?
4. Can you believe in God and evolution at the same time?

Religious and philosophical questions

THE EXISTENCE OF GOD

THE STARTING POINT

IS THERE AN ANSWER TO THE QUESTION?

Let's think first if there is an answer to the question of whether or not God exists.

Reason for believing there is an answer	Reason for believing there might not be an answer	The current position
The Universe is set up in such a way that it provides evidence for a cause and a design.	Just because the Universe looks like it was created and designed, that doesn't mean it was.	Most religious and non-religious groups accept that the answer depends on the evidence and strength of the conflicting arguments.
Our instincts tell us that everything that exists must have a cause and a design.	Our instincts may not be 100% reliable.	
Our reasoning is that there cannot be an infinite chain of causes, and that such complexity requires an intelligent designer.	We could just be conditioned to see things this way. There could be other possible explanations.	
The alternative of there being no explanation makes no sense.	We have convinced ourselves that God exists because the alternative is so unpleasant: a pointless Universe without a reason for existence.	

Questioning the existence of God means thinking about how *likely* it is that God exists. However, the question of whether or not God exists is unlikely to be answered by God knocking at your front door. Making a judgement about the existence of God requires evaluation of the evidence on whether or not it is more or less *likely* that he exists.

There are three main responses to arguments about the existence of God:

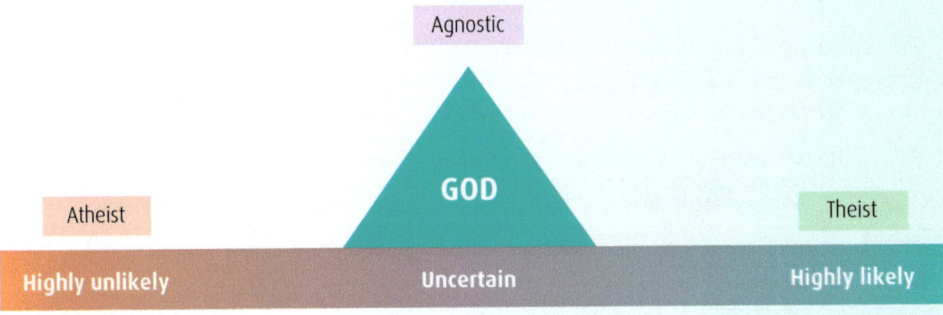

What we are doing here is looking at the evidence which supports belief in the God of Classical Theism (GCT). Check the RPQ toolkit on page 116 for an explanation of this concept of God.

contd

The existence of God – The starting point

We will start by wondering how you can prove the existence of God when...

- You can't see Him
- Nobody has seen Him

...and you won't get an answer by...

- Demanding a special appearance
- Travelling to space
- Demanding a sign

...but religions still believe in God. There are two main approaches:

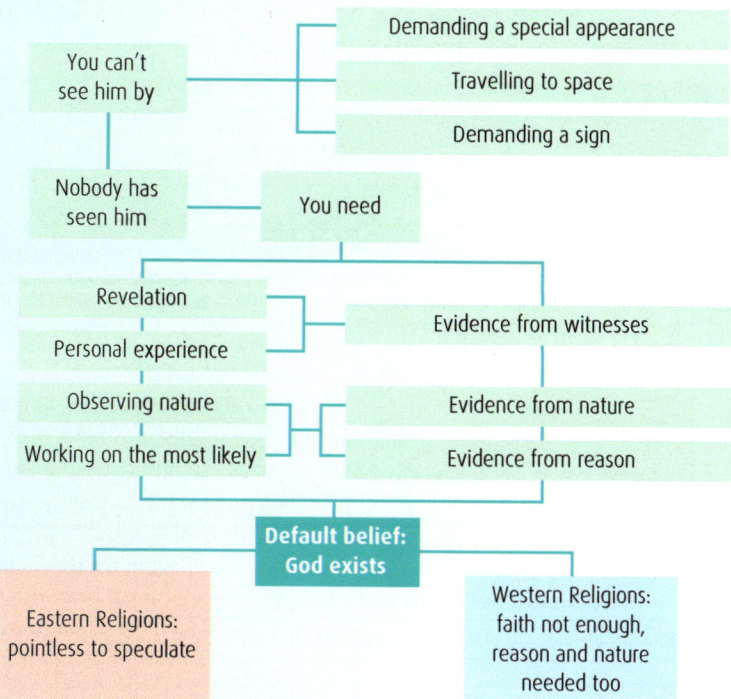

What Western thinkers were doing was to use reason (our ability to work things out), the natural world and sacred scripture to prove the existence of their God. They did not want to start with the sacred scripture and claim that because God is mentioned in it that he must exist. They wanted to look at the Universe and the natural world and use reason to show that God's existence could be proved.

When they looked at the Universe and the natural world they made various observations which, when pieced together, provided evidence for the existence of God. The two main parts of this evidence are shown in the tables below:

The Universe exists	The Universe is complex
Since the Universe exists, where did it come from?	Since the Universe is so complex, how was it created?
There are two possible answers: • It has always been here • something started it.	There are two possible answers: • It occurred naturally • something designed it.
We need to show that the most likely explanation is that God started it, and therefore God exists.	We need to show that the most likely explanation is that God designed it, and therefore God exists.
We also need to show that other explanations are less likely.	We also need to show that other explanations are less likely.

DON'T FORGET

To argue about God's existence you need evidence. He is unlikely to make an actual appearance.

VIDEO LINK

Learn more about the GCT by watching the clips at the Digital Zone.

ONLINE TEST

Test yourself on the existence of God at www.brightredbooks.net

THINGS TO DO AND THINK ABOUT

1. What is the biggest weakness of the view that God's existence can be proven?
2. What is the biggest strength of the view that God's existence can be proven?
3. Overall, explain whether you think the view that God's existence cannot be proven is weak or strong.

THE EXISTENCE OF GOD

THE COSMOLOGICAL ARGUMENT: AQUINAS

Aquinas wanted to prove that God existed from the fact that the Universe existed. That is why it is called the cosmological argument. He needed to prove that the only explanation for the Universe's existence was that God created it, and therefore he must exist. To prove that God existed he looked at how the Universe worked. Refer to Aquinas' cosmological argument in the RPQ toolkit on page 115.

St Thomas Aquinas, 1476

Everything that moves is moved by something else.
There isn't an infinite chain of movers.
There is an unmoved Mover.
The unmoved Mover is God.

	Support	Criticism
Is the argument based on facts?	It is true that everything we have experienced in the Universe changes or, as Aquinas put it, moves. So, from our perspective, this is a fact. It is also a fact, so far as we know, that things do not change or move on their own. Something has to make something change or make it move. Scientists work on the principle that it is reasonable to expect the laws which govern movement to be the same wherever you go in the Universe, which would mean that everything needs to be moved by something else. Looking at things moving it then becomes clear that something has to be the Prime Mover.	Our experience is limited to our part of the Universe and our knowledge is limited to the laws which govern it. We cannot be certain that things do not change or move on their own in other parts of the Universe. We can only make observations about things inside the Universe, we cannot really say anything much about things outside the Universe because we know nothing of them. Even if there is a Prime Mover, that is all we can say about it.
Is the argument based on our intuition?	Our intuition tells us that things do not change or move on their own, and therefore a Prime Mover is necessary. For believers, the Prime Mover is God, and therefore the cosmological argument is based on their intuition. Scientists' intuition tells them that everything exists for a reason, and that this can be seen by observing the natural world. However, their intuition tells them that the Prime Mover need not necessarily be God, and could be something else.	It is obvious that the Universe exists, and that things move and change in the Universe, but our intuition can take us no further. If there is a Prime Mover then this must be proven using the available evidence. The evidence is highly debatable.
Is the argument based on our experience?	Our experience tells us that there is a Prime Mover because we can see that everything seems to be moved or changed by something else, and if it is true for some things then it must be true for all things. It does not make sense to say that all the individual parts of the Universe have an explanation but that the entire Universe doesn't.	Our experience of things which move other things is that they do it automatically. This takes place without a divine purpose, such as that supplied by God. It is automatic and nothing more. Our experience of the Universe is incomplete. We can only claim that everything is moved or caused by something else if the evidence is complete. We know only a tiny part of the Universe and are therefore in no position to make claims about how the entire Universe appeared.

contd

The existence of God – The cosmological argument: Aquinas

	Everything that moves is moved by something else. *There isn't an infinite chain of movers.* *There is an unmoved Mover.* *The unmoved Mover is God.*	
	Support	**Criticism**
Is the argument supported by experts?	One of its strengths is its simplicity, say some philosophers. To claim that there is a Prime Mover is easier to accept than there being no Prime Mover. **Aristotle** said: 'There's a block of marble. It could be carved into a statue so it is a potential statue. It is not an actual statue until the sculptor sets about it. The sculptor changes it from a potential statue into an actual statue. The block of marble cannot do it on its own.' In other words, the Universe cannot change itself from a potential Universe to an actual Universe: there must be a Prime Mover to make that happen. Scientists have yet to prove what caused the Big Bang, which means that the cosmological argument cannot be ruled out until it is.	Some scientists believe that in the early stages of the Universe energy and matter simply came into existence (without being moved by anything) because the laws which governed the Universe at that point were so chaotic. The philosopher David Hume argued that we are conditioned to see a universe where things cannot move unless moved by something else. Hume also said that the most the Prime Mover argument establishes is that there might be a Prime Mover. It says nothing else about it other than it exists.
Does the argument contradict itself?	There is nothing in the argument that is contradictory. It is a simple straightforward description of what we see, what we experience, and what our instincts tell us.	The big **contradiction** is this: What caused the Prime Mover to move? If the answer is nothing then the first line of the cosmological argument is incorrect. If the answer is something then that something is the real Prime Mover, and therefore God isn't. An infinite Universe would remove the need for a Prime Mover: The Prime Mover would be replaced by an infinite chain of movers, but then the second line of the cosmological argument would be incorrect.
Is the argument the best possible answer?	We need to think about how likely it is that nothing can move or change by itself, and what the alternatives are.	It is difficult to prove without more evidence.

DON'T FORGET

The Cosmological argument and First Cause argument are different names for the same thing.

VIDEO LINK

Watch the video about the cosmological argument at the Digital Zone.

ONLINE TEST

Test yourself on this topic at www.brightredbooks.net

THINGS TO DO AND THINK ABOUT

1. What is more reliable, your senses or your gut feeling?

2. What's more important about the cosmological argument – that it is based on experience or that it is not contradictory?

3. Does it make any sense to argue against the idea that everything that moves is moved by something else?

Plato and Aristotle

THE EXISTENCE OF GOD
THE COSMOLOGICAL ARGUMENT: KALAM

The Kalam cosmological argument is a modern formulation of the cosmological argument for the existence of God. It was proposed by William Lane Craig in 1979 and is based on Muslim developments of this argument over a thousand years ago. It claims that everything that **begins** to exist has a cause.

> Everything that begins to exist has a cause.
> The Universe began to exist so it has a cause.
> An infinite chain of causes is impossible.
> There must be an Uncaused Cause.
> The Uncaused Cause is God.

	Support	Criticism
Is the argument based on facts?	It is a fact that everything we have experienced in the Universe has been caused. We are also assuming that the laws which govern the Universe are the same throughout the Universe, in which case the argument is based on facts.	Our experience is limited to our part of the Universe and our knowledge is limited to the laws which govern it. We cannot be certain that everything in the Universe has a cause. Even if there is an Uncaused Cause, that is all we can say about it. The Uncaused Cause need not be the GCT.
Is the argument based on our **intuition**?	Our intuition tells us that something caused the start of the Universe. The alternative would be an infinite Universe, an idea we struggle with and certainly don't grasp intuitively. Scientists' intuition tells them that there is a cause for everything, and that the explanations can be found by observing the natural world. However, their intuition tells them that the cause of everything need not necessarily be God, and could be something else.	The people who intuitively say this is obvious do so because they believe in God. They see the Universe as created by God. It is obvious that the Universe exists, and that something must have caused it to exist, but our intuition can take us no further. If there is an Uncaused Cause then this must be proven using the available evidence.
Is the argument based on our experience?	Our experience tells us that everything that exists has a cause and appears to have been caused by something else, and so it is reasonable to state that if this is true for some things it must be true for all things. To argue that only each part of the Universe has a cause for its existence, but that the entire Universe doesn't, contradicts our experience. Given that we have never experienced an Uncaused Cause, this viewpoint is entirely theoretical. Scientists are open to the possibility of there being uncaused causes but won't state that the Uncaused Cause is God without evidence that can be observed.	Our experience of the Universe is incomplete. We can only claim that everything has been caused by something else once the evidence is complete. We know only a tiny part of the Universe and are therefore in no position to make claims about what caused the entire Universe to appear.
Is the argument supported by experts?	One of its strengths is its simplicity, say some philosophers. To claim that there is an Uncaused Cause is easier to accept than the alternative of no cause at all.	There are scientists who believe that in the early stages of the Universe energy and matter simply came into existence because the laws which governed the Universe at that point were so chaotic.
Does the argument contradict itself?	There is nothing in the argument that is contradictory. It is a simple straightforward description of what we see, what we experience and what our instincts tell us.	The big contradiction is this: What caused the Uncaused Cause? If the answer is nothing then the first line of the Kalam cosmological argument is incorrect. If the answer is something then that something is the real Uncaused Cause, and therefore God isn't.
Is the argument the best possible answer?	We need to think about how likely it is that nothing is uncaused and what the alternatives are. It is more likely than unlikely that there will be a first cause.	It is difficult to disprove without more evidence.

DON'T FORGET

The Kalam cosmological argument claims that things that begin to exist have a cause. God never began to exist. He has always existed and does not need a cause.

VIDEO LINK

Watch the clip at the Digital Zone to learn more about the Kalam cosmological argument.

ONLINE TEST

Test yourself on this topic at www.brightredbooks.net

The existence of God – The cosmological argument: Kalam

 THINGS TO DO AND THINK ABOUT

1. The Kalam cosmological argument is in a hail of questions. Five questions are listed below. Which one would be the hardest to answer and why?

    a) Can you give two facts that support this belief?

    b) Can you give one thing from your experience that would support this belief?

    c) Can you give two reasons why God would not want to make His existence more obvious?

    d) Can you give two reasons why the Uncaused Cause of the Universe has to be God?

    e) Can you give two reasons why it makes sense to believe that God is the Uncaused Cause?

2. Is believing that the Universe happened for no reason at all any more unreasonable than saying that God was its Uncaused Cause?

3. Is believing that the Universe just popped into existence out of nothing any more unreasonable than saying that God caused it?

4. Is the existence of the Universe strong evidence that God exists?

THE EXISTENCE OF GOD

THE TELEOLOGICAL ARGUMENT 1

AQUINAS AND PALEY

Aquinas and Paley wanted to prove that God existed from observing that the Universe appeared to be designed. This is the teleological or design argument. Refer to the teleological argument in the RPQ toolkit.

	There is an order and purpose in the Universe. Order and purpose are the result of intelligence not chance. Therefore nature is guided by an intelligent designer. The Designer is God.	
	Support	**Criticism**
Is the argument based on facts?	There is evidence of design and purpose. Remember that in The Goldilocks Zone any slight change to the necessary 'constants' would spell disaster, and life and the Universe would not exist. Think also of our five senses and what they are able to do, how they complement each other, and how they are linked to our brains which make sense of the data they produce. The laws of mathematics are so well ordered that they appear to have been designed. There's also the Golden Ratio of 1.618 which appears in art, architecture, geometry and nature. It could just be coincidence and how the natural world works, but the precision involved raises the possibility of a creative intelligent designer.	Apparent design is when things appear to be designed, and **authentic design** is when they have actually been designed. The Universe has apparent design but that does not mean that it has actually been designed. There are many things in the Universe that are evidence of bad design. For example, the tube you use for breathing is also the tube that you use for consuming food, so there is an increased risk of choking. Our bodies are made up of hundreds of millions of cells but it only needs one of them to cause cancer. We live in a Universe which displays some order. What we do not know is how much order there is. It could be that this is the most ordered that any universe can ever be, or it might be that there are universes where there is perfect order and life is substantially more orderly than in our Universe.
Is the argument based on our intuition?	If our intuition is that complexity can only be explained by having a designer, then the Universe is sufficiently complex to require one. If the purpose of things can only be explained by giving something purpose, then everything in the Universe appears to have a purpose so must require a designer to give them purpose.	You would think that a designer would want to create the best model possible. All of the problems on Earth do not suggest a designer who really knows what he is doing. It is not obvious that the design, if there is one, is actually intelligent. For example, tectonic plates can be seen as design flaws since they cause earthquakes. Or perhaps the Universe was designed to have both good and bad features, in which case it could be claimed to have been very well designed.
Is the argument based on our experience?	We have experience of complex things and can define something as complex. The Universe is the most complex thing we know. It is not unreasonable to argue that there needed to be a designer. Our experience tells us that different things in the Universe each have a purpose. Purposes are given to things, they do not produce a purpose by themselves. Therefore, something has to provide the purpose and that something is the designer. Everything in the Universe can be explained. Our experience tells us that we do not have all the explanations just now. Our experience tells us that many of our theories have turned out to be correct so there is a chance that the theory that God is the Universe's designer could also turn out to be correct.	David Hume says that our experience of complexity and design doesn't just involve one person from start to finish. For example, take building a house, you need several different tradesmen. When you see a house, you know that it was designed, and you also know that several people were involved in building it. So, if the Universe was designed in a similar way then the conclusion is that a team of gods put it together. The teleological argument insists on an intelligent designer. Those who argue that the Universe is badly designed don't see the work of an intelligent designer. Hume also questioned whether or not the Universe was complex. We could look at the Universe and say it is complex but we have got nothing to compare it to. For all we know we might be experiencing a very simple universe that only looks complex to us.

DON'T FORGET

Teleological and design arguments are the same argument.

VIDEO LINK

Learn more about these arguments by watching the clips at the Digital Zone.

ONLINE TEST

Test your knowledge on the existence of God at www.brightredbooks.net

The existence of God – The teleological argument 1

 THINGS TO DO AND THINK ABOUT

The Cosmological and Teleological Arguments.

Do these arguments prove that the God of Classical Theism exists?

- Copy the table below onto a decent-sized piece of paper.
- In the **Yes or No?** column write in your view of whether or not the cosmological or teleological arguments demonstrate the attribute listed in the first column.
- In the **Support** column write in the reason for your choice.
- In the **Counter-argument** column write in one argument against your choice.
- Do this for all the attributes of the God of Classical Theism.
- Finally, answer the question in the box at the bottom.

Attributes	Yes or No?	Support	Counter-argument
Eternal			
Omnipotent			
Omniscient			
Loving			
Good			
Spirit			
Personal			
Immanent			
God of History			
Transcendent			
Just			

Is it reasonable to believe that the God of Classical Theism exists?

THE EXISTENCE OF GOD
THE TELEOLOGICAL ARGUMENT 2

TESTING THE VIEWPOINT

	Support	Criticism
Is the argument supported by experts?	Comparing the Universe to a watch and the conclusions we can draw from that are common sense. The Universe's laws are regular. If the Universe was chaotic then there could be no dependable regular laws. We can actually understand the Universe because it is a rational place which suggests design. It is unlikely that life could appear at all. The requirements are so specific that it looks as though things were fixed to allow life to develop. Perhaps the most famous philosophical support for the Intelligent Design (ID) argument came from the former atheist Professor Antony Flew in 2004, who became a believer when he saw that the intricate nature of the Universe pointed to an infinite intelligence that revealed itself in the intricate workings of the Universe. Supporters of ID believe that the Universe is designed but they are not Creationists. What they are looking for is evidence that there are some things in the natural world which must be specially set up, that produce information and instructions, use programming and coding, and produce something as a result of this. ID supporters argue that our DNA does all of this and that it demonstrates there is intelligence behind its design. Physicist Freeman Dyson said: 'As we look out into the Universe and identify the many accidents of physics and astronomy that have worked together for our benefit, it almost seems as if the universe must in some sense have known that we were coming.'[1] [1] John D. Barrow and Frank J. Tipler, *The Anthropic Cosmological Principle* (1986)	David Hume said that apparent design does not mean authentic design. Comparing the Universe to a man-made object is not valid. It is like comparing the growth of a cabbage to the building of a model ship. He also pointed out design flaws in the Universe such as suffering and questioned how an intelligent designer could build in such terrible flaws. Some philosophers question Aquinas' analogy of the archer and the arrow: the archer guides the arrow to its target by firing it in the right direction. In a similar way, the designer guides the Universe towards its target. What target, though, ask the philosophers, and what is the actual purpose of the Universe? The writer Douglas Adams wasn't quite so sure about ID or the Anthropic Principle: 'This is rather as if you imagine a puddle waking up one morning and thinking, "This is an interesting world I find myself in — an interesting hole I find myself in — fits me rather neatly, doesn't it? In fact, it fits me staggeringly well, must have been made to have me in it!" This is such a powerful idea that as the sun rises in the sky and the air heats up and as, gradually, the puddle gets smaller and smaller, frantically hanging on to the notion that everything's going to be alright, because this world was meant to have him in it, was built to have him in it; so, the moment he disappears catches him rather by surprise. I think this may be something we need to be on the watch out for.'[2] Theories of evolution suggest that there is no design in the universe. The process is driven by the survival of the fittest and the will to survive. It is not designed. Our understanding of evolution is far from complete. However, all the research done on evolution demonstrates that the recurring theme is **natural selection** driven by mutation, adaptation and survival. This is not design, it is the operation of the laws of the natural world. [2] Douglas Adams, *The Salmon of Doubt*
Does the argument contradict itself?	One of the problems facing the ID argument is the problem of evil. God is not only the designer but also good. Philosopher John Stuart Mill claimed that the evidence we see '…does not seem to show that. It shows us a creation that is full of cruelty, malfunction and waste. Take evolution, for example. It is very wasteful. It kills off creatures that will struggle to survive. It makes species extinct. It is a creation that is "red in tooth and claw" and creatures eat each other to survive. It is hard to imagine a more cruel design.'	In response to accusations of poor design there is the **free will defence**. This is the argument that God designed a Universe which had a combination of free will and natural laws. Free will without natural laws would result in a Universe that could not be understood by anyone because it is only when you have laws that you can make sense of things. There are other defences like this and they are all called **theodicies** and they all try to explain why a good God would build so much suffering into his design. They all revolve around the idea of free will giving the Universe meaning and purpose so that the lives of intelligent beings are meaningful.

DON'T FORGET

Remember the three approaches to the Design Argument: Aquinas, Paley, Behe.

VIDEO LINK

Learn more about these approaches by watching the clips on the Digital Zone.

contd

The existence of God – The teleological argument 2

	Support	Criticism
Is the argument the best possible proof?	The design argument is firmly rooted in our experience and science confirms extraordinary levels of complexity in the natural world.	It is not. It leaves too many questions unanswered. Above all else it cannot identify who the designer is.
	Like the cosmological argument, the ID argument struggles to prove that the GCT is the designer, but there is always the possibility that the ID argument is right up to the point where it says a very specific type of God designed it.	

ONLINE TEST

Test yourself on this topic at www.brightredbooks.net

THINGS TO DO AND THINK ABOUT

1. This belief is facing a tirade of questions. Five questions are listed below. Which one would be the hardest to answer and why?

    a) Can you give two facts that support this belief?

    b) Can you give one thing from your experience that would support this belief?

    c) Can you give two reasons why God would not want to make his existence more obvious?

    d) Can you give two reasons why the designer of the Universe has to be God?

    e) Can you give two reasons why it makes sense to believe that God is the designer?

2. Is believing that nature designed the Universe any more unreasonable than saying that God is its Designer?

3. Is believing that the Universe was caused by chance any more unreasonable than saying that God designed it?

4. Is the apparent design of the Universe strong evidence that God exists?

GLOSSARY

abolitionists countries or individuals which want the death penalty stopped

actual infinity the concept of there being something without beginning or end

Advance Directive document stating the end-of-life wishes of an individual

agnostic an individual who believes that there is insufficient proof to prove or disprove the existence of God

Allah Arabic word for God

anatta no soul

anicca impermanence

Anthropic Principle the idea that the Universe was designed to produce intelligent life

antisocial personality disorder psychological condition of many criminals

Apparent Design the supposed existence of God by citing as evidence the appearance of design or purpose in the natural world

arhat an individual who has attained nibbana

Aristotle Greek philosopher

ascetic an individual who lives a very simple life in a monastery

Ashoka the king who made Buddhism his empire's religion

assisted suicide the act of assisting someone to commit suicide

atheist an individual who believes that the existence of God is highly unlikely

atonement the act of doing something to make up for wrongdoing

atonement theories different theories used by Christians as to what Jesus' death achieved

Augustine (of Hippo) influential theologian who lived over 1500 years ago

authentic design something that is actually designed

baptising religious rite of sprinkling water on to a person's forehead or of immersing them in water, symbolising purification or regeneration and admission to the Christian Church

bhikkhuni Buddhist nun

bhikku Buddhist monk

Big Bang theory the theory that there was an explosion just before the Universe expanded

bodhisatta an individual who delays entry into nibbana to help others achieve enlightenment

Brahman the Hindu word for God

brutalises to make someone or society brutal

Buddha any enlightened person

Caiaphas the chief priest who tried Jesus

capital punishment putting an individual to death for committing a crime

caste system hereditary divisions in Hindu society based on karma

Christmas Christian celebration remembering the birth of Jesus and that God became human

Christology the study of who and what Jesus was

cloning copying DNA

communion the name of a special meal had by Christians to remember the sacrifice of Jesus

communion elements the bread and the wine

compassionate to care deeply

conservatives traditionalists who are reluctant to engage in new ways of thinking

contradiction two statements that say the opposite of each other

cosmological relating to the origin and development of the Universe

counter-argument a response to an argument

covenant an agreement/deal

Creation the making of the Universe, usually regarded as an act of God.

Creation Science a form of science which supports the belief that God made the Universe by scientific means

Creator a supernatural being that has the ability to create the Universe and life

criminology the study of crime

criticism comments, positive or negative, on a point of view

culpable homicide responsible for the death of someone either accidentally or without intent

custodial sentence prison

Dalai Lama the leader of Tibetan Buddhism

David Hume an eighteenth century Scottish philosopher

deterrence to put people off

Dhamma The Law as set down by Buddha

dhammakaya part of the Trikaya – the truth body

discretionary a decision made based on circumstances

DNACPR an instruction, often for the chronically ill: Do Not Attempt Cardio-Pulmonary Resuscitation

double effect the motive to do one thing and it results in another – for example, giving a drug to relieve pain which results in the patient's death

dukkha suffering

Easter Christian celebration of the resurrection of Jesus

economic to do with wealth and poverty

Eightfold Path Buddha's plan for achieving enlightenment

embryo an unborn or unhatched offspring in the process of development

embryo research research information from embryos

environmental to do with nature

eternal something that has no beginning and no end

euthanasia the painless killing of a patient suffering from an incurable and painful disease or in an irreversible coma

Evolution the theory of how life developed

First Cause a supposed ultimate cause of all events, which does not itself have a cause, identified with God

Five Precepts Buddhist ideals for lay people

Four Noble Truths the Buddha's explanation of the human condition

Four Sights the sights the Buddha saw when he left the Temple

free will the concept that humans have a free choice rather than being programmed

free will defence the use of free will to defend God against accusations of cruelty in the world

fundamentalist individuals who read sacred scripture as literally true

galaxy a cluster of stars

GCT God of Classical Theism

Genesis the first book in the Bible, which contains Christian creationism

God of the Gaps the idea that when things cannot be explained then God is the explanation

Goldilocks Zone the name given to the very favourable position of the Earth in the Universe

Good Friday the day when Jesus was executed

Glossary

Gospels the main sources of information about Jesus in the Bible

gunas an individual's characteristics in eastern religions

hadiths collections of the teachings of Muhummad not in the Qur'an

Heaven a state of being with God for all time

Hell a state of being separated from God for all time

Herod the King during Jesus' life

HFEA UK Government body checking on embryo research and use

holy something that is seen as special by God

hospices units (often run by charities) for terminally ill patients

immanent present all around

immortal cannot die

incarceration another word for imprisonment

Incarnation when a god or God takes on the form of a human

infertility when a couple cannot conceive a child

instrumental value something that is valuable in relation to its usefulness

Intelligent Designer supernatural being (usually God) perceived to be the Creator of the Universe

intrinsic value something that is valuable in itself

intuition similar to instinct

Isaiah a prophet in the Bible

Islam the religion of Muslims

IVF in-vitro fertilisation (test tube babies)

Jesus' Temptations the time when Jesus was tempted by the Devil

Jews the people who follow the religion of Judaism

Joseph Jesus' father

Judaeo-Christian description for shared ideas between Jews, Christians and Muslims

Judaism the religion of the Jews

Judas Iscariot the disciple that betrayed Jesus

judgement the idea that God judges the lives of humans – found in Judaeo-Christian traditions

kamma action (karma for Hindus)

kammalokha the Earth

Kantian a method of deciding right from wrong proposed by the philosopher Immanuel Kant

Kingdom of God Jesus' vision of how life should be lived

laity people who are not priests, monks or nuns

liberals individuals who are open to new ideas

literalists individuals who read sacred scripture as true

Mahayana the form of Buddhism which has most followers

mainstream science science that is accepted by the scientific community

mandalas geometric designs

mantras chants

Mary Jesus' mother

Mary Magdalene Jesus' closest female friend and the first to meet Jesus after his death

materialism prizing possessions and money

meditation deep calm thought

Messiah the Hebrew word for a person chosen by God for a special mission

Metteyya the successor to the Buddha

Milinda a king who was very influential in Buddhism

miscarriage of justice when the jury gets the wrong verdict

monastery a place where monks study and live

monotheistic belief in one God

multiverse the idea that this Universe is one of many

Muslims the people whose religion is Islam

mutations changes that take place in living beings from generation to generation

Nagasena a Buddhist teacher

natural selection part of the theory of evolution where nature selects those most likely to survive

New Testament the part of the Bible containing information about Jesus and Christian teaching

NHS National Health Service

Nibbana liberation

nirmanakaya part of the Trikaya – the Buddha in the flesh

non-custodial sentence a punishment not involving prison, e.g. fines

non-integration not becoming involved with others

non-voluntary active euthanasia consent to end an individual's life is given by another because the individual cannot give consent by taking direct action

non-voluntary euthanasia consent to end an individual's life is given by another because the individual cannot give consent

non-voluntary passive euthanasia consent to end an individual's life is given by another because the individual cannot give consent by allowing the person to die

NTD non-treatment decisions

Old Testament The first part of the Bible which is very similar to the Jewish Bible

omnipotence all powerful

omnipresent present everywhere

omniscience all knowing

Original sin the idea of the first ever sin committed by Eve – Augustine developed it

origins of life how life began

origins of the Universe how the Universe began

Orthodox Church the main church in Eastern Europe which has several different branches

oscillating universe the idea that the Universe is in a cycle of birth and rebirth

Pali the language used in many Buddhist scared texts

palliative care end-of-life care given to relieve symptoms and cope with the stress

palliative sedation drugs given to an individual near the end of their life to keep them sleeping

Palm Sunday the first day of Jesus' last week of life

parinibbana this is nibbana after death

PAS physician-assisted suicide

passive euthanasia when euthanasia occurs by taking no action to save the patient

Patanjali Hindu philosopher who developed yoga

personal autonomy the right to make decisions for oneself

Peter Jesus' closest male friend

PGD Preimplantation Genetic Diagnosis

Pontius Pilate Roman Governor of Palestine in Jesus' time

GLOSSARY

potential infinity something that has a beginning but no end

Power of Attorney a legal document permitting individuals to make decisions on your behalf if or when you are no longer able to make decisions

prescribed punishments for crimes forbidden by Allah

pro-choice organisations or individuals in favour of letting people choose over abortion or euthanasia

pro-life organisations or individuals in favour of preserving life

Promised Land the land that God promised Abraham and his descendants

prophet an individual who can foretell the future

prosecution a lawyer who has to prove a person's guilt

Protestant Church part of the Christian church – it has many branches

psychological to do with the mind

psychopath a mental illness where individuals are extremely violent

puja worship

Redeemer a name given to Jesus

reformation a purpose of punishment designed to make criminals better people

rehabilitation a purpose of punishment designed to make criminals better people

restorative justice an action whereby offenders try to put right what they did wrong

resurrection Jesus rising from the dead

retentionists individuals or countries in favour of keeping the death penalty

retribution the view that criminals deserved to be punished

revelation God revealing himself to humanity

rituals religious ceremonies or actions

Roman Catholic Church a branch of Christianity

sacred something that has been set aside by God for special treatment

sacrifice to give something up for your faith

salvation believing that you have a soul and that you are going to suffer the consequences of your sins

samatha a type of meditation

sambhogyakaya part of the Trikaya – the divine enjoyment body

samkhya a Hindu philosophy

samsara rebirth

sanctity set aside by God for special treatment

Sangha the Buddhist community

Sanhedrin the Jewish Council that tried Jesus

Sanskrit an ancient Hindu language

Saviour a name given to Jesus

saviour siblings embryos that are selected to help other children in families

scientific foreknowledge the idea that scripture contains scientific knowledge

scientific method the method used by scientists to make discoveries

scripture sacred books

self-delusion kidding yourself on

self-denial denying yourself something for a purpose

self-revealing to reveal yourself – God is self-revealing

Shakyamuni a name given to Buddha

shramanas groups of religious people that Buddha joined

Siddhatta Gautama Buddha's name

sin to disobey God's laws

singularity when everything in the Universe was gathered together in one tiny space

skandhas Buddhist teaching about what humans are made of

skilful actions Buddhist belief about how to live properly

slippery slope an argument which says that if you permit a thing to happen once it opens the door to even worse things being done

Son of God a name used for Jesus

Son of Man a name used for Jesus

steady state theory the idea that the Universe has always existed

sunatta everything is empty

supernatural being a being like God, angels or demons

tanha craving

Tathagata a name given to the Buddha

teleological the belief that causes, design and purpose exist in nature

Ten Precepts rules for living as a monk in Buddhism

The Fall when Adam and Eve sinned

theist an individual who believes the existence of God is highly likely

theodicies arguments used to defend belief in the GCT

Therevada a form of Buddhism split into several branches

Thomas Aquinas an influential Christian thinker associated with the cosmological argument

Three Jewels the Sangha, the Buddha and the Dhamma

Three Marks of Existence anicca, anatta and dukha

Three Poisons hate, greed and ignorance in Buddhism

transcendent the idea that God is beyond many of the Universe's definitions

Trikaya the three bodies of the Buddha

Trinity the Father, Son and Holy Spirit in Christianity

tripitaka Buddhist sacred scriptures

tusita a Buddhist heaven

Universe everything that we experience

unskilful actions bad ways to behave according to Buddhism

utilitarianism the belief that right and wrong should be judges on the consequences of an act

vajryana a branch of Buddhism

Vedic religion the religion which produced Hinduism and Buddhism

vipissana a type of meditation

voluntary active euthanasia when a person volunteers to have the doctor give them something to kill them

voluntary euthanasia when a person volunteers to have the doctor end their life

voluntary passive euthanasia when a person volunteers to have the doctor end their life by doing nothing to save them

vulnerable individuals people who have mental or physical incapacity through age, circumstances or disease

Wesak a Buddhist festival

whole life term when a person is imprisoned until they day they die

William Paley an English philosopher associated with the Design Argument

without capacity an individual who is no longer able to make informed decisions about their health and welfare

worldview how people see the world

yoga part of the process of meditation